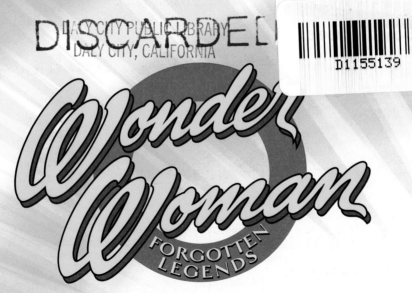

Wonder Woman
FORGOTTEN LEGENDS

KURT BUSIEK
LEE MARRS
GEORGE PÉREZ
writers

TRINA ROBBINS
IRV NOVICK
RICK MAGYAR
RAMONA FRADON
artists

NANSI HOOLAHAN
SHELLEY EIBER
colorists

L. LOIS BUHALIS
PHIL FELIX
CARRIE SPIEGLE
letterers

TRINA ROBBINS
cover artist

TRINA ROBBINS
EDUARDO BARRETO
original series covers

WONDER WOMAN created by **WILLIAM MOULTON MARSTON**

S

ALAN GOLD Editor - Original Series
JEB WOODARD Group Editor - Collected Editions • **SCOTT NYBAKKEN** Editor - Collected Edition
STEVE COOK Design Director - Books • **SHANNON STEWART** Publication Design

BOB HARRAS Senior VP - Editor-in-Chief, DC Comics • **PAT McCALLUM** Executive Editor, DC Comics

WONDER WOMAN: FORGOTTEN LEGENDS

DC Comics, 2900 West Alameda Ave., Burbank, CA 91505.
Printed by LSC Communications, Owensville, MO, USA. 2/16/18. First Printing.
ISBN: 978-1-4012-7795-6

Library of Congress Cataloging-in-Publication Data is available.

FSC www.fsc.org MIX Paper from responsible sources FSC® C132124

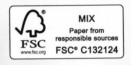

The following essay by Trina Robbins originally appeared in issue #2 of THE LEGEND OF WONDER WOMAN.

THE LEGEND OF
THE LEGEND OF WONDER WOMAN

Once upon a time in the 1950s, there was a little girl who avidly read Wonder Woman. Every week, when she got her 25¢ allowance (we got much smaller allowances in those days!), she would run down to the corner drugstore to find the latest SENSATION COMICS, WONDER WOMAN, COMIC CAVALCADE—anything that featured the lovely Amazon princess, beautiful as Aphrodite, wise as Athena, swifter than Mercury and...well, you get the picture.

Dear readers, can you guess who that little girl was? Well, no, not Jenette Kahn...No, not Gloria Steinem...Okay, it's true—I was only one of *thousands* of little girls who ardently *gobbled up* all Wonder Woman comics in the fifties. In those days Wonder Woman was still being drawn by her original artist, the great Harry G. Peter, and although her creator, William Moulton Marston, had died a few years earlier, the books still retained the colorful element of fantasy that had so endeared them to the hearts of America's young female population in the 1940s. Young girls aren't too crazy about cops and robbers, which was the theme of the average action comic from that period. We also didn't relate a whole lot to all those costumed heroes running around and flexing their muscles. That was boy stuff. But the intrepid Amazon was for us—a superior female character who had the kind of adventures we liked: trips to fantastic lost kingdoms and meetings with beautiful (and often evil) queens and empresses.

Here's where the story gets sad. The little girl became a teenager, and her mother convinced her to *give away* her Wonder Woman collection (because "comics are just for kids," right?). Well, shortly after I gave away what must have been thousands of dollars' worth of comics (thanks, Mom), Harry G. Peter passed away to that great artist's studio in the sky, and other artists took over WONDER WOMAN. But I didn't know this. I was busy trying to be a grown-up, so I didn't look at another comic for about ten years.

Finally, in the mid-sixties I gave up on trying to be a grown-up, and went back to my comics. (I even started *drawing* them!) To my horror I found that some new artist was drawing Wonder Woman, and she no longer looked like the Amazon I had known and loved in the fifties! (Actually, for a brief period in 1966, writer Bob Kanigher and artists Ross Andru and Mike Esposito *did* attempt to do a Golden Age Wonder Woman, but although the art worked, the stories were missing that wonderful fantasy element, and veered dangerously close to camp.)

Fast-forward to 1985. The little girl, now all grown up, is *still* avidly reading Wonder Woman—all the Golden Age Wonder Woman books I can find at comic book stores and conventions. Then the phone rings, and out of the blue I hear that DC wants me to do a special four-issue Wonder Woman miniseries. After recovering, I start worrying. There *must* be some catch. "You understand," I tell Alan Gold, "that I don't *want* to do the contemporary Wonder Woman? If I draw Wonder Woman, I want to draw her in the Golden Age style of H.G. Peter." And Alan tells me that this is *exactly* what DC wants!

Now things get even better: Kurt Busiek, another Golden Age fan, turns out to be a dream to work with. He accepts all the concepts I come up with without a murmur, and then does the hard part of taking my ideas and fleshing them out into a workable story. And then, to my cast of recycled Golden Age characters, Kurt adds a character of his own: little Suzie, the engaging brat who shares Wonder Woman's adventures in the Land of Mirrors and the Atom Galaxy.

From the very beginning Suzie worked just fine as a character; I knew just where to take her in the plot, and I even knew immediately what she looked like. In fact, Suzie felt *so* familiar, for a character that someone *else* had created, that around about the first half of the second book I started getting strange feelings of *déjà vu* as I drew her. I had seen this girl somewhere before—but where? And then it came to me! There, on top of my file cabinet, still in its original frame, sat a photo of a little girl in a traditional "little-girl dress" from the fifties, with a white Peter Pan collar and little puffed sleeves. Her blond hair is neatly pulled into two braids—no big hair ribbons, but it's close enough. There stands Suzie, in a picture frame on a file cabinet—only it's *not* Suzie! The girl in the photo is *me*, in 1950, seven years old. A little younger than Suzie, and a couple of years earlier than our story, but it's her all right, or she's me! Subconsciously, I'd been putting *myself* into the story, thereby making my childhood dream come true.

So the legend has a happy ending. The little girl who avidly read Wonder Woman in the 1950s finally got to travel with her idol to the Land of Mirrors and the Atom Galaxy, and even to Paradise Island, and to have adventures that she will never forget!

—Trina Robbins
1986

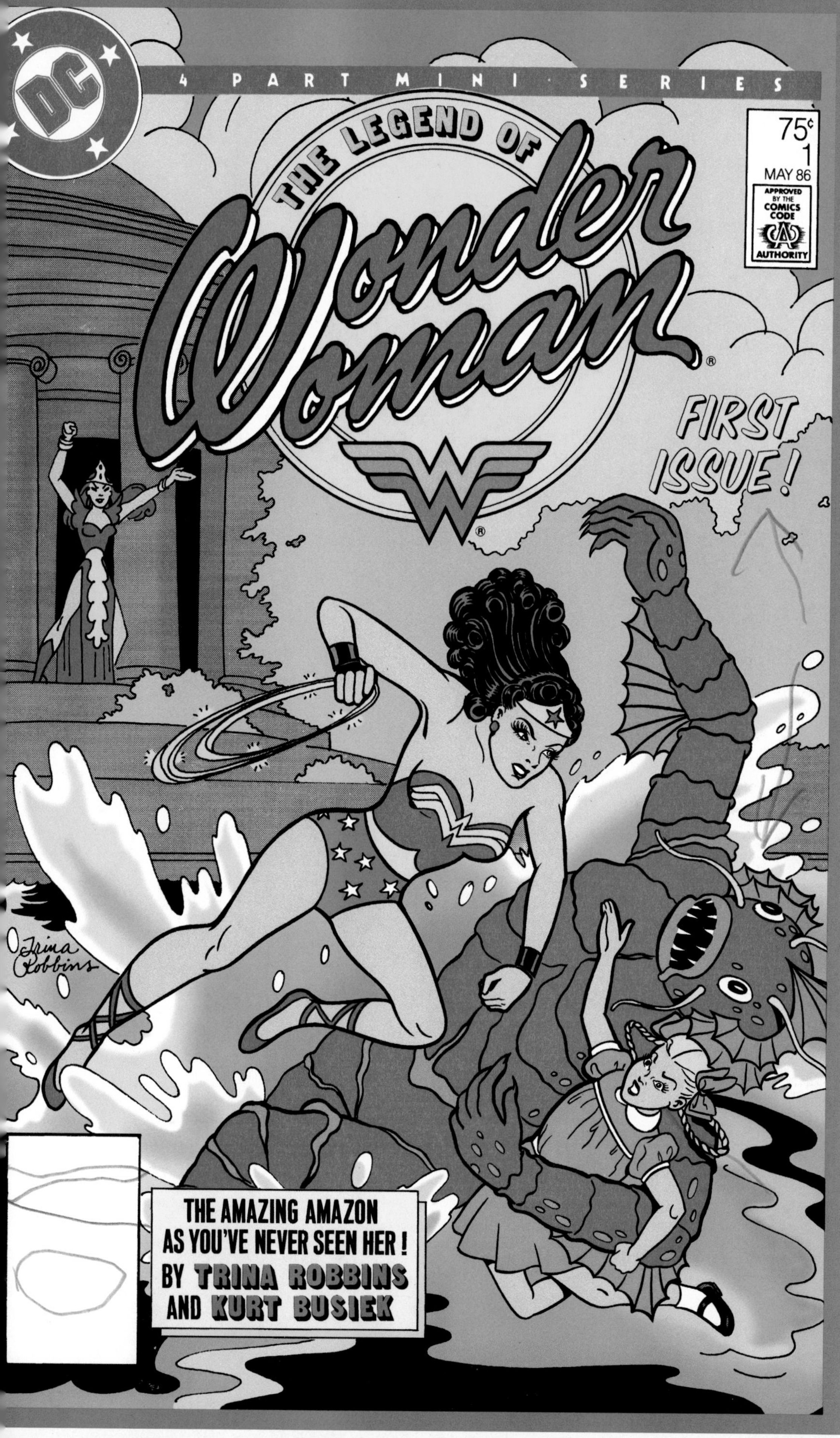
DC
4 PART MINI-SERIES
75¢
1
MAY 86
APPROVED BY THE COMICS CODE AUTHORITY
THE LEGEND OF
Wonder Woman®
FIRST ISSUE!
Trina Robbins
THE AMAZING AMAZON
AS YOU'VE NEVER SEEN HER!
BY TRINA ROBBINS
AND KURT BUSIEK

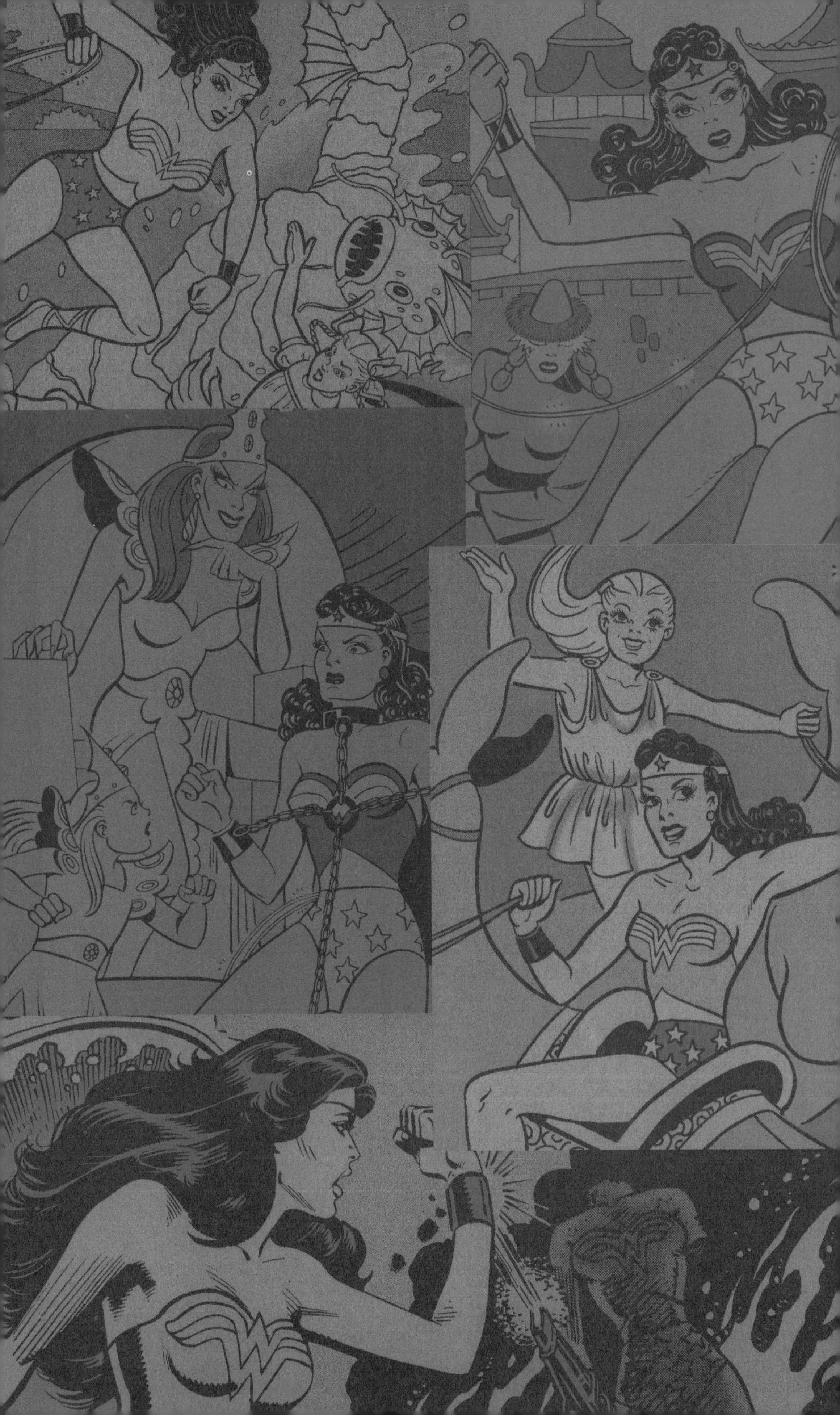

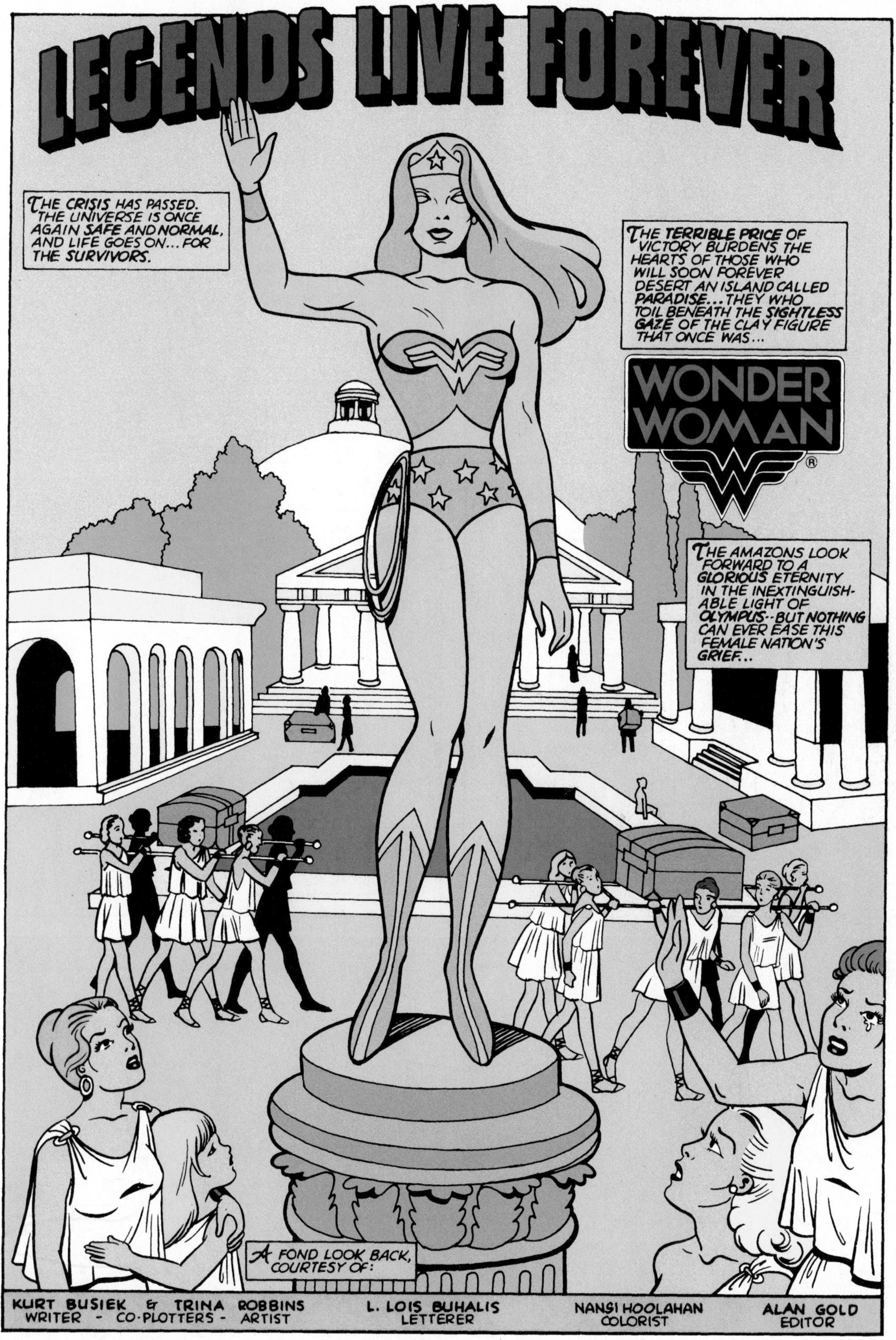
LEGENDS LIVE FOREVER
THE CRISIS HAS PASSED. THE UNIVERSE IS ONCE AGAIN SAFE AND NORMAL, AND LIFE GOES ON... FOR THE SURVIVORS.
THE TERRIBLE PRICE OF VICTORY BURDENS THE HEARTS OF THOSE WHO WILL SOON FOREVER DESERT AN ISLAND CALLED PARADISE... THEY WHO TOIL BENEATH THE SIGHTLESS GAZE OF THE CLAY FIGURE THAT ONCE WAS...
WONDER WOMAN
THE AMAZONS LOOK FORWARD TO A GLORIOUS ETERNITY IN THE INEXTINGUISH-ABLE LIGHT OF OLYMPUS--BUT NOTHING CAN EVER EASE THIS FEMALE NATION'S GRIEF...
A FOND LOOK BACK, COURTESY OF:
KURT BUSIEK & TRINA ROBBINS
WRITER - CO-PLOTTERS - ARTIST
L. LOIS BUHALIS
LETTERER
NANSI HOOLAHAN
COLORIST
ALAN GOLD
EDITOR

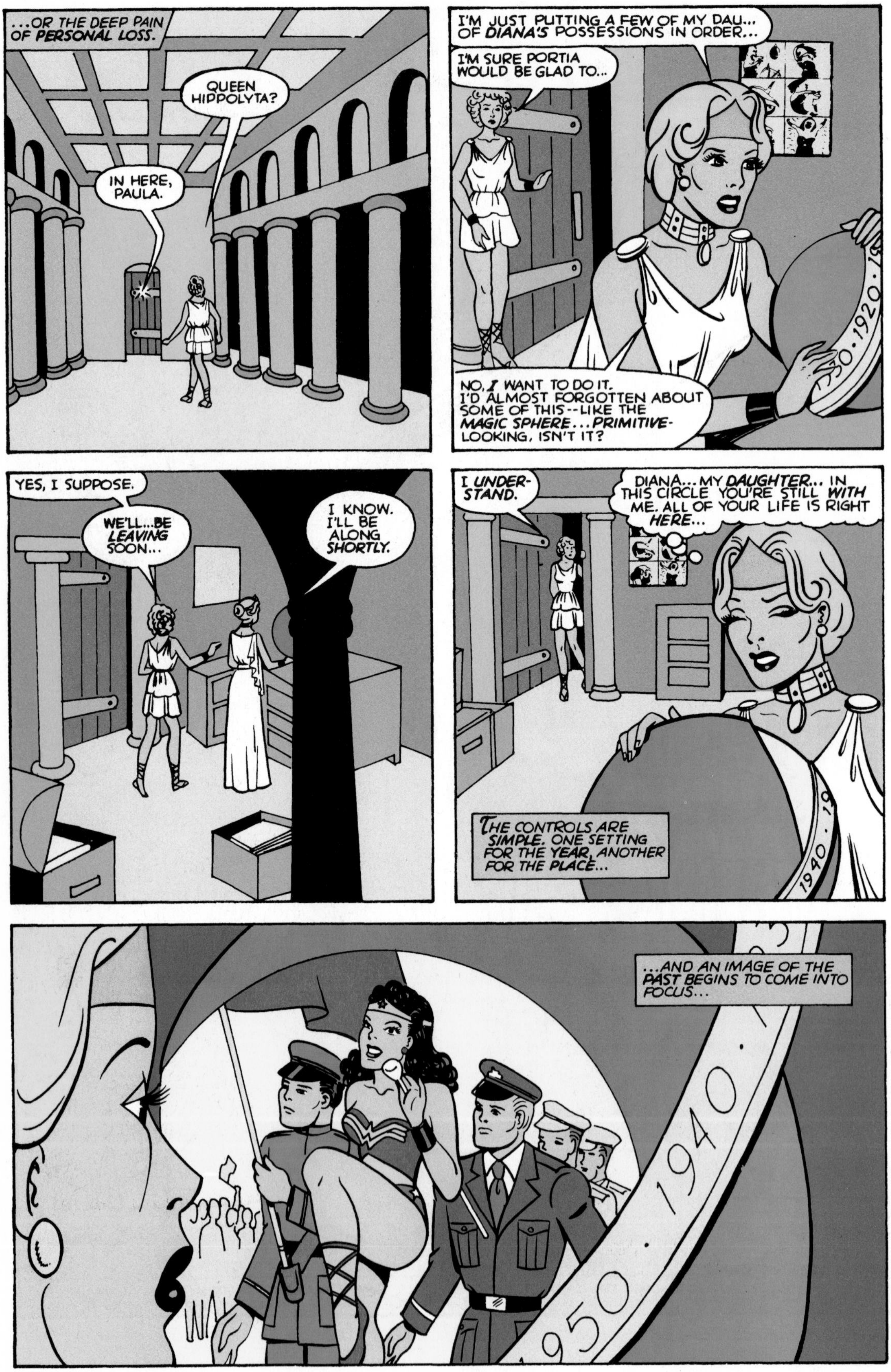
...OR THE DEEP PAIN OF PERSONAL LOSS.
QUEEN HIPPOLYTA?
IN HERE, PAULA.
I'M JUST PUTTING A FEW OF MY DAU... OF DIANA'S POSSESSIONS IN ORDER...
I'M SURE PORTIA WOULD BE GLAD TO...
NO, I WANT TO DO IT. I'D ALMOST FORGOTTEN ABOUT SOME OF THIS--LIKE THE MAGIC SPHERE...PRIMITIVE-LOOKING, ISN'T IT?
YES, I SUPPOSE.
WE'LL...BE LEAVING SOON...
I KNOW. I'LL BE ALONG SHORTLY.
I UNDERSTAND.
DIANA... MY DAUGHTER... IN THIS CIRCLE YOU'RE STILL WITH ME. ALL OF YOUR LIFE IS RIGHT HERE...
THE CONTROLS ARE SIMPLE. ONE SETTING FOR THE YEAR, ANOTHER FOR THE PLACE...
...AND AN IMAGE OF THE PAST BEGINS TO COME INTO FOCUS...
1950 · 1940 ·

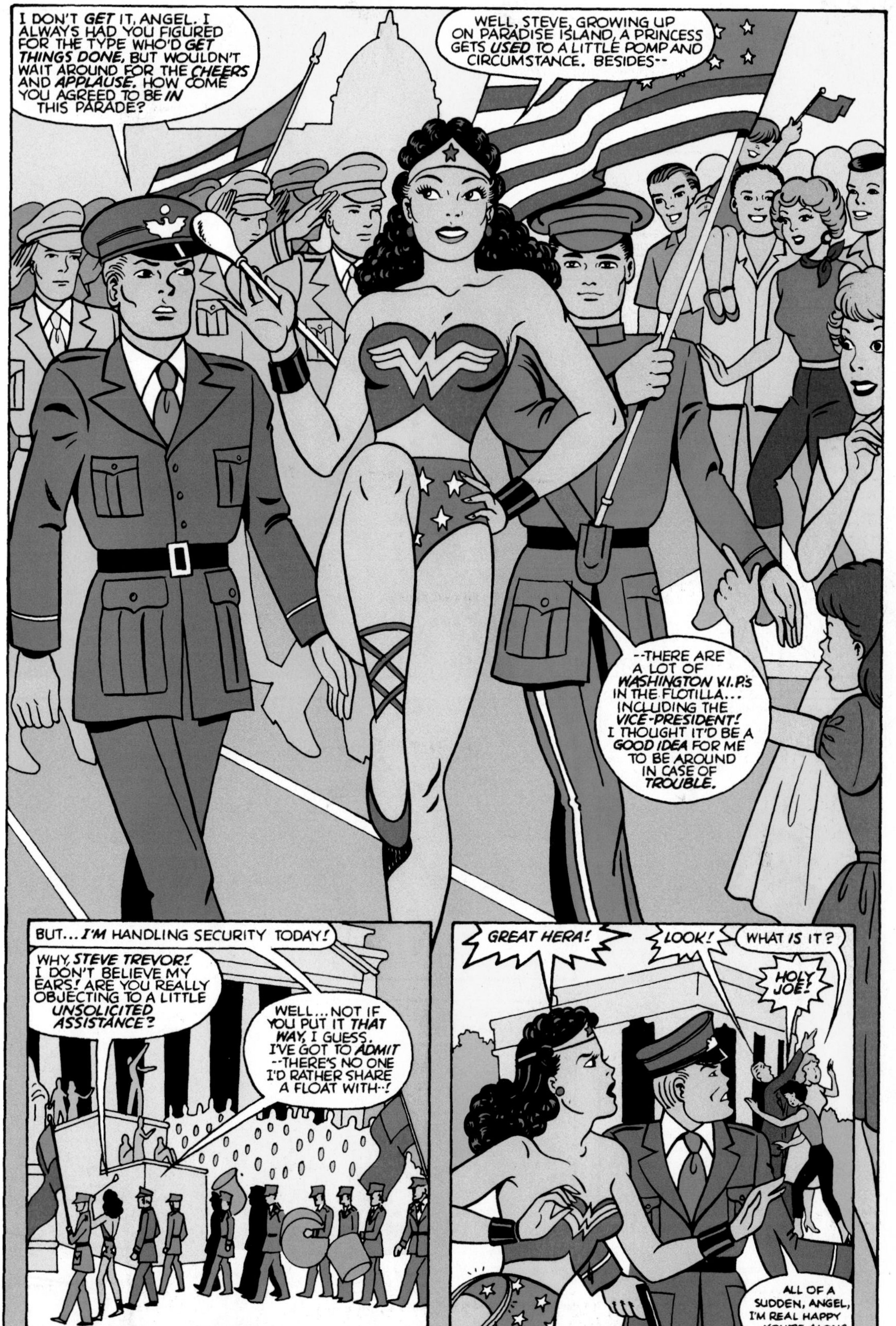
I DON'T GET IT, ANGEL. I ALWAYS HAD YOU FIGURED FOR THE TYPE WHO'D GET THINGS DONE, BUT WOULDN'T WAIT AROUND FOR THE CHEERS AND APPLAUSE. HOW COME YOU AGREED TO BE IN THIS PARADE?
WELL, STEVE, GROWING UP ON PARADISE ISLAND, A PRINCESS GETS USED TO A LITTLE POMP AND CIRCUMSTANCE. BESIDES--
--THERE ARE A LOT OF WASHINGTON V.I.P.'s IN THE FLOTILLA... INCLUDING THE VICE-PRESIDENT! I THOUGHT IT'D BE A GOOD IDEA FOR ME TO BE AROUND IN CASE OF TROUBLE.
BUT... I'M HANDLING SECURITY TODAY!
WHY, STEVE TREVOR! I DON'T BELIEVE MY EARS! ARE YOU REALLY OBJECTING TO A LITTLE UNSOLICITED ASSISTANCE?
WELL... NOT IF YOU PUT IT THAT WAY, I GUESS. I'VE GOT TO ADMIT --THERE'S NO ONE I'D RATHER SHARE A FLOAT WITH--!
GREAT HERA!
LOOK!
WHAT IS IT?
HOLY JOE!
ALL OF A SUDDEN, ANGEL, I'M REAL HAPPY YOU'RE ALONG.

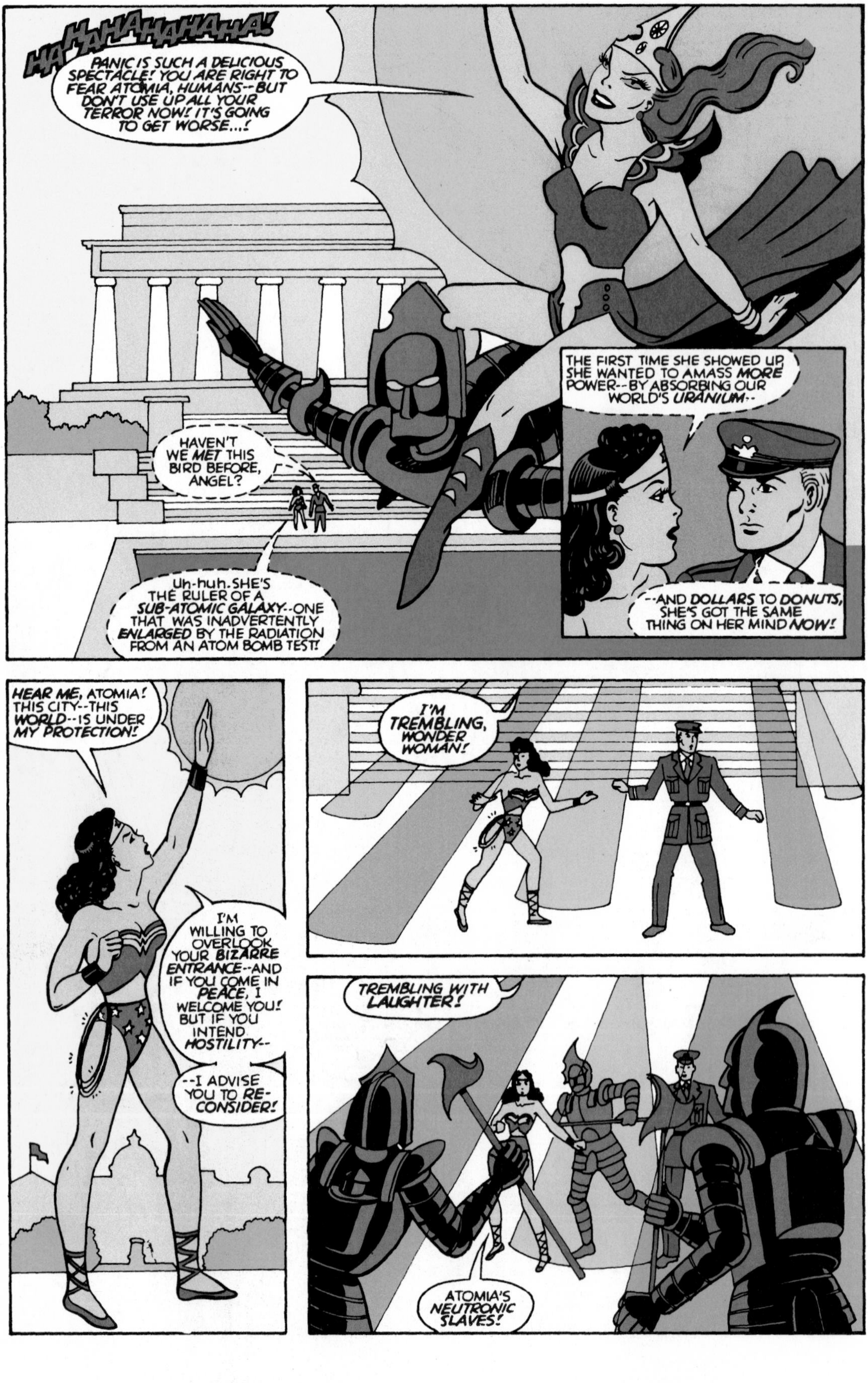
HAHAHAHAHAHAHA!
PANIC IS SUCH A DELICIOUS SPECTACLE! YOU ARE RIGHT TO FEAR ATOMIA, HUMANS--BUT DON'T USE UP ALL YOUR TERROR NOW! IT'S GOING TO GET WORSE...!
HAVEN'T WE MET THIS BIRD BEFORE, ANGEL?
Uh-huh. SHE'S THE RULER OF A SUB-ATOMIC GALAXY--ONE THAT WAS INADVERTENTLY ENLARGED BY THE RADIATION FROM AN ATOM BOMB TEST!
THE FIRST TIME SHE SHOWED UP, SHE WANTED TO AMASS MORE POWER--BY ABSORBING OUR WORLD'S URANIUM--
--AND DOLLARS TO DONUTS, SHE'S GOT THE SAME THING ON HER MIND NOW!
HEAR ME, ATOMIA! THIS CITY--THIS WORLD--IS UNDER MY PROTECTION!
I'M WILLING TO OVERLOOK YOUR BIZARRE ENTRANCE--AND IF YOU COME IN PEACE, I WELCOME YOU! BUT IF YOU INTEND HOSTILITY--
--I ADVISE YOU TO RE-CONSIDER!
I'M TREMBLING, WONDER WOMAN!
TREMBLING WITH LAUGHTER!
ATOMIA'S NEUTRONIC SLAVES!

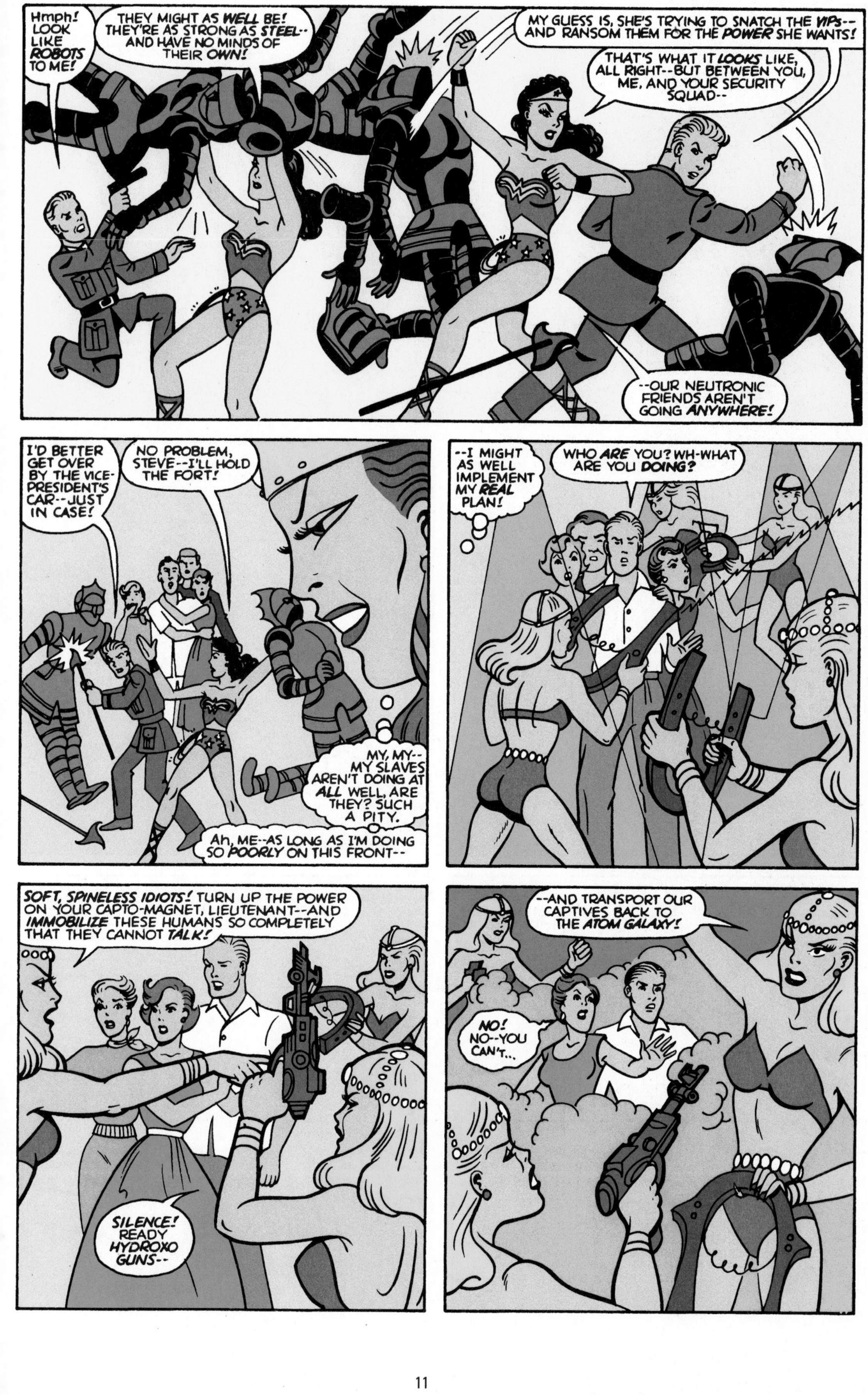

Hmph! LOOK LIKE ROBOTS TO ME!
THEY MIGHT AS WELL BE! THEY'RE AS STRONG AS STEEL--AND HAVE NO MINDS OF THEIR OWN!
MY GUESS IS, SHE'S TRYING TO SNATCH THE VIPs--AND RANSOM THEM FOR THE POWER SHE WANTS!
THAT'S WHAT IT LOOKS LIKE, ALL RIGHT--BUT BETWEEN YOU, ME, AND YOUR SECURITY SQUAD--
--OUR NEUTRONIC FRIENDS AREN'T GOING ANYWHERE!
I'D BETTER GET OVER BY THE VICE-PRESIDENT'S CAR--JUST IN CASE!
NO PROBLEM, STEVE--I'LL HOLD THE FORT!
MY, MY--MY SLAVES AREN'T DOING AT ALL WELL, ARE THEY? SUCH A PITY.
Ah, ME--AS LONG AS I'M DOING SO POORLY ON THIS FRONT--
--I MIGHT AS WELL IMPLEMENT MY REAL PLAN!
WHO ARE YOU? WH-WHAT ARE YOU DOING?
SOFT, SPINELESS IDIOTS! TURN UP THE POWER ON YOUR CAPTO-MAGNET, LIEUTENANT--AND IMMOBILIZE THESE HUMANS SO COMPLETELY THAT THEY CANNOT TALK!
SILENCE! READY HYDROXO GUNS--
--AND TRANSPORT OUR CAPTIVES BACK TO THE ATOM GALAXY!
NO! NO--YOU CAN'T...

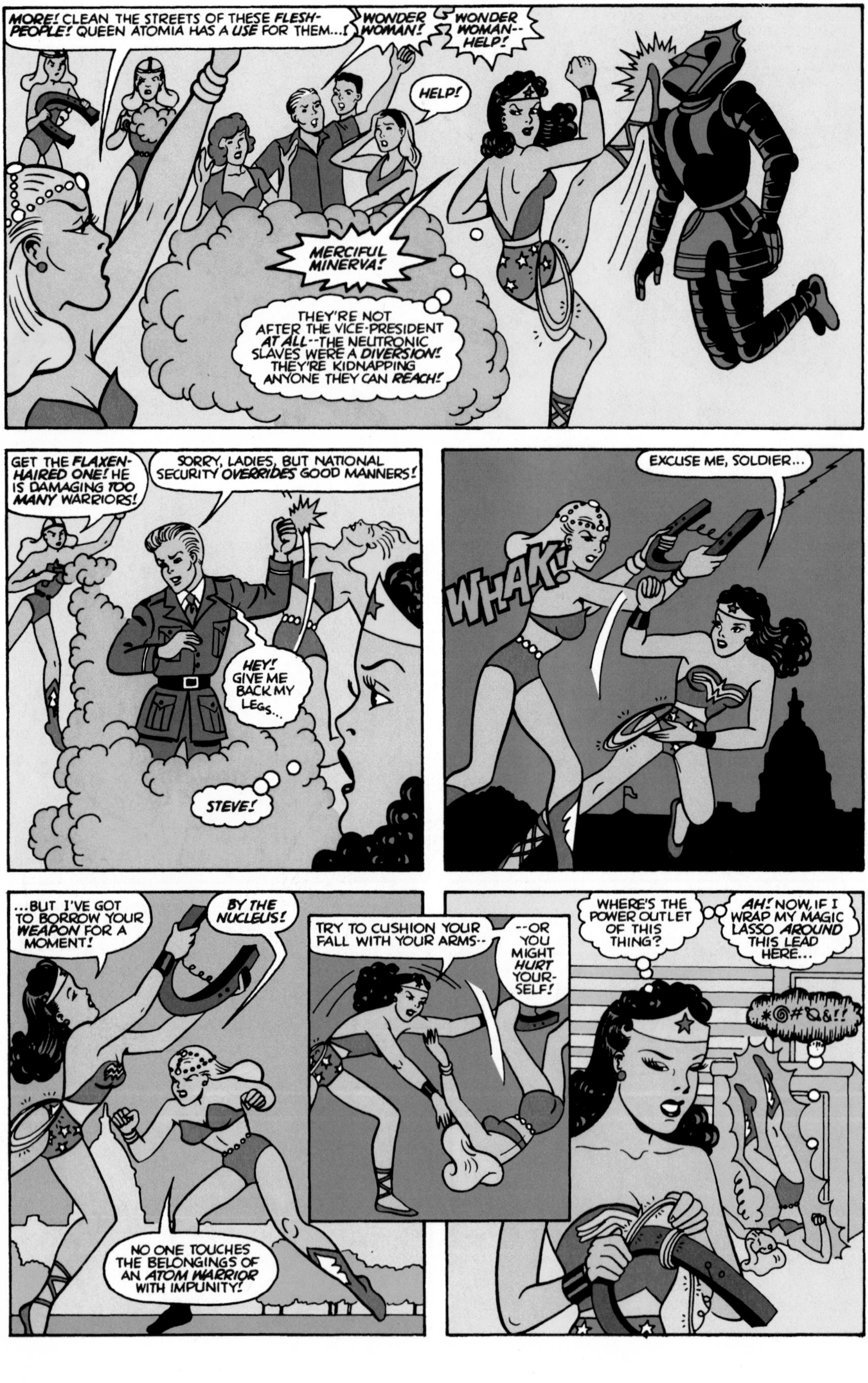

MORE! CLEAN THE STREETS OF THESE FLESH-PEOPLE! QUEEN ATOMIA HAS A USE FOR THEM...!
WONDER WOMAN!
WONDER WOMAN--HELP!
HELP!
MERCIFUL MINERVA!
THEY'RE NOT AFTER THE VICE-PRESIDENT AT ALL--THE NEUTRONIC SLAVES WERE A DIVERSION! THEY'RE KIDNAPPING ANYONE THEY CAN REACH!
GET THE FLAXEN-HAIRED ONE! HE IS DAMAGING TOO MANY WARRIORS!
SORRY, LADIES, BUT NATIONAL SECURITY OVERRIDES GOOD MANNERS!
HEY! GIVE ME BACK MY LEGS...
STEVE!
EXCUSE ME, SOLDIER...
WHAK!
...BUT I'VE GOT TO BORROW YOUR WEAPON FOR A MOMENT!
BY THE NUCLEUS!
NO ONE TOUCHES THE BELONGINGS OF AN ATOM WARRIOR WITH IMPUNITY!
TRY TO CUSHION YOUR FALL WITH YOUR ARMS--
--OR YOU MIGHT HURT YOUR-SELF!
WHERE'S THE POWER OUTLET OF THIS THING?
AH! NOW, IF I WRAP MY MAGIC LASSO AROUND THIS LEAD HERE...
*@#&!!

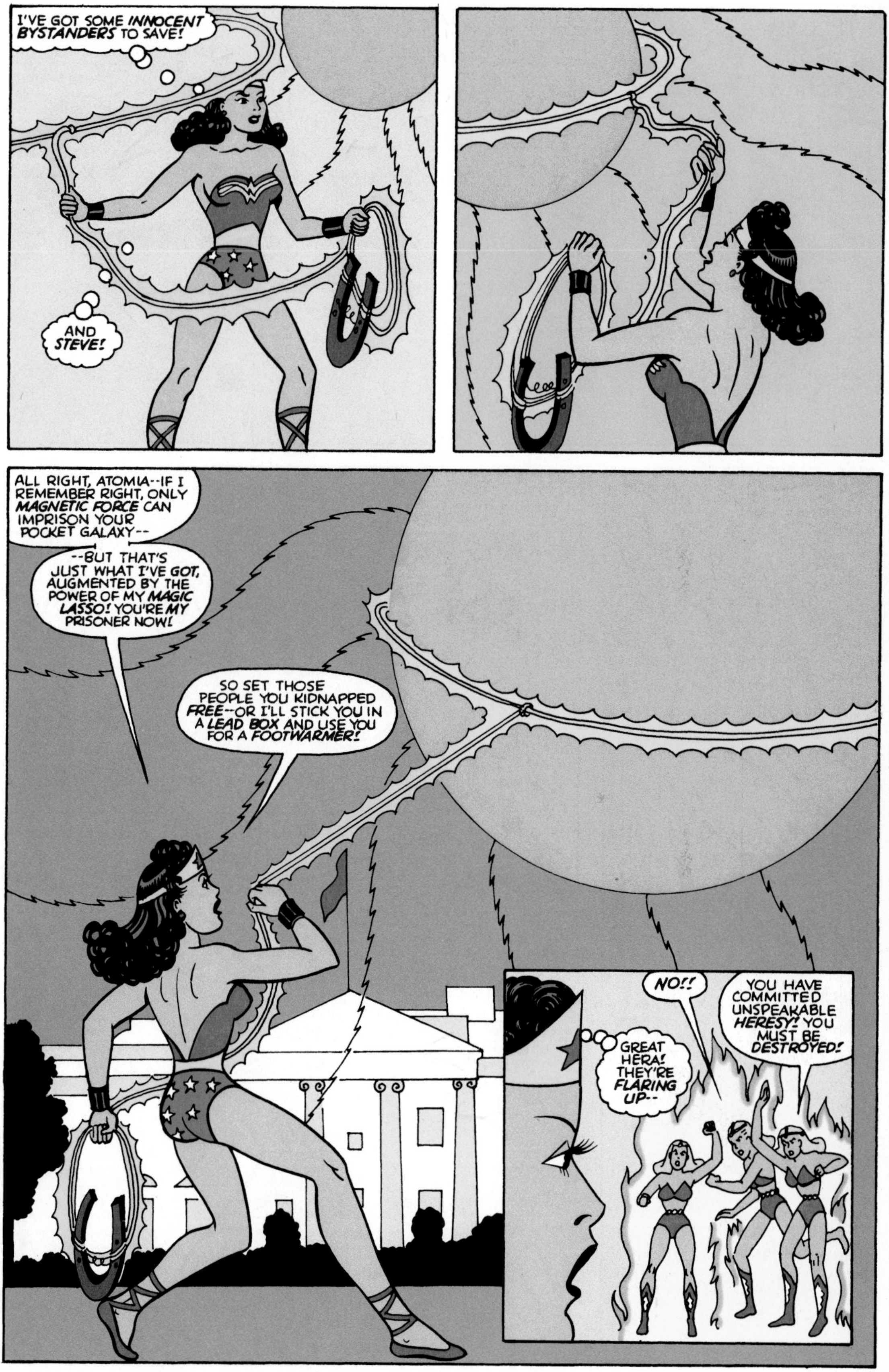

I'VE GOT SOME INNOCENT BYSTANDERS TO SAVE!
AND STEVE!
ALL RIGHT, ATOMIA--IF I REMEMBER RIGHT, ONLY MAGNETIC FORCE CAN IMPRISON YOUR POCKET GALAXY--
--BUT THAT'S JUST WHAT I'VE GOT, AUGMENTED BY THE POWER OF MY MAGIC LASSO! YOU'RE MY PRISONER NOW!
SO SET THOSE PEOPLE YOU KIDNAPPED FREE--OR I'LL STICK YOU IN A LEAD BOX AND USE YOU FOR A FOOTWARMER!
GREAT HERA! THEY'RE FLARING UP--
NO!!
YOU HAVE COMMITTED UNSPEAKABLE HERESY! YOU MUST BE DESTROYED!

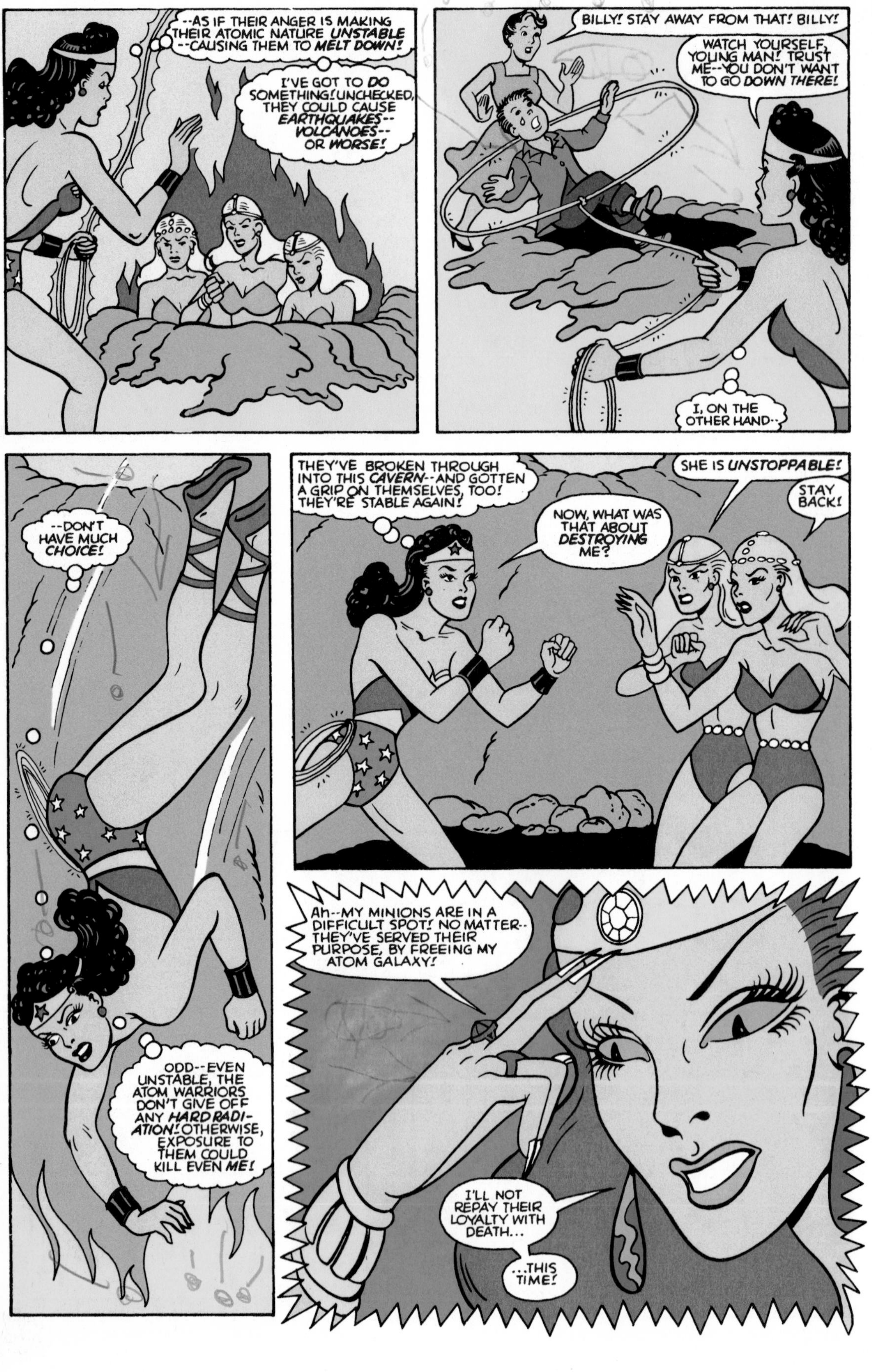

--AS IF THEIR ANGER IS MAKING THEIR ATOMIC NATURE UNSTABLE --CAUSING THEM TO MELT DOWN!
I'VE GOT TO DO SOMETHING! UNCHECKED, THEY COULD CAUSE EARTHQUAKES-- VOLCANOES-- OR WORSE!
BILLY! STAY AWAY FROM THAT! BILLY!
WATCH YOURSELF, YOUNG MAN! TRUST ME--YOU DON'T WANT TO GO DOWN THERE!
I, ON THE OTHER HAND--
--DON'T HAVE MUCH CHOICE!
ODD--EVEN UNSTABLE, THE ATOM WARRIORS DON'T GIVE OFF ANY HARD RADI-ATION! OTHERWISE, EXPOSURE TO THEM COULD KILL EVEN ME!
THEY'VE BROKEN THROUGH INTO THIS CAVERN--AND GOTTEN A GRIP ON THEMSELVES, TOO! THEY'RE STABLE AGAIN!
NOW, WHAT WAS THAT ABOUT DESTROYING ME?
SHE IS UNSTOPPABLE!
STAY BACK!
Ah--MY MINIONS ARE IN A DIFFICULT SPOT! NO MATTER-- THEY'VE SERVED THEIR PURPOSE, BY FREEING MY ATOM GALAXY!
I'LL NOT REPAY THEIR LOYALTY WITH DEATH...
...THIS TIME!

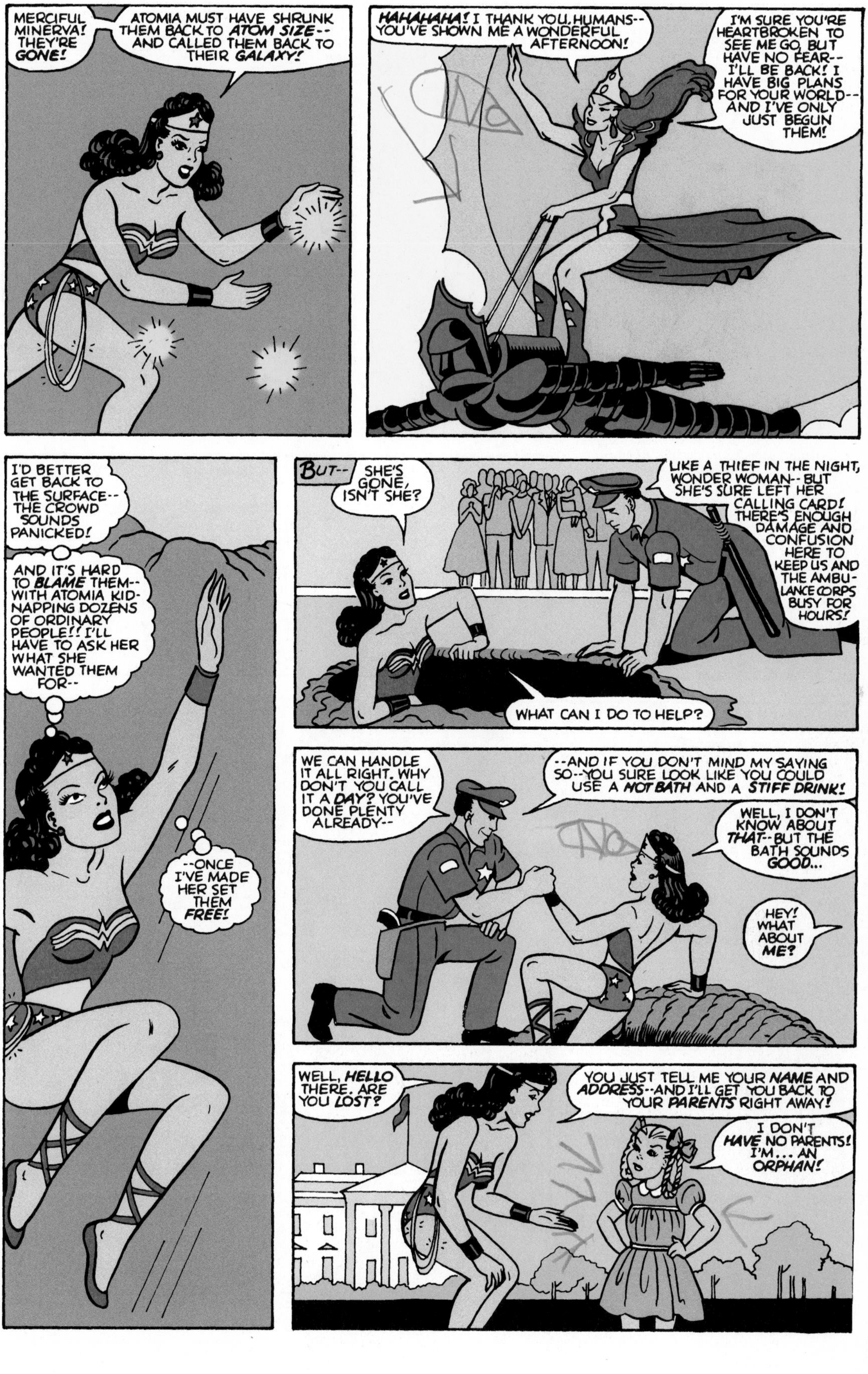
MERCIFUL MINERVA! THEY'RE GONE!
ATOMIA MUST HAVE SHRUNK THEM BACK TO ATOM SIZE-- AND CALLED THEM BACK TO THEIR GALAXY!
HAHAHAHA! I THANK YOU, HUMANS-- YOU'VE SHOWN ME A WONDERFUL AFTERNOON!
I'M SURE YOU'RE HEARTBROKEN TO SEE ME GO, BUT HAVE NO FEAR-- I'LL BE BACK! I HAVE BIG PLANS FOR YOUR WORLD-- AND I'VE ONLY JUST BEGUN THEM!
I'D BETTER GET BACK TO THE SURFACE-- THE CROWD SOUNDS PANICKED!
AND IT'S HARD TO BLAME THEM-- WITH ATOMIA KIDNAPPING DOZENS OF ORDINARY PEOPLE!! I'LL HAVE TO ASK HER WHAT SHE WANTED THEM FOR--
--ONCE I'VE MADE HER SET THEM FREE!
BUT--
SHE'S GONE, ISN'T SHE?
LIKE A THIEF IN THE NIGHT, WONDER WOMAN-- BUT SHE'S SURE LEFT HER CALLING CARD! THERE'S ENOUGH DAMAGE AND CONFUSION HERE TO KEEP US AND THE AMBULANCE CORPS BUSY FOR HOURS!
WHAT CAN I DO TO HELP?
WE CAN HANDLE IT ALL RIGHT. WHY DON'T YOU CALL IT A DAY? YOU'VE DONE PLENTY ALREADY--
--AND IF YOU DON'T MIND MY SAYING SO--YOU SURE LOOK LIKE YOU COULD USE A HOT BATH AND A STIFF DRINK!
WELL, I DON'T KNOW ABOUT THAT--BUT THE BATH SOUNDS GOOD...
HEY! WHAT ABOUT ME?
WELL, HELLO THERE. ARE YOU LOST?
YOU JUST TELL ME YOUR NAME AND ADDRESS--AND I'LL GET YOU BACK TO YOUR PARENTS RIGHT AWAY!
I DON'T HAVE NO PARENTS! I'M... AN ORPHAN!

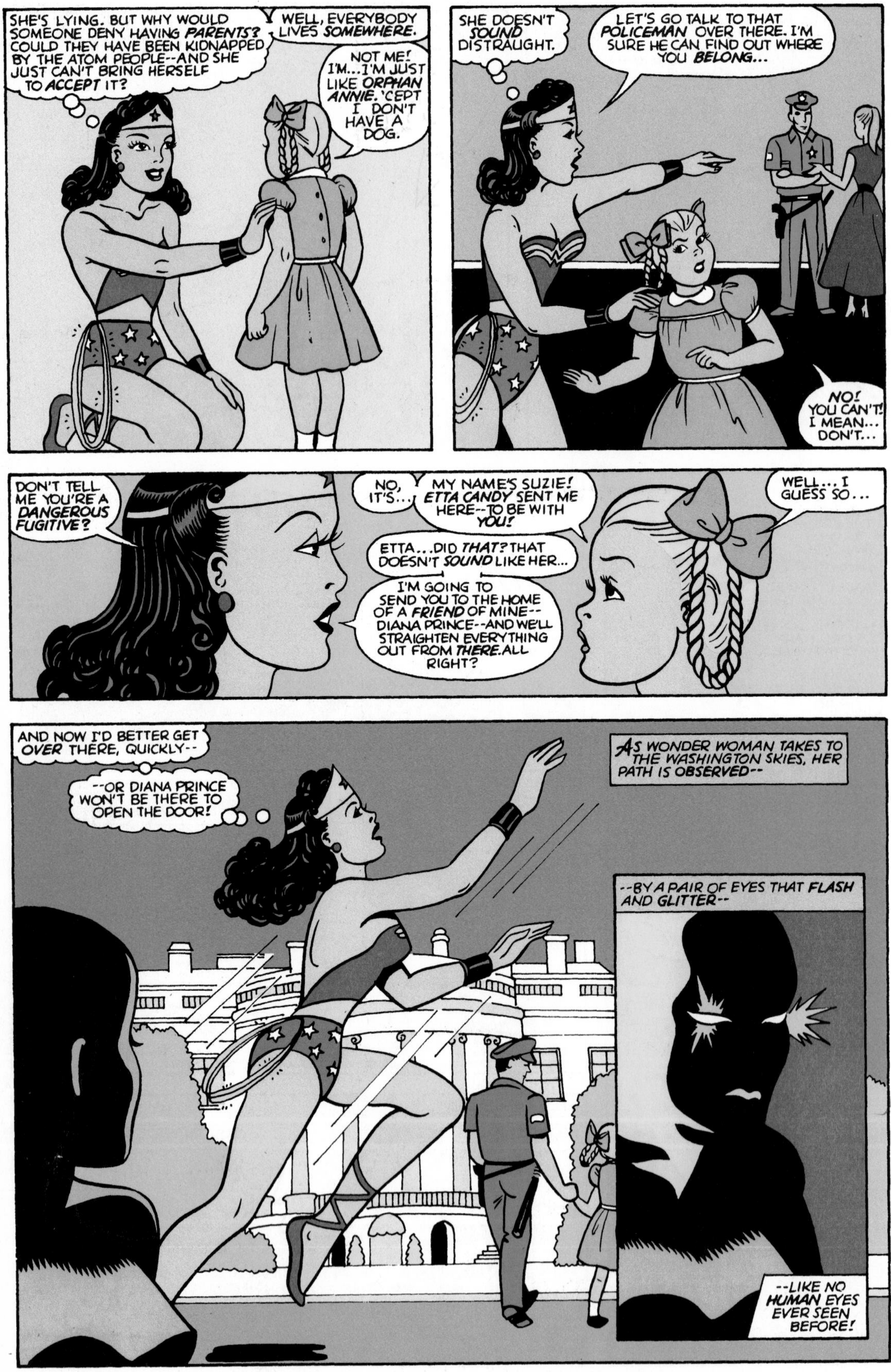
SHE'S LYING. BUT WHY WOULD SOMEONE DENY HAVING PARENTS? COULD THEY HAVE BEEN KIDNAPPED BY THE ATOM PEOPLE--AND SHE JUST CAN'T BRING HERSELF TO ACCEPT IT?
WELL, EVERYBODY LIVES SOMEWHERE.
NOT ME! I'M...I'M JUST LIKE ORPHAN ANNIE. 'CEPT I DON'T HAVE A DOG.
SHE DOESN'T SOUND DISTRAUGHT.
LET'S GO TALK TO THAT POLICEMAN OVER THERE. I'M SURE HE CAN FIND OUT WHERE YOU BELONG...
NO! YOU CAN'T! I MEAN... DON'T...
DON'T TELL ME YOU'RE A DANGEROUS FUGITIVE?
NO, IT'S...
MY NAME'S SUZIE! ETTA CANDY SENT ME HERE--TO BE WITH YOU!
ETTA...DID THAT? THAT DOESN'T SOUND LIKE HER...
I'M GOING TO SEND YOU TO THE HOME OF A FRIEND OF MINE--DIANA PRINCE--AND WE'LL STRAIGHTEN EVERYTHING OUT FROM THERE. ALL RIGHT?
WELL... I GUESS SO...
AND NOW I'D BETTER GET OVER THERE, QUICKLY--
--OR DIANA PRINCE WON'T BE THERE TO OPEN THE DOOR!
AS WONDER WOMAN TAKES TO THE WASHINGTON SKIES, HER PATH IS OBSERVED--
--BY A PAIR OF EYES THAT FLASH AND GLITTER--
--LIKE NO HUMAN EYES EVER SEEN BEFORE!

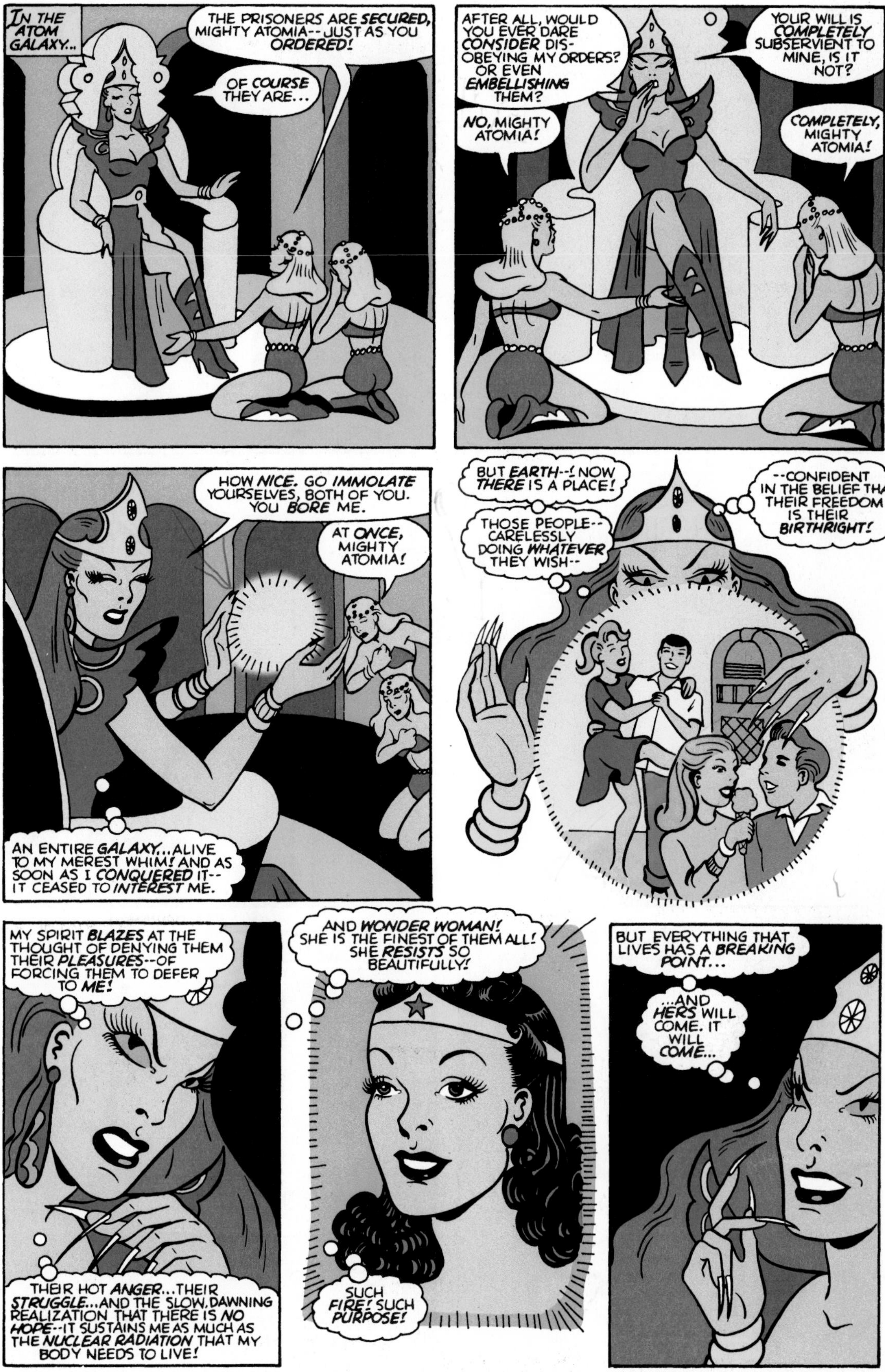

IN THE ATOM GALAXY...
THE PRISONERS ARE SECURED, MIGHTY ATOMIA-- JUST AS YOU ORDERED!
OF COURSE THEY ARE...
AFTER ALL, WOULD YOU EVER DARE CONSIDER DIS-OBEYING MY ORDERS? OR EVEN EMBELLISHING THEM?
NO, MIGHTY ATOMIA!
YOUR WILL IS COMPLETELY SUBSERVIENT TO MINE, IS IT NOT?
COMPLETELY, MIGHTY ATOMIA!
HOW NICE. GO IMMOLATE YOURSELVES, BOTH OF YOU. YOU BORE ME.
AT ONCE, MIGHTY ATOMIA!
AN ENTIRE GALAXY...ALIVE TO MY MEREST WHIM! AND AS SOON AS I CONQUERED IT-- IT CEASED TO INTEREST ME.
BUT EARTH--! NOW THERE IS A PLACE!
THOSE PEOPLE-- CARELESSLY DOING WHATEVER THEY WISH--
--CONFIDENT IN THE BELIEF THAT THEIR FREEDOM IS THEIR BIRTHRIGHT!
MY SPIRIT BLAZES AT THE THOUGHT OF DENYING THEM THEIR PLEASURES--OF FORCING THEM TO DEFER TO ME!
THEIR HOT ANGER...THEIR STRUGGLE...AND THE SLOW, DAWNING REALIZATION THAT THERE IS NO HOPE--IT SUSTAINS ME AS MUCH AS THE NUCLEAR RADIATION THAT MY BODY NEEDS TO LIVE!
AND WONDER WOMAN! SHE IS THE FINEST OF THEM ALL! SHE RESISTS SO BEAUTIFULLY!
SUCH FIRE! SUCH PURPOSE!
BUT EVERYTHING THAT LIVES HAS A BREAKING POINT...
...AND HERS WILL COME. IT WILL COME...

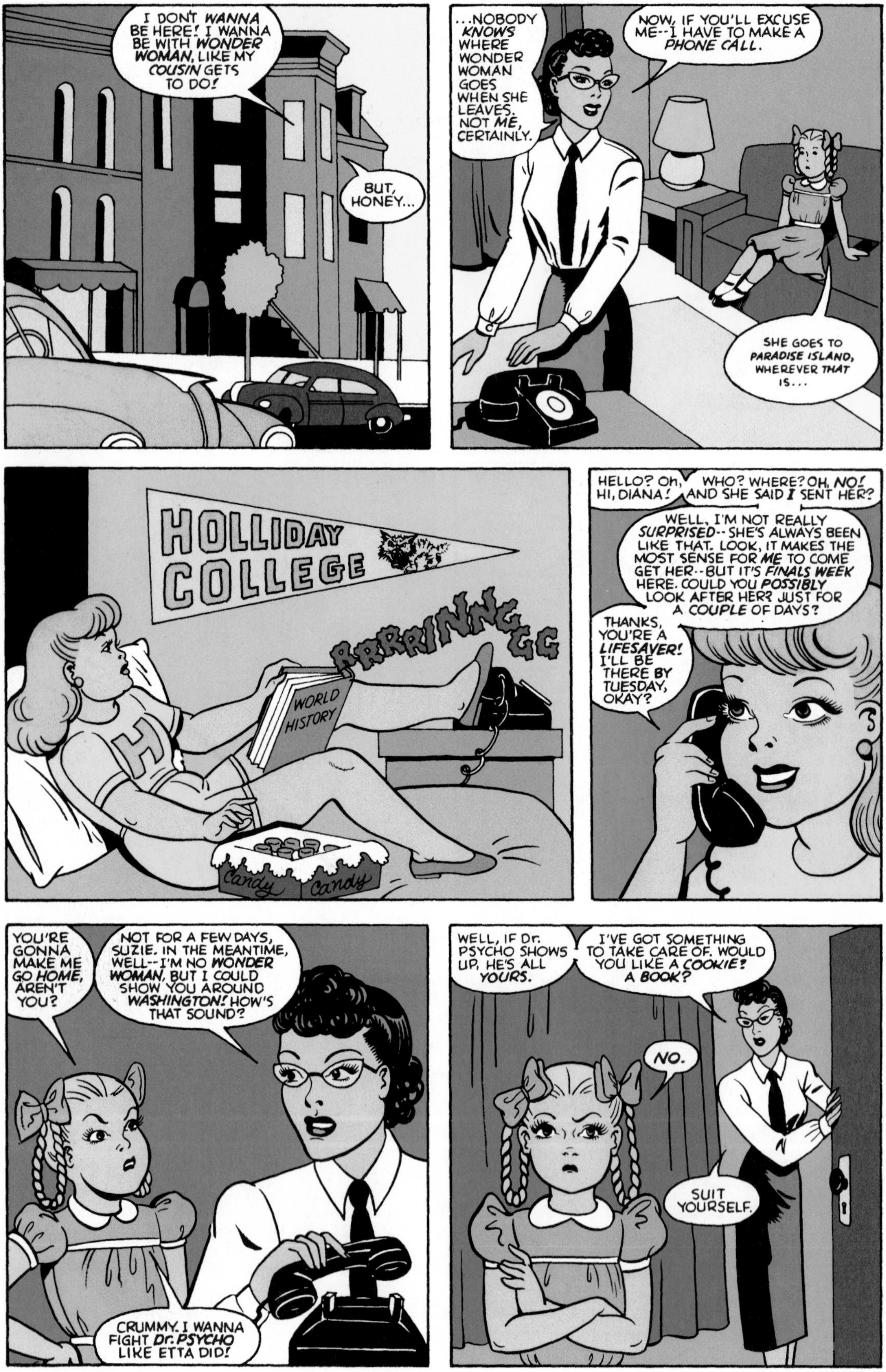

I DON'T WANNA BE HERE! I WANNA BE WITH WONDER WOMAN, LIKE MY COUSIN GETS TO DO!
BUT, HONEY...
...NOBODY KNOWS WHERE WONDER WOMAN GOES WHEN SHE LEAVES. NOT ME, CERTAINLY.
NOW, IF YOU'LL EXCUSE ME--I HAVE TO MAKE A PHONE CALL.
SHE GOES TO PARADISE ISLAND, WHEREVER THAT IS...
HOLLIDAY COLLEGE
RRRRINNGGG
WORLD HISTORY
Candy
Candy
HELLO? Oh, HI, DIANA!
WHO? WHERE? OH, NO! AND SHE SAID I SENT HER?
WELL, I'M NOT REALLY SURPRISED-- SHE'S ALWAYS BEEN LIKE THAT. LOOK, IT MAKES THE MOST SENSE FOR ME TO COME GET HER--BUT IT'S FINALS WEEK HERE. COULD YOU POSSIBLY LOOK AFTER HER? JUST FOR A COUPLE OF DAYS?
THANKS, YOU'RE A LIFESAVER! I'LL BE THERE BY TUESDAY, OKAY?
YOU'RE GONNA MAKE ME GO HOME, AREN'T YOU?
NOT FOR A FEW DAYS, SUZIE. IN THE MEANTIME, WELL--I'M NO WONDER WOMAN, BUT I COULD SHOW YOU AROUND WASHINGTON! HOW'S THAT SOUND?
CRUMMY. I WANNA FIGHT Dr. PSYCHO LIKE ETTA DID!
WELL, IF Dr. PSYCHO SHOWS UP, HE'S ALL YOURS.
I'VE GOT SOMETHING TO TAKE CARE OF. WOULD YOU LIKE A COOKIE? A BOOK?
NO.
SUIT YOURSELF.

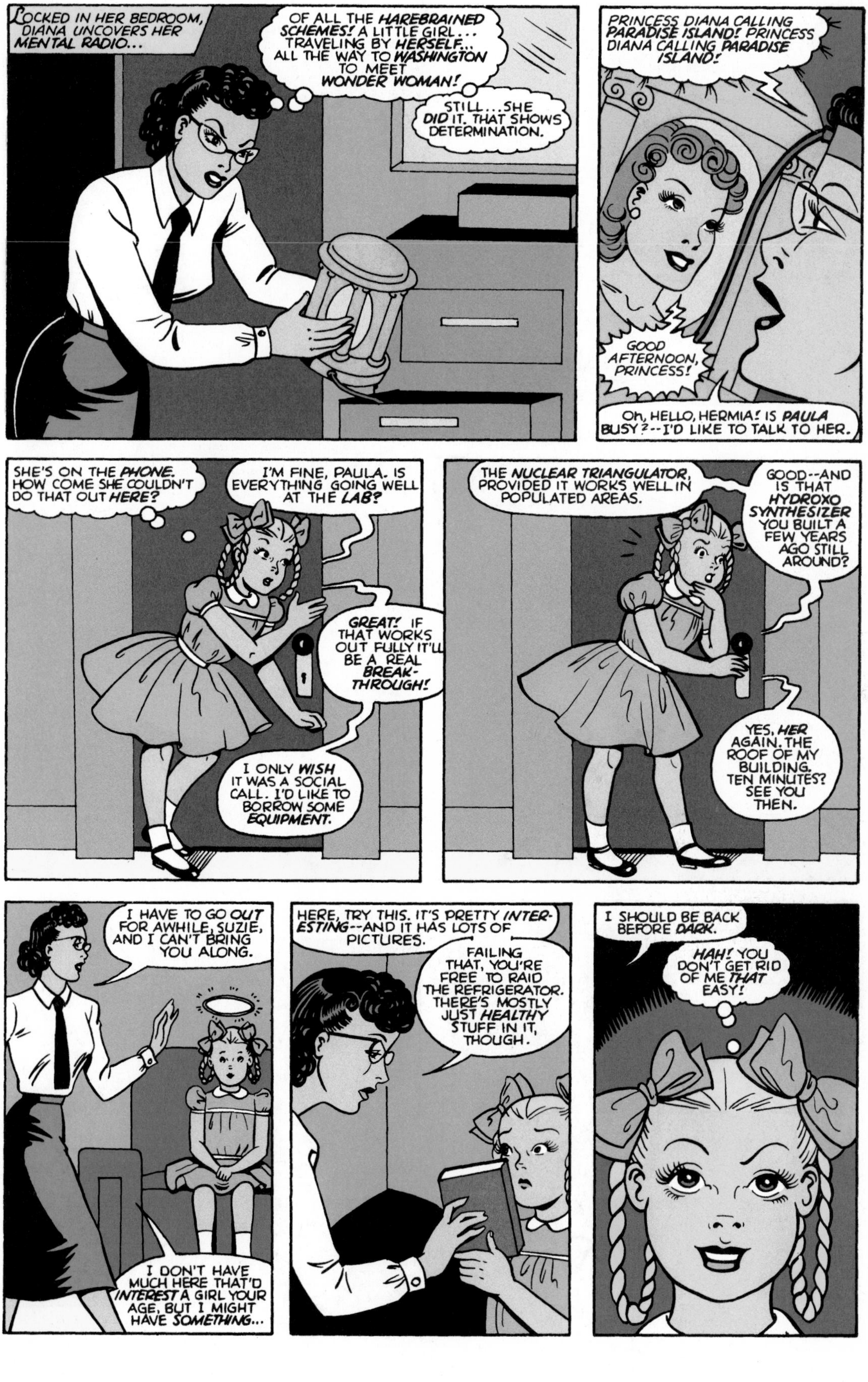
LOCKED IN HER BEDROOM, DIANA UNCOVERS HER MENTAL RADIO...
OF ALL THE HAREBRAINED SCHEMES! A LITTLE GIRL... TRAVELING BY HERSELF... ALL THE WAY TO WASHINGTON TO MEET WONDER WOMAN!
STILL...SHE DID IT. THAT SHOWS DETERMINATION.
PRINCESS DIANA CALLING PARADISE ISLAND! PRINCESS DIANA CALLING PARADISE ISLAND!
GOOD AFTERNOON, PRINCESS!
Oh, HELLO, HERMIA! IS PAULA BUSY?--I'D LIKE TO TALK TO HER.
SHE'S ON THE PHONE. HOW COME SHE COULDN'T DO THAT OUT HERE?
I'M FINE, PAULA. IS EVERYTHING GOING WELL AT THE LAB?
GREAT! IF THAT WORKS OUT FULLY IT'LL BE A REAL BREAK-THROUGH!
I ONLY WISH IT WAS A SOCIAL CALL. I'D LIKE TO BORROW SOME EQUIPMENT.
THE NUCLEAR TRIANGULATOR, PROVIDED IT WORKS WELL IN POPULATED AREAS.
GOOD--AND IS THAT HYDROXO SYNTHESIZER YOU BUILT A FEW YEARS AGO STILL AROUND?
YES, HER AGAIN. THE ROOF OF MY BUILDING. TEN MINUTES? SEE YOU THEN.
I HAVE TO GO OUT FOR AWHILE, SUZIE, AND I CAN'T BRING YOU ALONG.
I DON'T HAVE MUCH HERE THAT'D INTEREST A GIRL YOUR AGE, BUT I MIGHT HAVE SOMETHING...
HERE, TRY THIS. IT'S PRETTY INTER-ESTING--AND IT HAS LOTS OF PICTURES.
FAILING THAT, YOU'RE FREE TO RAID THE REFRIGERATOR. THERE'S MOSTLY JUST HEALTHY STUFF IN IT, THOUGH.
I SHOULD BE BACK BEFORE DARK.
HAH! YOU DON'T GET RID OF ME THAT EASY!

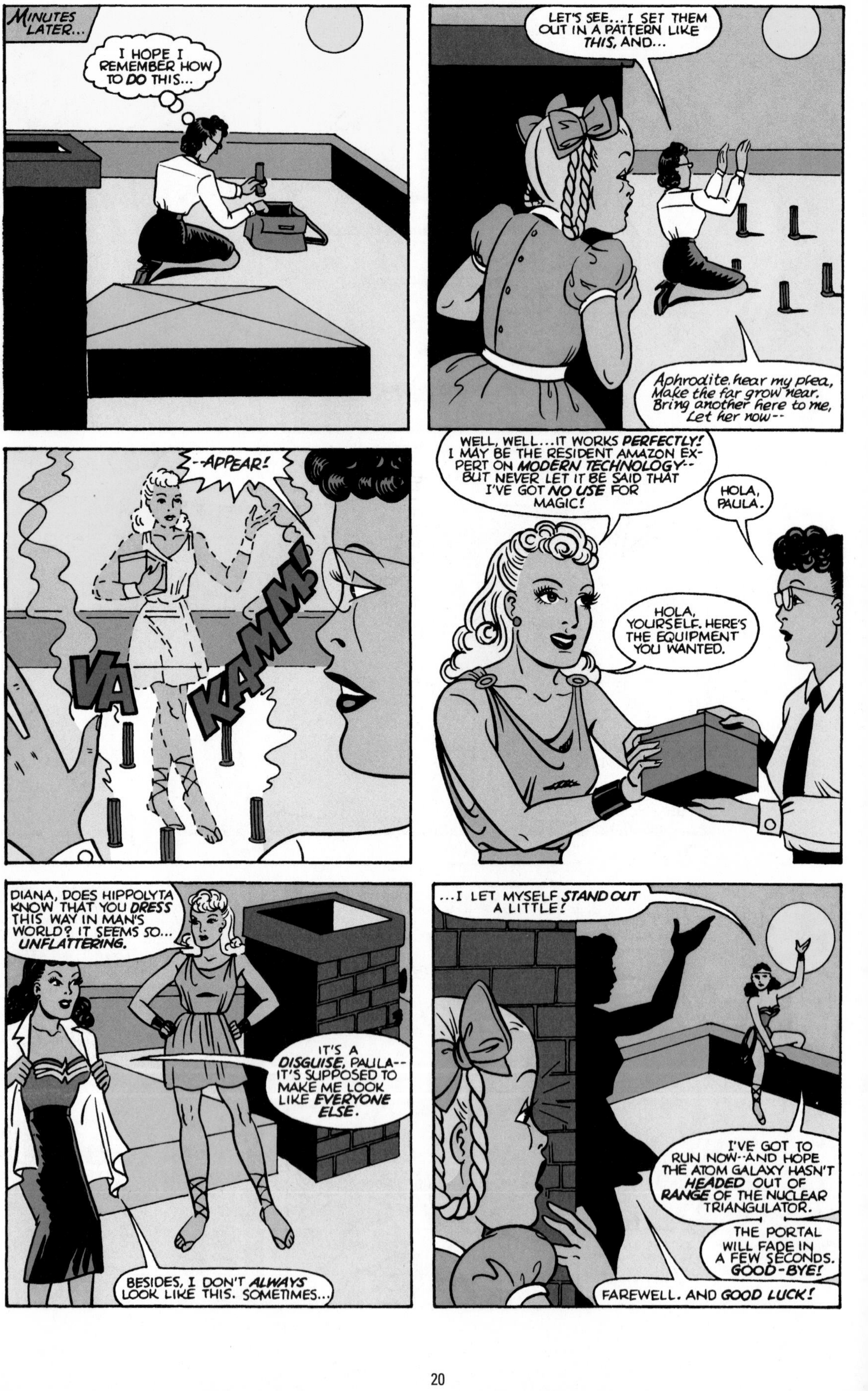

MINUTES LATER...
I HOPE I REMEMBER HOW TO DO THIS...
LET'S SEE... I SET THEM OUT IN A PATTERN LIKE THIS, AND...
Aphrodite, hear my plea, Make the far grow near. Bring another here to me, Let her now--
--APPEAR!
VA KAMM!
WELL, WELL... IT WORKS PERFECTLY! I MAY BE THE RESIDENT AMAZON EXPERT ON MODERN TECHNOLOGY-- BUT NEVER LET IT BE SAID THAT I'VE GOT NO USE FOR MAGIC!
HOLA, PAULA.
HOLA, YOURSELF. HERE'S THE EQUIPMENT YOU WANTED.
DIANA, DOES HIPPOLYTA KNOW THAT YOU DRESS THIS WAY IN MAN'S WORLD? IT SEEMS SO... UNFLATTERING.
IT'S A DISGUISE, PAULA-- IT'S SUPPOSED TO MAKE ME LOOK LIKE EVERYONE ELSE.
BESIDES, I DON'T ALWAYS LOOK LIKE THIS. SOMETIMES...
...I LET MYSELF STAND OUT A LITTLE!
I'VE GOT TO RUN NOW--AND HOPE THE ATOM GALAXY HASN'T HEADED OUT OF RANGE OF THE NUCLEAR TRIANGULATOR.
THE PORTAL WILL FADE IN A FEW SECONDS. GOOD-BYE!
FAREWELL. AND GOOD LUCK!

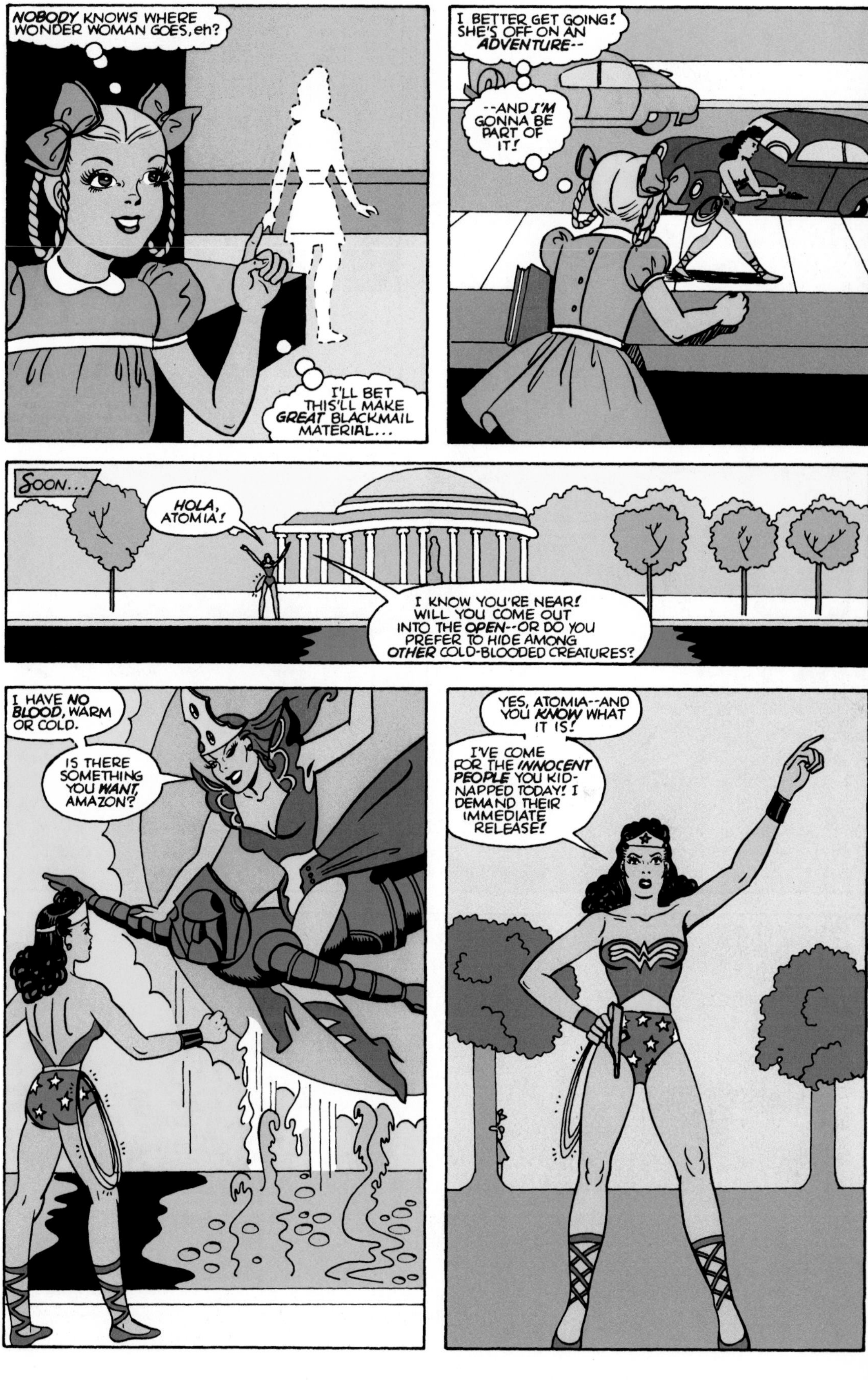
NOBODY KNOWS WHERE WONDER WOMAN GOES, eh?
I'LL BET THIS'LL MAKE GREAT BLACKMAIL MATERIAL...
I BETTER GET GOING! SHE'S OFF ON AN ADVENTURE--
--AND I'M GONNA BE PART OF IT!
SOON...
HOLA, ATOMIA!
I KNOW YOU'RE NEAR! WILL YOU COME OUT INTO THE OPEN--OR DO YOU PREFER TO HIDE AMONG OTHER COLD-BLOODED CREATURES?
I HAVE NO BLOOD, WARM OR COLD.
IS THERE SOMETHING YOU WANT, AMAZON?
YES, ATOMIA--AND YOU KNOW WHAT IT IS!
I'VE COME FOR THE INNOCENT PEOPLE YOU KID-NAPPED TODAY! I DEMAND THEIR IMMEDIATE RELEASE!

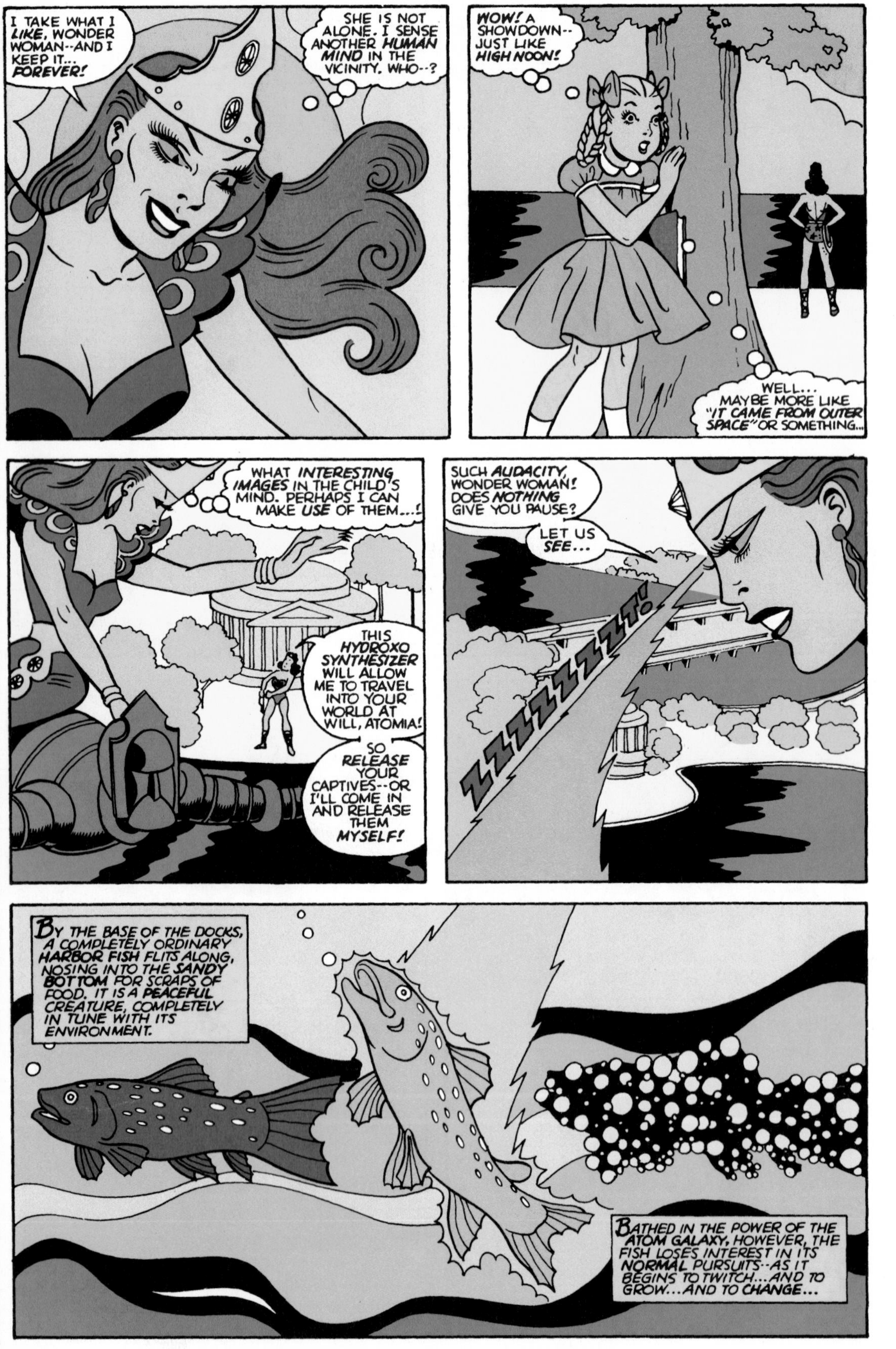

I TAKE WHAT I LIKE, WONDER WOMAN--AND I KEEP IT... FOREVER!
SHE IS NOT ALONE. I SENSE ANOTHER HUMAN MIND IN THE VICINITY. WHO--?
WOW! A SHOWDOWN-- JUST LIKE HIGH NOON!
WELL... MAYBE MORE LIKE "IT CAME FROM OUTER SPACE" OR SOMETHING...
WHAT INTERESTING IMAGES IN THE CHILD'S MIND. PERHAPS I CAN MAKE USE OF THEM...!
THIS HYDROXO SYNTHESIZER WILL ALLOW ME TO TRAVEL INTO YOUR WORLD AT WILL, ATOMIA!
SO RELEASE YOUR CAPTIVES--OR I'LL COME IN AND RELEASE THEM MYSELF!
SUCH AUDACITY, WONDER WOMAN! DOES NOTHING GIVE YOU PAUSE?
LET US SEE...
ZZZZZZZZZT!
BY THE BASE OF THE DOCKS, A COMPLETELY ORDINARY HARBOR FISH FLITS ALONG, NOSING INTO THE SANDY BOTTOM FOR SCRAPS OF FOOD. IT IS A PEACEFUL CREATURE, COMPLETELY IN TUNE WITH ITS ENVIRONMENT.
BATHED IN THE POWER OF THE ATOM GALAXY, HOWEVER, THE FISH LOSES INTEREST IN ITS NORMAL PURSUITS--AS IT BEGINS TO TWITCH... AND TO GROW... AND TO CHANGE...

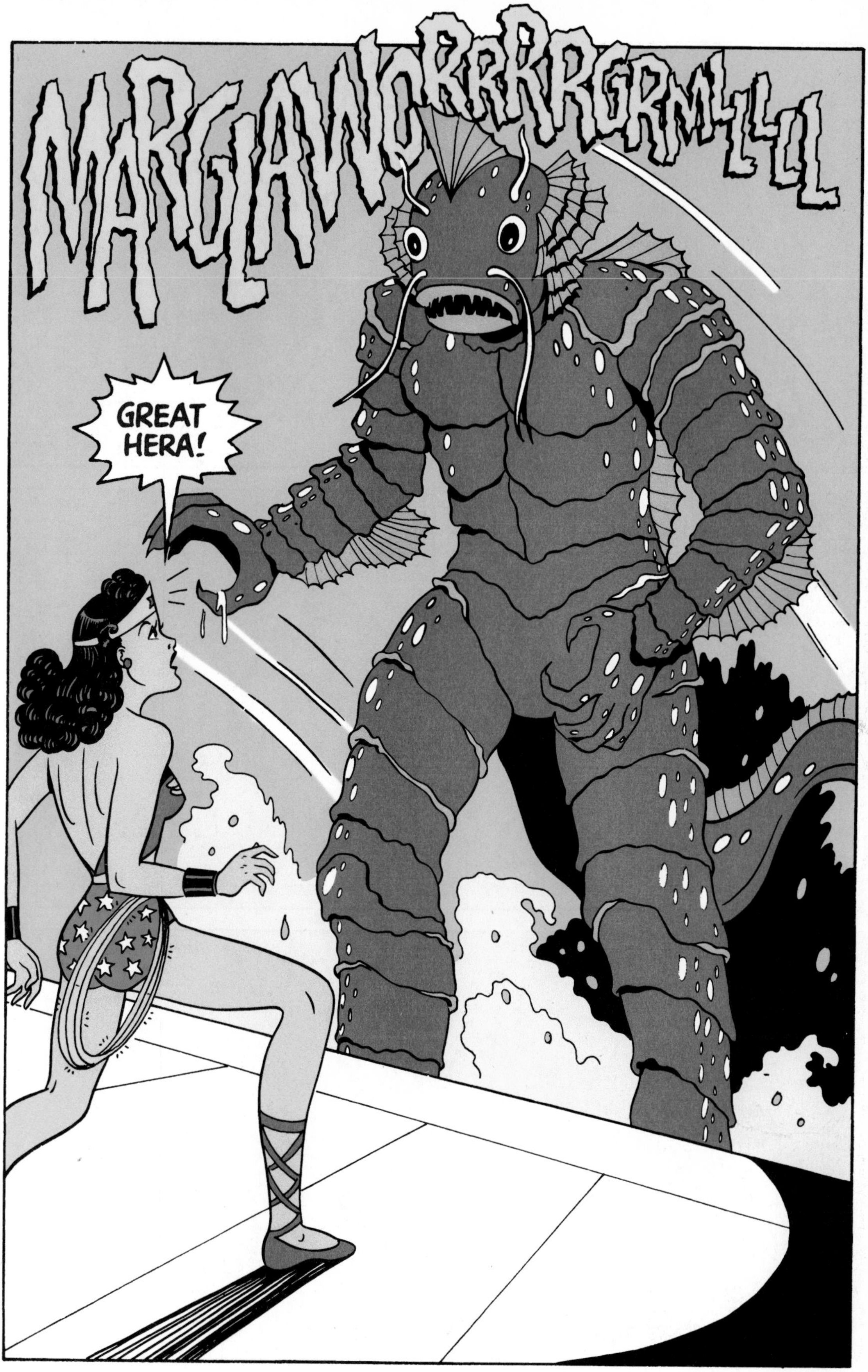
MARGLAWORRRRRGRMLLLL
GREAT HERA!

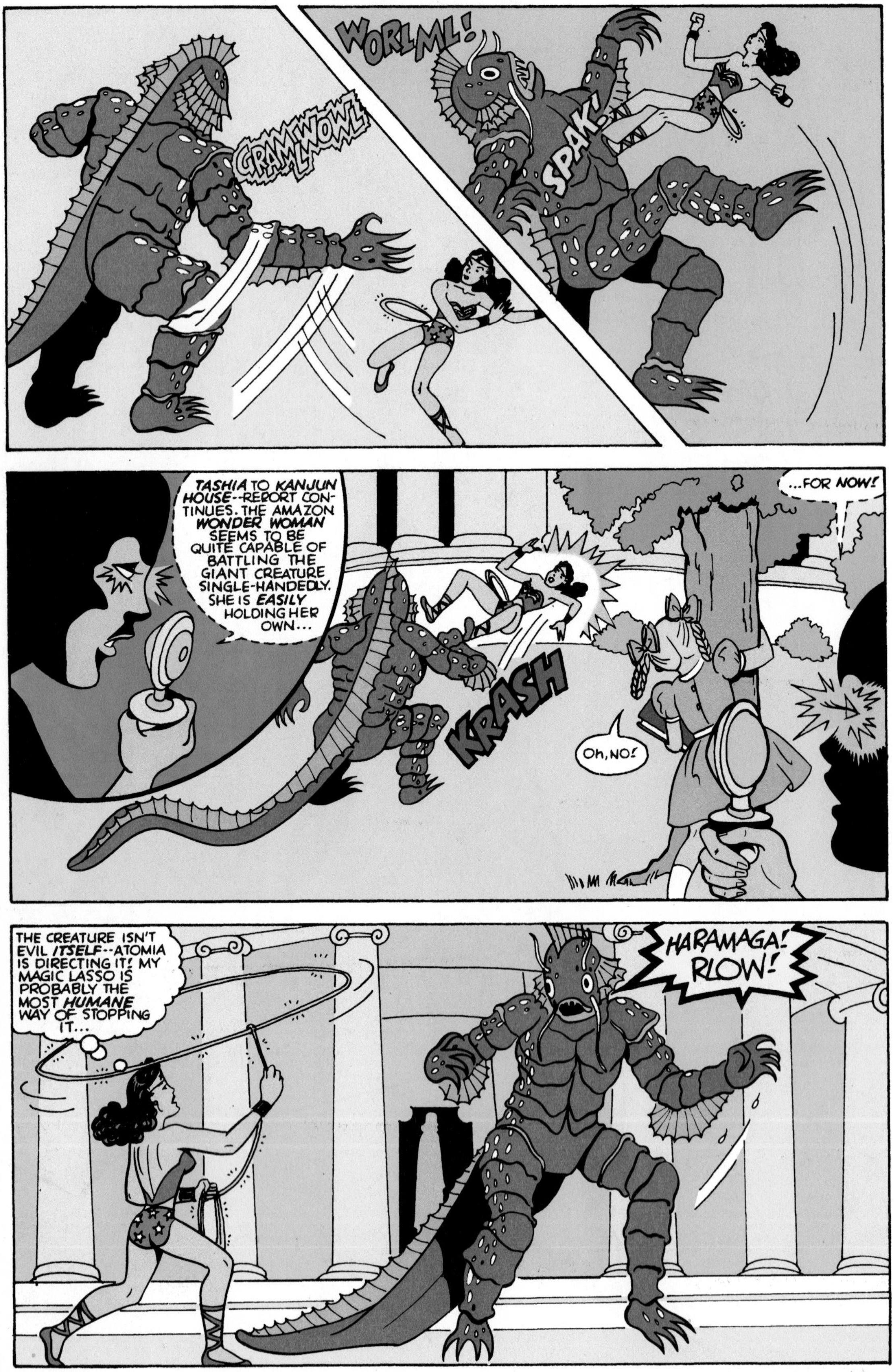
GRAMLWOWL
WORLML!
SPAK!
TASHIA TO KANJUN HOUSE--REPORT CONTINUES. THE AMAZON WONDER WOMAN SEEMS TO BE QUITE CAPABLE OF BATTLING THE GIANT CREATURE SINGLE-HANDEDLY. SHE IS EASILY HOLDING HER OWN...
...FOR NOW!
KRASH
Oh, NO!
THE CREATURE ISN'T EVIL ITSELF--ATOMIA IS DIRECTING IT! MY MAGIC LASSO IS PROBABLY THE MOST HUMANE WAY OF STOPPING IT...
HARAMAGA! RLOW!

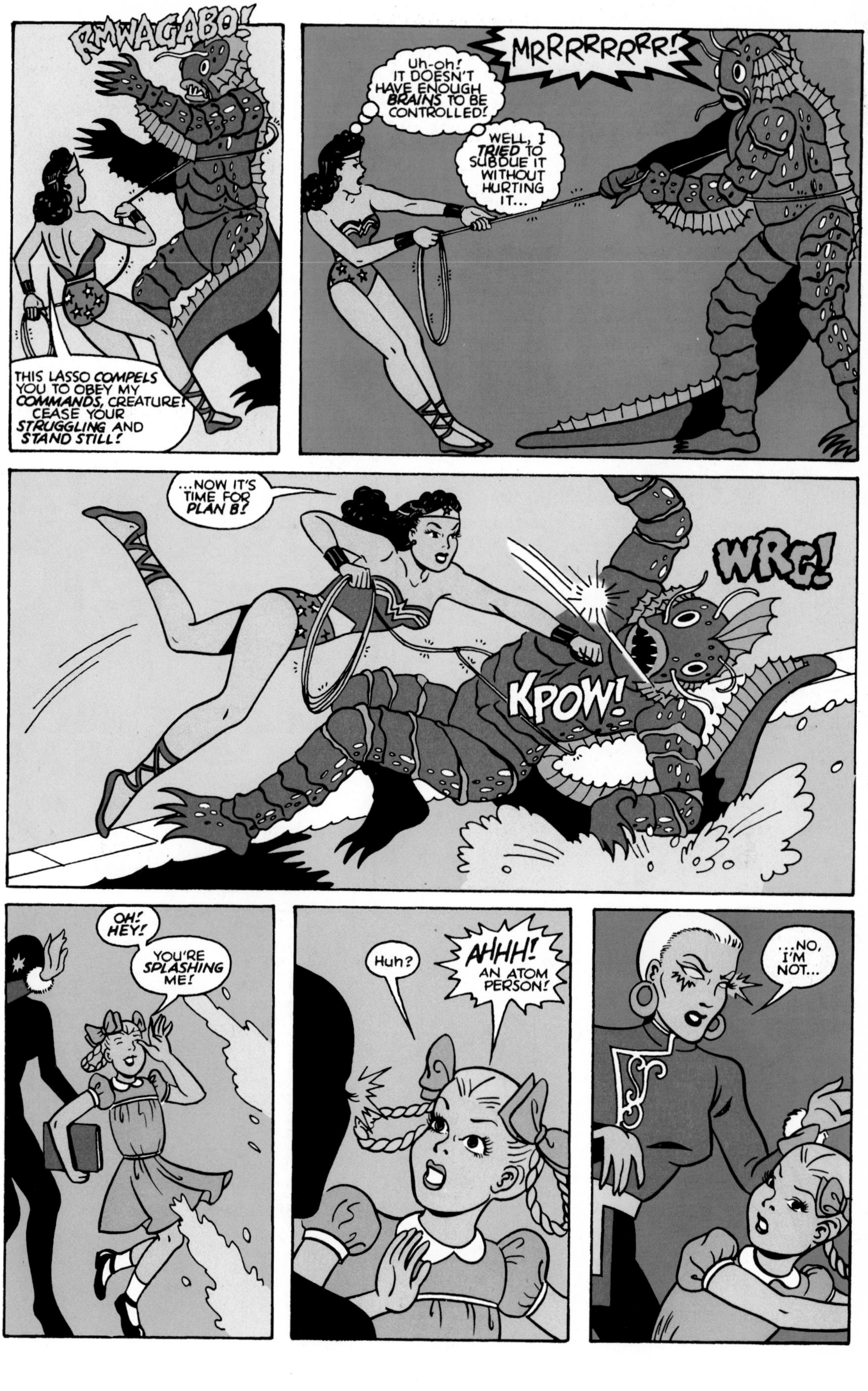
RMWAGABO!
THIS LASSO COMPELS YOU TO OBEY MY COMMANDS, CREATURE! CEASE YOUR STRUGGLING AND STAND STILL!
MRRRRRRRR!
Uh-oh! IT DOESN'T HAVE ENOUGH BRAINS TO BE CONTROLLED!
WELL, I TRIED TO SUBDUE IT WITHOUT HURTING IT...
...NOW IT'S TIME FOR PLAN B!
WRG!
KPOW!
OH! HEY!
YOU'RE SPLASHING ME!
Huh?
AHHH! AN ATOM PERSON!
...NO, I'M NOT...

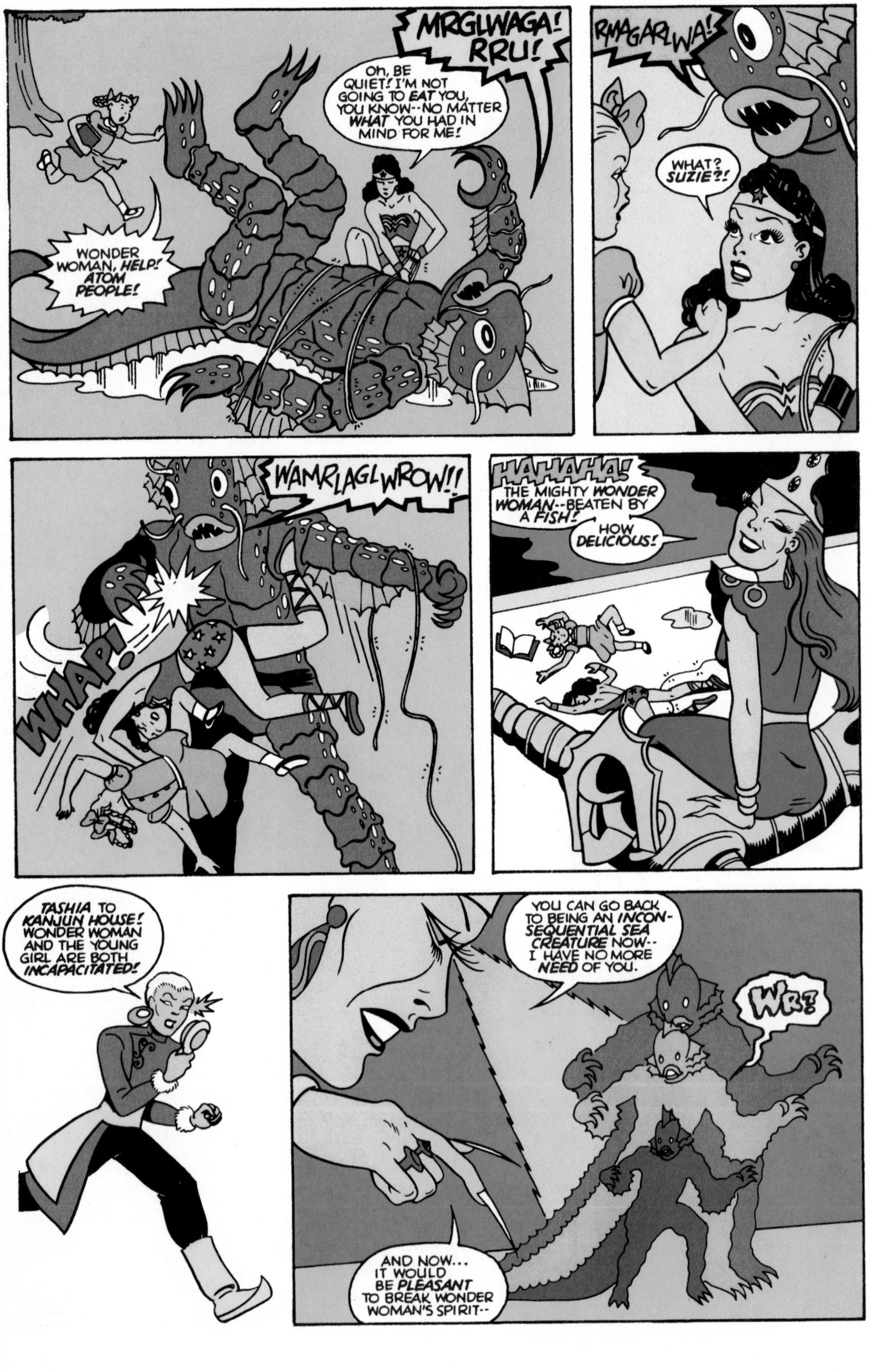
MRGLWAGA! RRU!
Oh, BE QUIET! I'M NOT GOING TO EAT YOU, YOU KNOW--NO MATTER WHAT YOU HAD IN MIND FOR ME!
WONDER WOMAN, HELP! ATOM PEOPLE!
RMAGARLWA!
WHAT? SUZIE?!
WAMRLAGLWROW!!
WHAP!
HAHAHA! THE MIGHTY WONDER WOMAN--BEATEN BY A FISH!
HOW DELICIOUS!
TASHIA TO KANJUN HOUSE! WONDER WOMAN AND THE YOUNG GIRL ARE BOTH INCAPACITATED!
YOU CAN GO BACK TO BEING AN INCON-SEQUENTIAL SEA CREATURE NOW-- I HAVE NO MORE NEED OF YOU.
WR?
AND NOW... IT WOULD BE PLEASANT TO BREAK WONDER WOMAN'S SPIRIT--

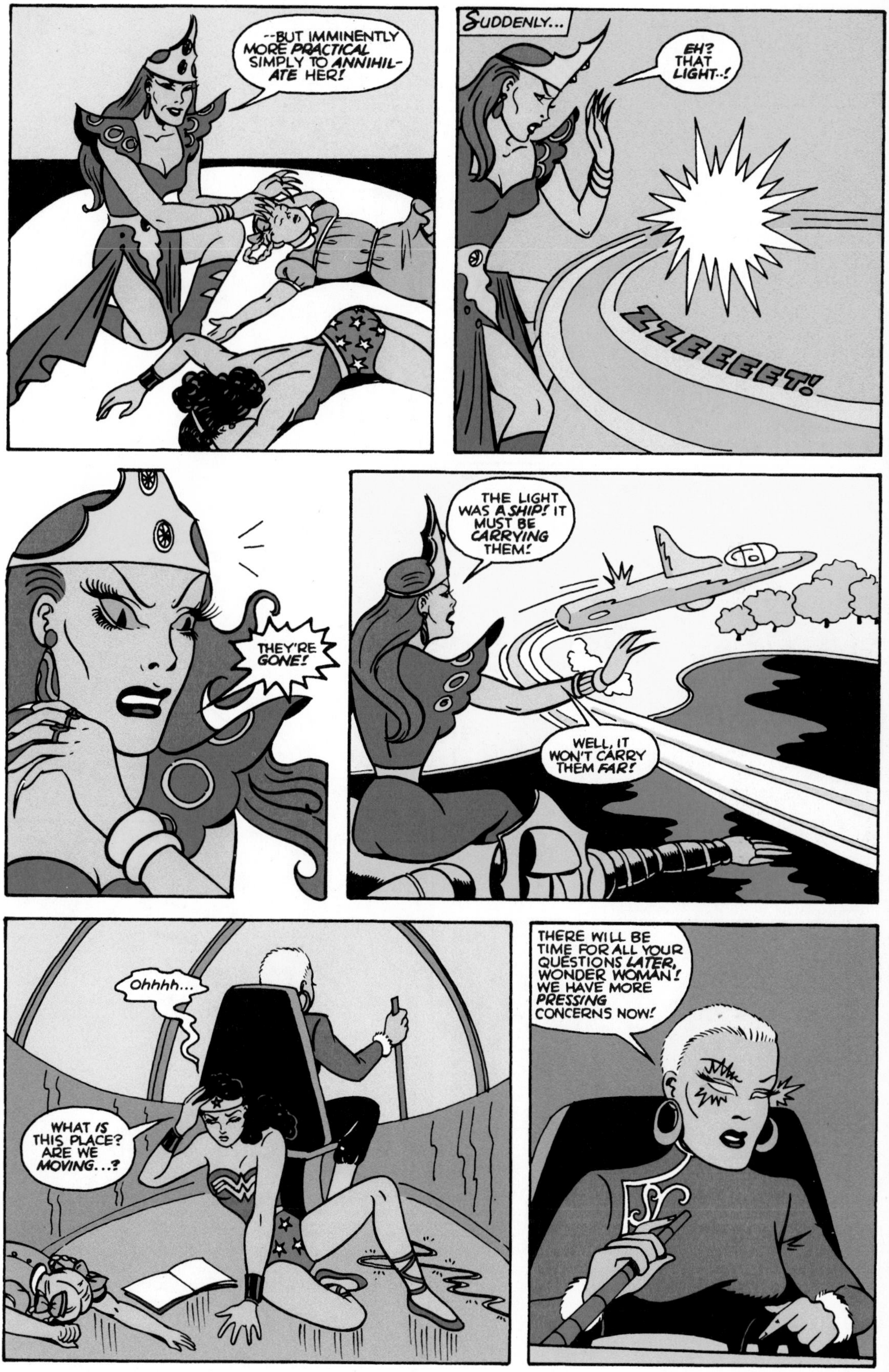
--BUT IMMINENTLY MORE PRACTICAL SIMPLY TO ANNIHILATE HER!
SUDDENLY...
EH? THAT LIGHT..!
ZZEEEET!
THEY'RE GONE!
THE LIGHT WAS A SHIP! IT MUST BE CARRYING THEM!
WELL, IT WON'T CARRY THEM FAR!
Ohhhh...
WHAT IS THIS PLACE? ARE WE MOVING...?
THERE WILL BE TIME FOR ALL YOUR QUESTIONS LATER, WONDER WOMAN! WE HAVE MORE PRESSING CONCERNS NOW!

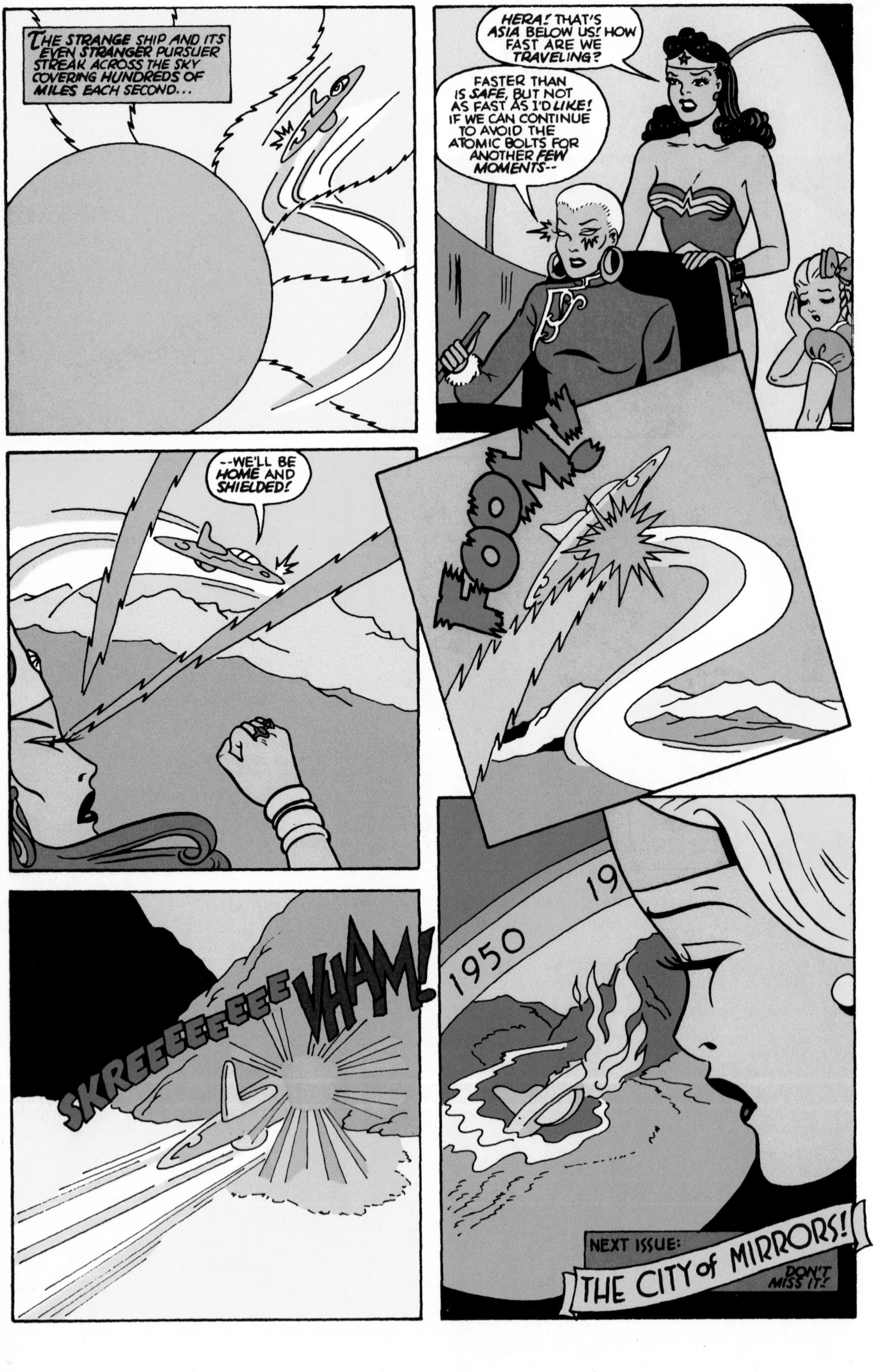

THE STRANGE SHIP AND ITS EVEN STRANGER PURSUER STREAK ACROSS THE SKY COVERING HUNDREDS OF MILES EACH SECOND...
HERA! THAT'S ASIA BELOW US! HOW FAST ARE WE TRAVELING?
FASTER THAN IS SAFE, BUT NOT AS FAST AS I'D LIKE! IF WE CAN CONTINUE TO AVOID THE ATOMIC BOLTS FOR ANOTHER FEW MOMENTS--
--WE'LL BE HOME AND SHIELDED!
FOOOM!
SKREEEEEEEEEE
WHAM!
1950
19
NEXT ISSUE:
THE CITY of MIRRORS!
DON'T MISS IT!

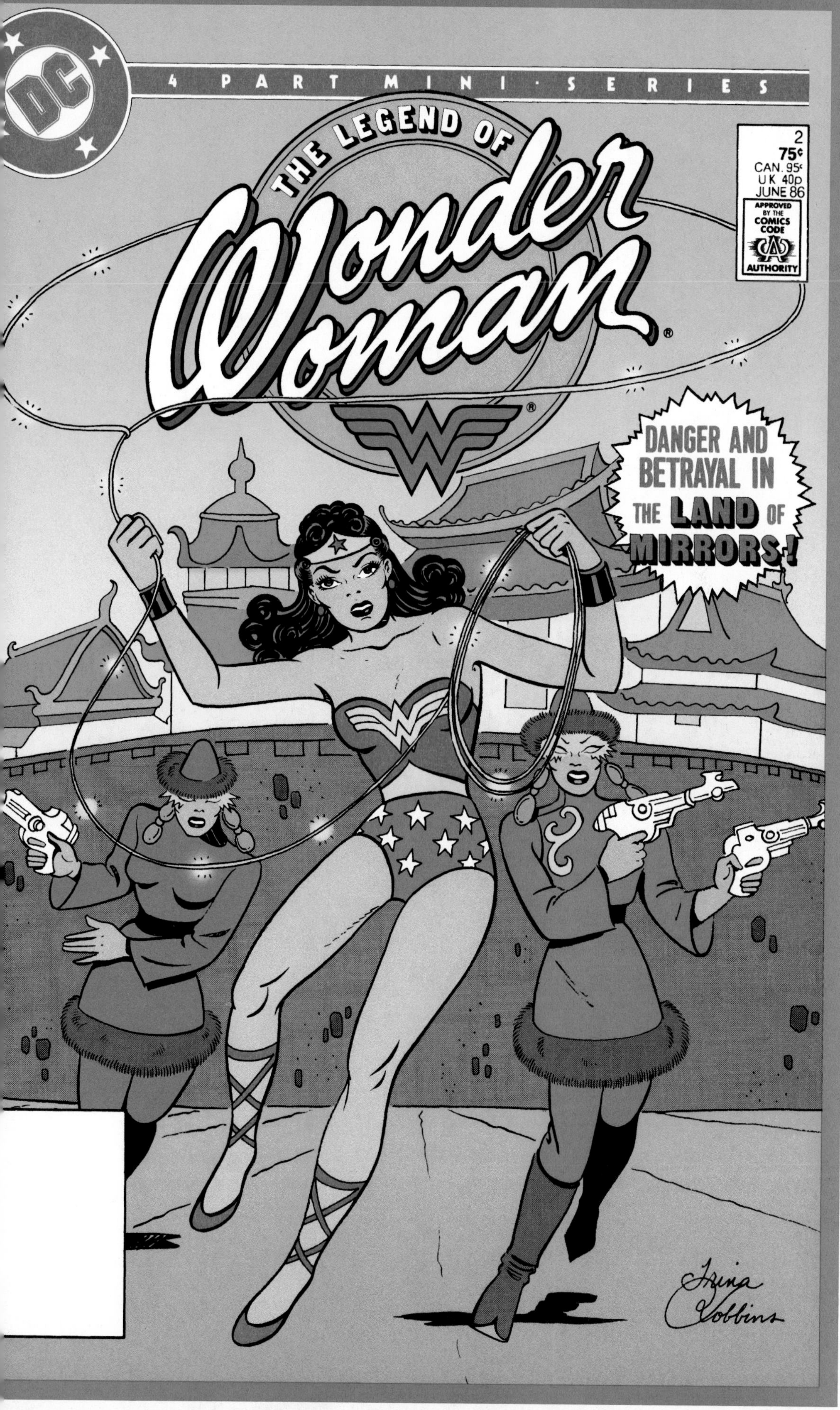
DC
4 PART MINI·SERIES
THE LEGEND OF
Wonder Woman®
2
75¢
CAN. 95¢
U K 40p
JUNE 86
APPROVED BY THE COMICS CODE AUTHORITY
DANGER AND BETRAYAL IN THE LAND OF MIRRORS!
Trina Robbins

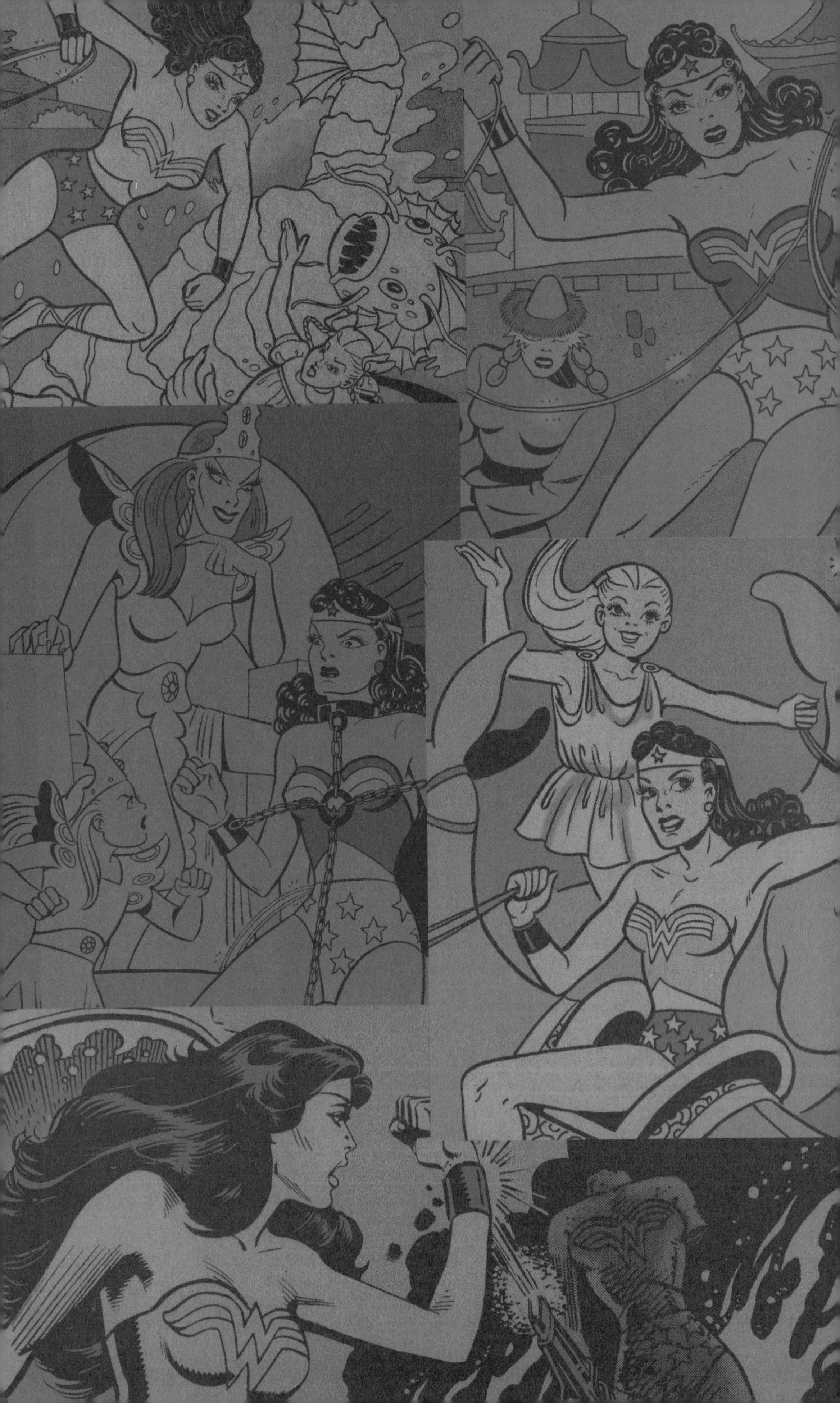

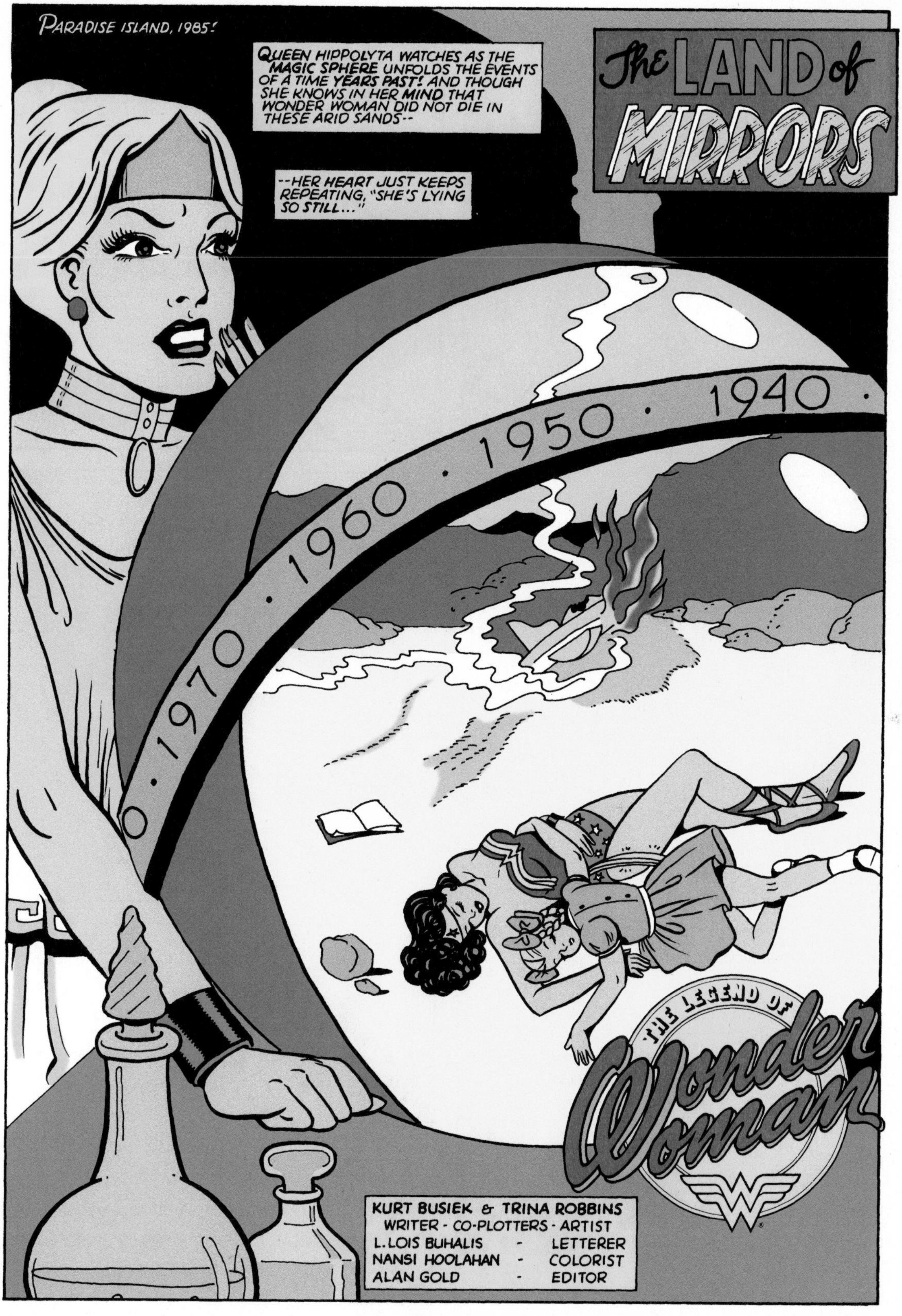

PARADISE ISLAND, 1985!
QUEEN HIPPOLYTA WATCHES AS THE MAGIC SPHERE UNFOLDS THE EVENTS OF A TIME YEARS PAST! AND THOUGH SHE KNOWS IN HER MIND THAT WONDER WOMAN DID NOT DIE IN THESE ARID SANDS--
--HER HEART JUST KEEPS REPEATING, "SHE'S LYING SO STILL..."
The LAND of MIRRORS
1940 · 1950 · 1960 · 1970 ·
THE LEGEND OF Wonder Woman
KURT BUSIEK & TRINA ROBBINS
WRITER - CO-PLOTTERS - ARTIST
L. LOIS BUHALIS - LETTERER
NANSI HOOLAHAN - COLORIST
ALAN GOLD - EDITOR

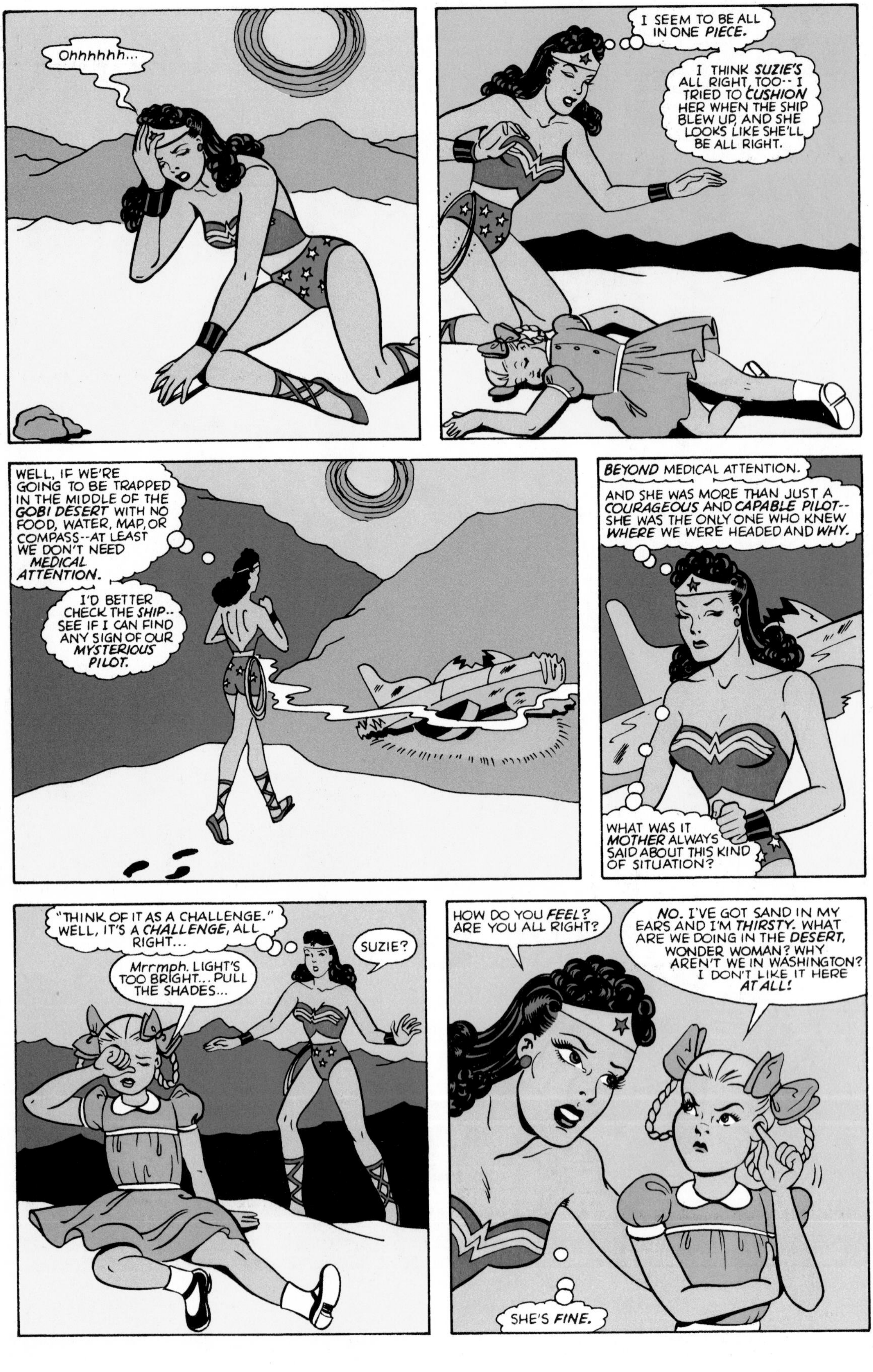

Ohhhhhh...
I SEEM TO BE ALL IN ONE PIECE.
I THINK SUZIE'S ALL RIGHT, TOO-- I TRIED TO CUSHION HER WHEN THE SHIP BLEW UP, AND SHE LOOKS LIKE SHE'LL BE ALL RIGHT.
WELL, IF WE'RE GOING TO BE TRAPPED IN THE MIDDLE OF THE GOBI DESERT WITH NO FOOD, WATER, MAP, OR COMPASS--AT LEAST WE DON'T NEED MEDICAL ATTENTION.
I'D BETTER CHECK THE SHIP.. SEE IF I CAN FIND ANY SIGN OF OUR MYSTERIOUS PILOT.
BEYOND MEDICAL ATTENTION.
AND SHE WAS MORE THAN JUST A COURAGEOUS AND CAPABLE PILOT-- SHE WAS THE ONLY ONE WHO KNEW WHERE WE WERE HEADED AND WHY.
WHAT WAS IT MOTHER ALWAYS SAID ABOUT THIS KIND OF SITUATION?
"THINK OF IT AS A CHALLENGE." WELL, IT'S A CHALLENGE, ALL RIGHT...
SUZIE?
Mrrmph. LIGHT'S TOO BRIGHT... PULL THE SHADES...
HOW DO YOU FEEL? ARE YOU ALL RIGHT?
NO. I'VE GOT SAND IN MY EARS AND I'M THIRSTY. WHAT ARE WE DOING IN THE DESERT, WONDER WOMAN? WHY AREN'T WE IN WASHINGTON? I DON'T LIKE IT HERE AT ALL!
SHE'S FINE.

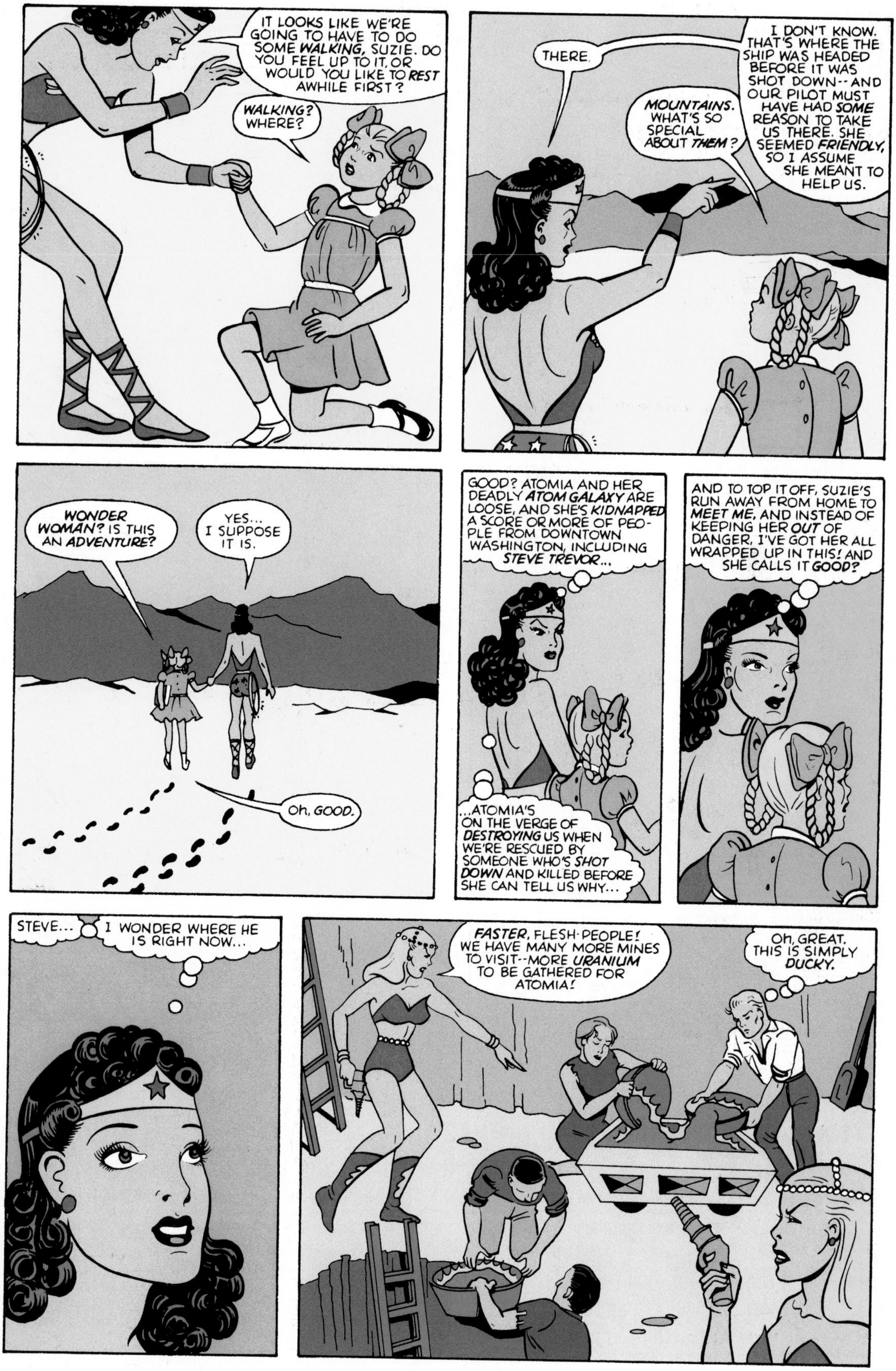
IT LOOKS LIKE WE'RE GOING TO HAVE TO DO SOME WALKING, SUZIE. DO YOU FEEL UP TO IT, OR WOULD YOU LIKE TO REST AWHILE FIRST?
WALKING? WHERE?
THERE.
MOUNTAINS. WHAT'S SO SPECIAL ABOUT THEM?
I DON'T KNOW. THAT'S WHERE THE SHIP WAS HEADED BEFORE IT WAS SHOT DOWN--AND OUR PILOT MUST HAVE HAD SOME REASON TO TAKE US THERE. SHE SEEMED FRIENDLY, SO I ASSUME SHE MEANT TO HELP US.
WONDER WOMAN? IS THIS AN ADVENTURE?
YES... I SUPPOSE IT IS.
Oh, GOOD.
GOOD? ATOMIA AND HER DEADLY ATOM GALAXY ARE LOOSE, AND SHE'S KIDNAPPED A SCORE OR MORE OF PEOPLE FROM DOWNTOWN WASHINGTON, INCLUDING STEVE TREVOR...
...ATOMIA'S ON THE VERGE OF DESTROYING US WHEN WE'RE RESCUED BY SOMEONE WHO'S SHOT DOWN AND KILLED BEFORE SHE CAN TELL US WHY...
AND TO TOP IT OFF, SUZIE'S RUN AWAY FROM HOME TO MEET ME, AND INSTEAD OF KEEPING HER OUT OF DANGER, I'VE GOT HER ALL WRAPPED UP IN THIS! AND SHE CALLS IT GOOD?
STEVE...
I WONDER WHERE HE IS RIGHT NOW...
FASTER, FLESH-PEOPLE! WE HAVE MANY MORE MINES TO VISIT--MORE URANIUM TO BE GATHERED FOR ATOMIA!
Oh, GREAT. THIS IS SIMPLY DUCKY.

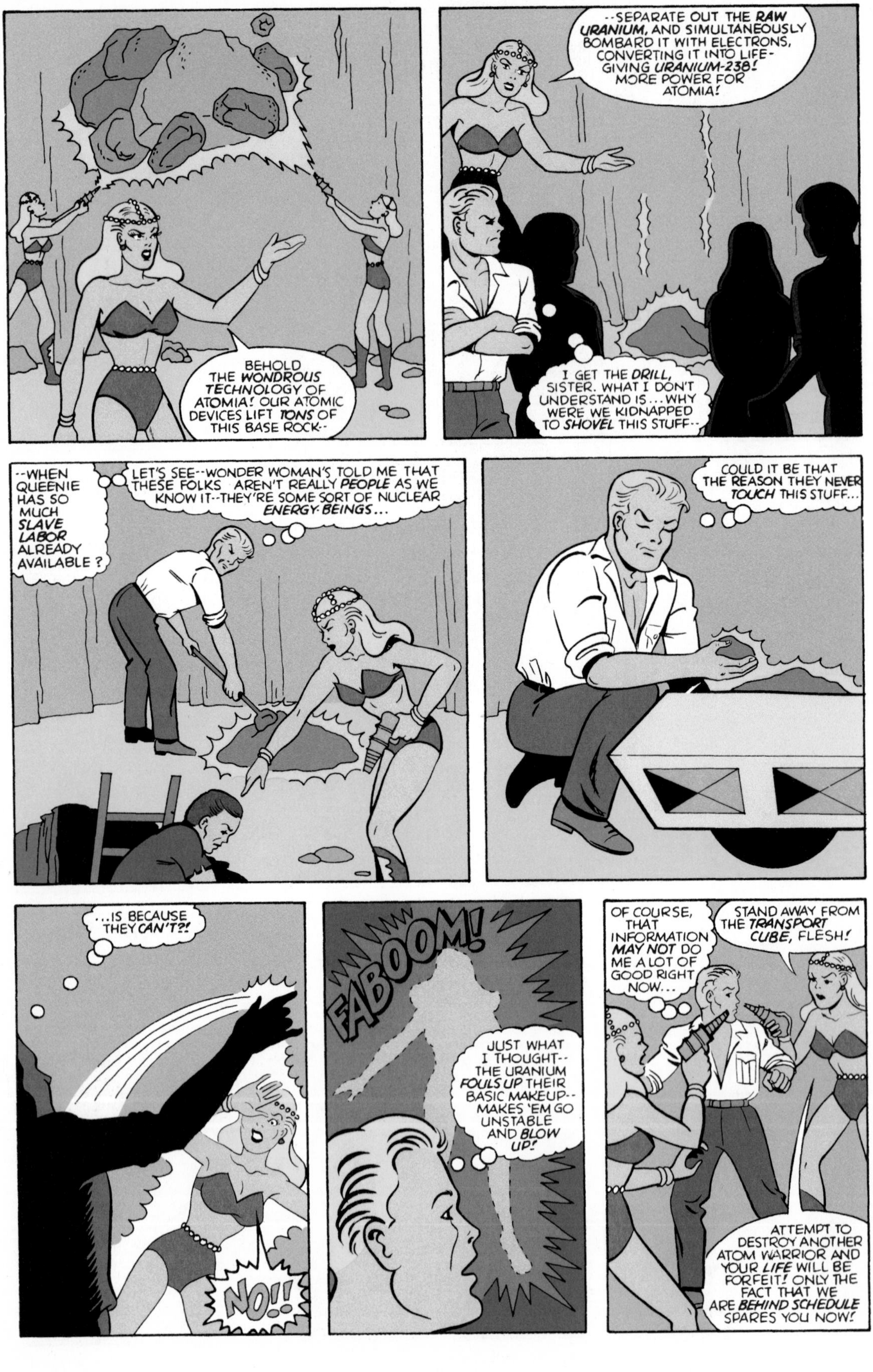
BEHOLD THE WONDROUS TECHNOLOGY OF ATOMIA! OUR ATOMIC DEVICES LIFT TONS OF THIS BASE ROCK--
--SEPARATE OUT THE RAW URANIUM, AND SIMULTANEOUSLY BOMBARD IT WITH ELECTRONS, CONVERTING IT INTO LIFE-GIVING URANIUM-238! MORE POWER FOR ATOMIA!
I GET THE DRILL, SISTER. WHAT I DON'T UNDERSTAND IS... WHY WERE WE KIDNAPPED TO SHOVEL THIS STUFF--
--WHEN QUEENIE HAS SO MUCH SLAVE LABOR ALREADY AVAILABLE?
LET'S SEE--WONDER WOMAN'S TOLD ME THAT THESE FOLKS AREN'T REALLY PEOPLE AS WE KNOW IT--THEY'RE SOME SORT OF NUCLEAR ENERGY-BEINGS...
COULD IT BE THAT THE REASON THEY NEVER TOUCH THIS STUFF...
...IS BECAUSE THEY CAN'T?!
NO!!
FABOOM!
JUST WHAT I THOUGHT-- THE URANIUM FOULS UP THEIR BASIC MAKEUP-- MAKES 'EM GO UNSTABLE AND BLOW UP!
OF COURSE, THAT INFORMATION MAY NOT DO ME A LOT OF GOOD RIGHT NOW...
STAND AWAY FROM THE TRANSPORT CUBE, FLESH!
ATTEMPT TO DESTROY ANOTHER ATOM WARRIOR AND YOUR LIFE WILL BE FORFEIT! ONLY THE FACT THAT WE ARE BEHIND SCHEDULE SPARES YOU NOW!

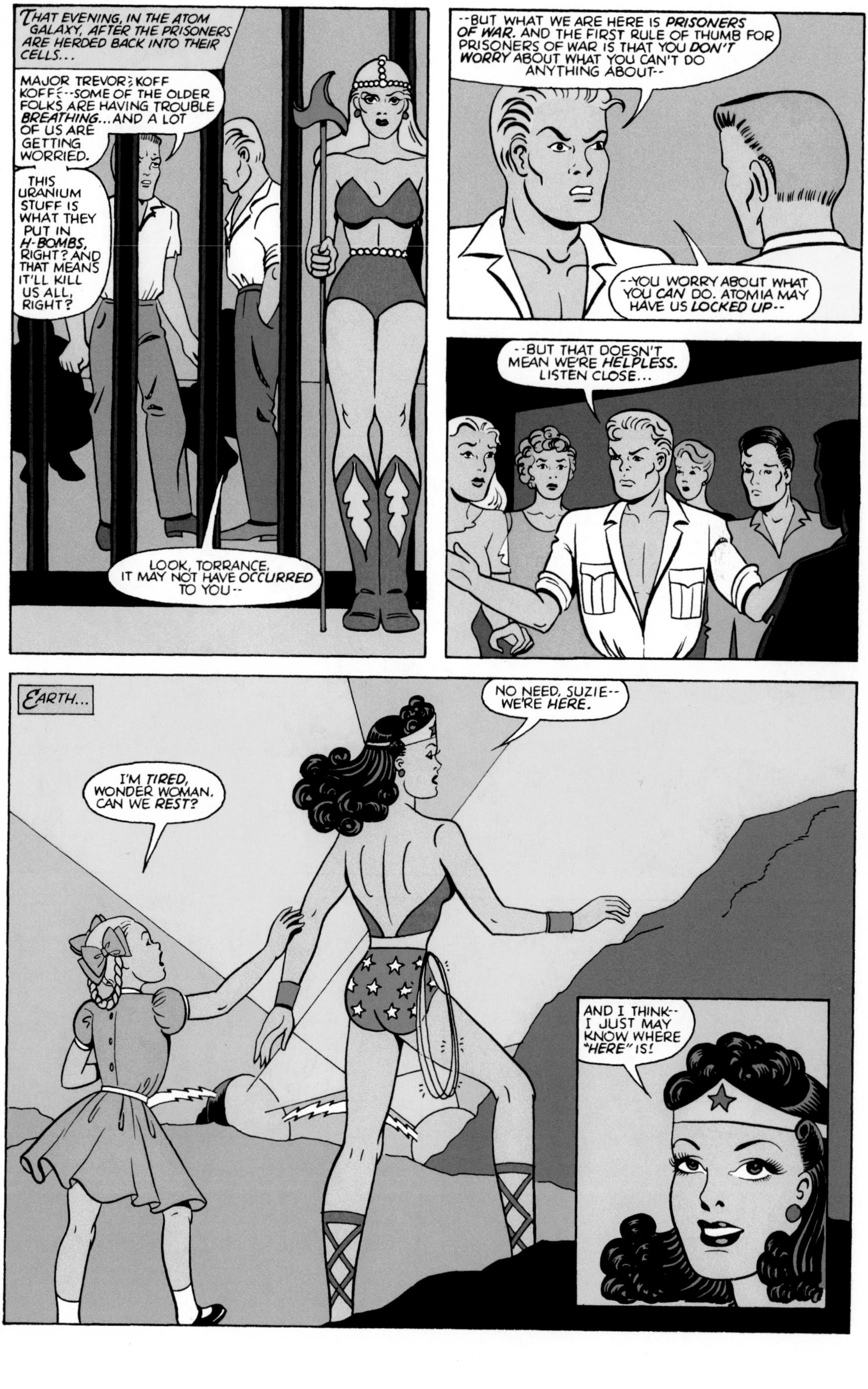
THAT EVENING, IN THE ATOM GALAXY, AFTER THE PRISONERS ARE HERDED BACK INTO THEIR CELLS...
MAJOR TREVOR--KOFF KOFF--SOME OF THE OLDER FOLKS ARE HAVING TROUBLE BREATHING... AND A LOT OF US ARE GETTING WORRIED.
THIS URANIUM STUFF IS WHAT THEY PUT IN H-BOMBS, RIGHT? AND THAT MEANS IT'LL KILL US ALL, RIGHT?
LOOK, TORRANCE, IT MAY NOT HAVE OCCURRED TO YOU--
--BUT WHAT WE ARE HERE IS PRISONERS OF WAR. AND THE FIRST RULE OF THUMB FOR PRISONERS OF WAR IS THAT YOU DON'T WORRY ABOUT WHAT YOU CAN'T DO ANYTHING ABOUT--
--YOU WORRY ABOUT WHAT YOU CAN DO. ATOMIA MAY HAVE US LOCKED UP--
--BUT THAT DOESN'T MEAN WE'RE HELPLESS. LISTEN CLOSE...
EARTH...
I'M TIRED, WONDER WOMAN. CAN WE REST?
NO NEED, SUZIE--WE'RE HERE.
AND I THINK--I JUST MAY KNOW WHERE "HERE" IS!

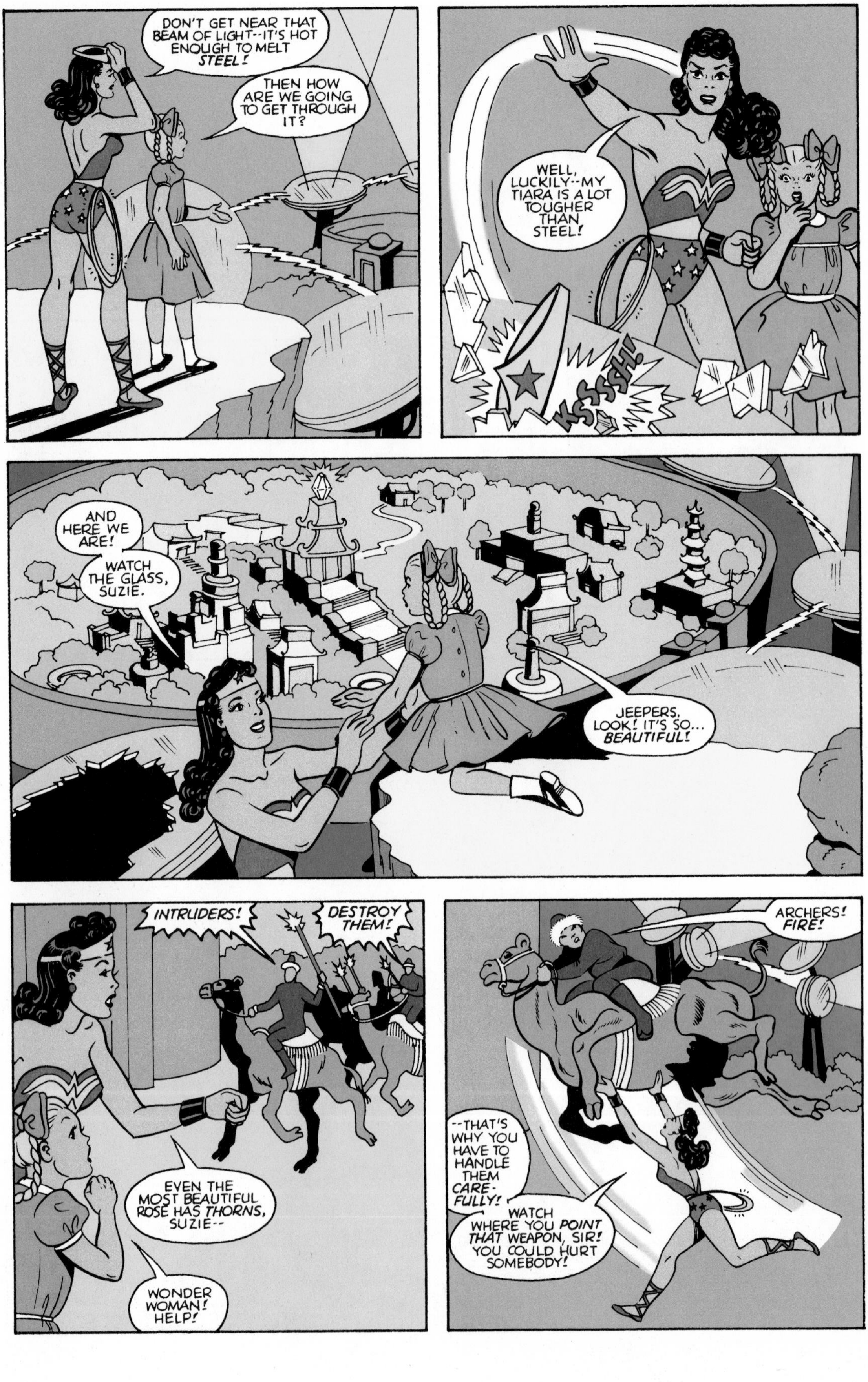
DON'T GET NEAR THAT BEAM OF LIGHT--IT'S HOT ENOUGH TO MELT STEEL!
THEN HOW ARE WE GOING TO GET THROUGH IT?
WELL, LUCKILY--MY TIARA IS A LOT TOUGHER THAN STEEL!
KSSSSH!
AND HERE WE ARE!
WATCH THE GLASS, SUZIE.
JEEPERS, LOOK! IT'S SO... BEAUTIFUL!
INTRUDERS!
DESTROY THEM!
EVEN THE MOST BEAUTIFUL ROSE HAS THORNS, SUZIE--
WONDER WOMAN! HELP!
ARCHERS! FIRE!
--THAT'S WHY YOU HAVE TO HANDLE THEM CARE-FULLY!
WATCH WHERE YOU POINT THAT WEAPON, SIR! YOU COULD HURT SOMEBODY!

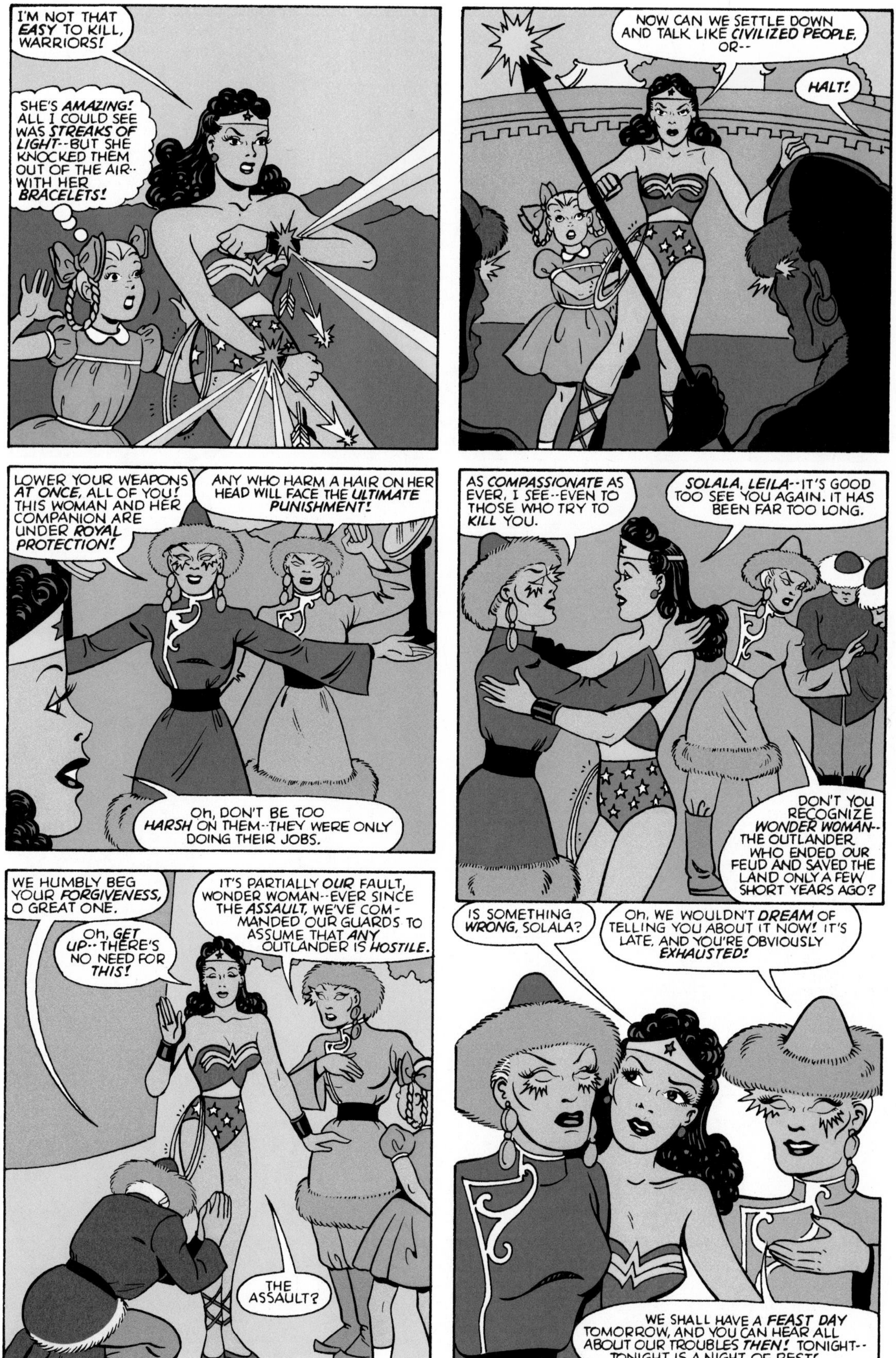

I'M NOT THAT EASY TO KILL, WARRIORS!
SHE'S AMAZING! ALL I COULD SEE WAS STREAKS OF LIGHT--BUT SHE KNOCKED THEM OUT OF THE AIR--WITH HER BRACELETS!
NOW CAN WE SETTLE DOWN AND TALK LIKE CIVILIZED PEOPLE, OR--
HALT!
LOWER YOUR WEAPONS AT ONCE, ALL OF YOU! THIS WOMAN AND HER COMPANION ARE UNDER ROYAL PROTECTION!
ANY WHO HARM A HAIR ON HER HEAD WILL FACE THE ULTIMATE PUNISHMENT!
Oh, DON'T BE TOO HARSH ON THEM--THEY WERE ONLY DOING THEIR JOBS.
AS COMPASSIONATE AS EVER, I SEE--EVEN TO THOSE WHO TRY TO KILL YOU.
SOLALA, LEILA--IT'S GOOD TOO SEE YOU AGAIN. IT HAS BEEN FAR TOO LONG.
DON'T YOU RECOGNIZE WONDER WOMAN--THE OUTLANDER WHO ENDED OUR FEUD AND SAVED THE LAND ONLY A FEW SHORT YEARS AGO?
WE HUMBLY BEG YOUR FORGIVENESS, O GREAT ONE.
Oh, GET UP--THERE'S NO NEED FOR THIS!
IT'S PARTIALLY OUR FAULT, WONDER WOMAN--EVER SINCE THE ASSAULT, WE'VE COMMANDED OUR GUARDS TO ASSUME THAT ANY OUTLANDER IS HOSTILE.
THE ASSAULT?
IS SOMETHING WRONG, SOLALA?
Oh, WE WOULDN'T DREAM OF TELLING YOU ABOUT IT NOW! IT'S LATE, AND YOU'RE OBVIOUSLY EXHAUSTED!
WE SHALL HAVE A FEAST DAY TOMORROW, AND YOU CAN HEAR ALL ABOUT OUR TROUBLES THEN! TONIGHT--TONIGHT IS A NIGHT OF REST!

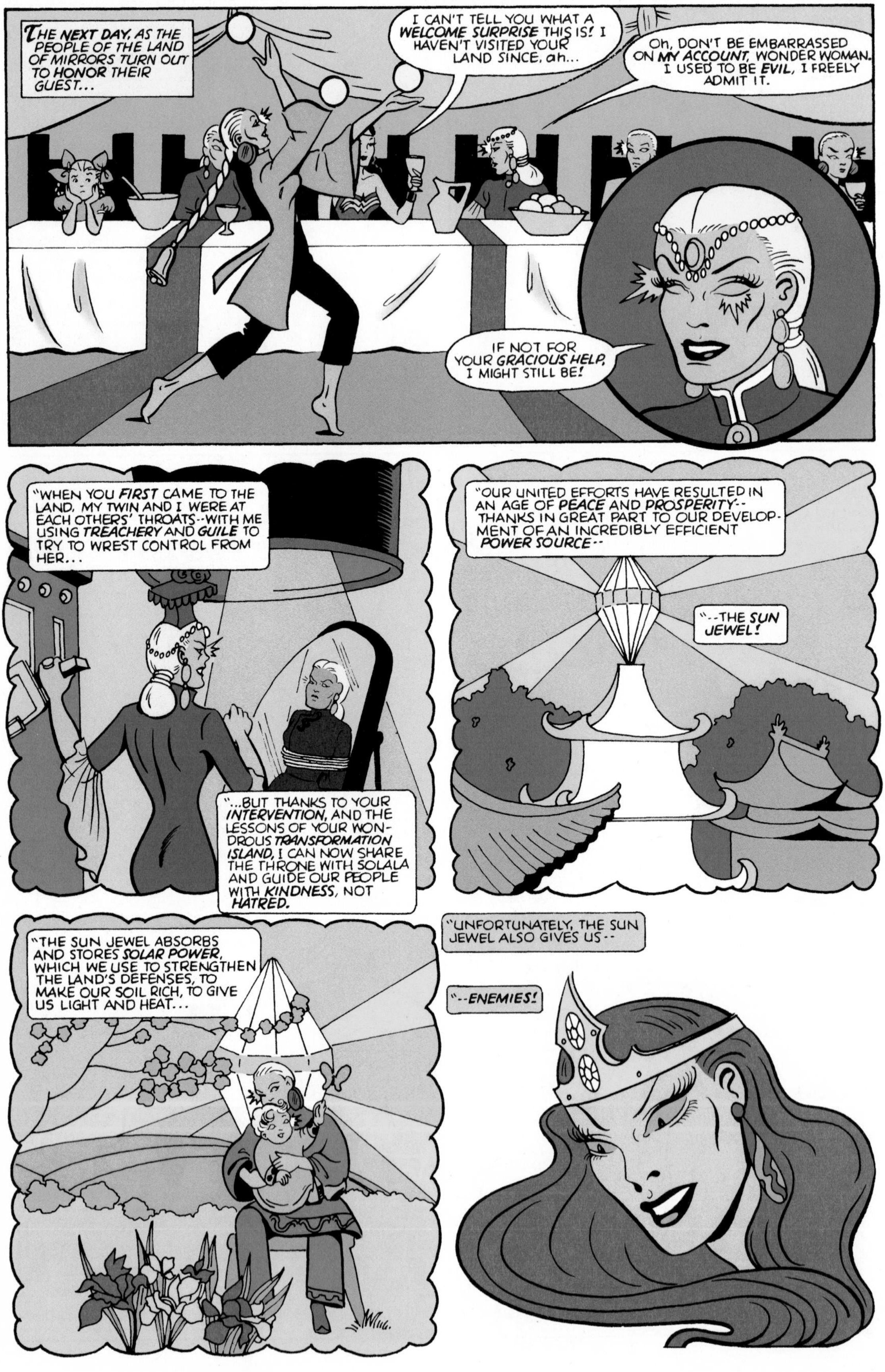
THE NEXT DAY, AS THE PEOPLE OF THE LAND OF MIRRORS TURN OUT TO HONOR THEIR GUEST...
I CAN'T TELL YOU WHAT A WELCOME SURPRISE THIS IS! I HAVEN'T VISITED YOUR LAND SINCE, ah...
Oh, DON'T BE EMBARRASSED ON MY ACCOUNT, WONDER WOMAN. I USED TO BE EVIL, I FREELY ADMIT IT.
IF NOT FOR YOUR GRACIOUS HELP, I MIGHT STILL BE!
"WHEN YOU FIRST CAME TO THE LAND, MY TWIN AND I WERE AT EACH OTHERS' THROATS--WITH ME USING TREACHERY AND GUILE TO TRY TO WREST CONTROL FROM HER...
"...BUT THANKS TO YOUR INTERVENTION, AND THE LESSONS OF YOUR WONDROUS TRANSFORMATION ISLAND, I CAN NOW SHARE THE THRONE WITH SOLALA AND GUIDE OUR PEOPLE WITH KINDNESS, NOT HATRED.
"OUR UNITED EFFORTS HAVE RESULTED IN AN AGE OF PEACE AND PROSPERITY-- THANKS IN GREAT PART TO OUR DEVELOPMENT OF AN INCREDIBLY EFFICIENT POWER SOURCE--
"--THE SUN JEWEL!
"THE SUN JEWEL ABSORBS AND STORES SOLAR POWER, WHICH WE USE TO STRENGTHEN THE LAND'S DEFENSES, TO MAKE OUR SOIL RICH, TO GIVE US LIGHT AND HEAT...
"UNFORTUNATELY, THE SUN JEWEL ALSO GIVES US--
"--ENEMIES!

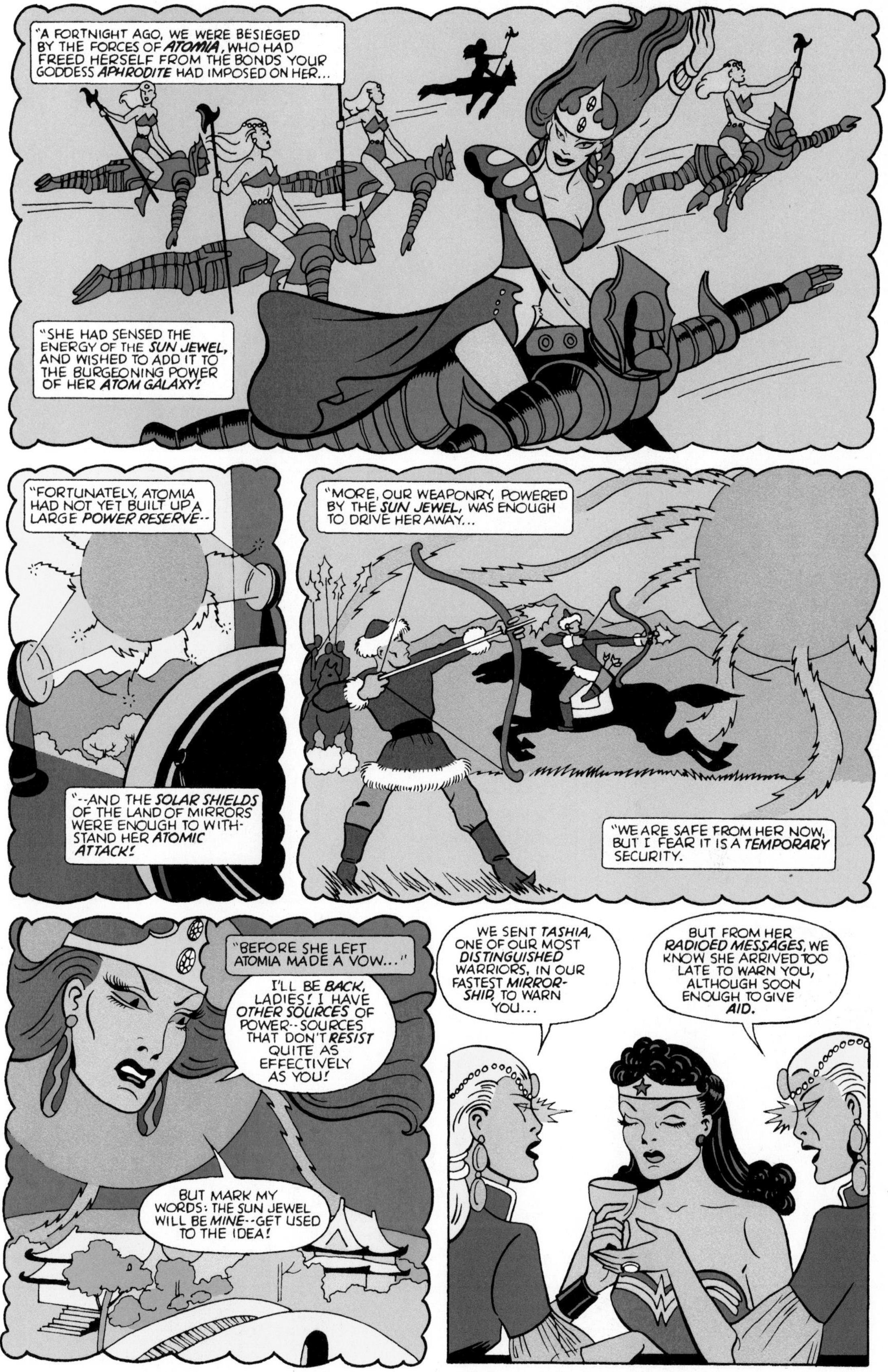
"A FORTNIGHT AGO, WE WERE BESIEGED BY THE FORCES OF ATOMIA, WHO HAD FREED HERSELF FROM THE BONDS YOUR GODDESS APHRODITE HAD IMPOSED ON HER...
"SHE HAD SENSED THE ENERGY OF THE SUN JEWEL, AND WISHED TO ADD IT TO THE BURGEONING POWER OF HER ATOM GALAXY!
"FORTUNATELY, ATOMIA HAD NOT YET BUILT UP A LARGE POWER RESERVE--
"--AND THE SOLAR SHIELDS OF THE LAND OF MIRRORS WERE ENOUGH TO WITH-STAND HER ATOMIC ATTACK!
"MORE, OUR WEAPONRY, POWERED BY THE SUN JEWEL, WAS ENOUGH TO DRIVE HER AWAY...
"WE ARE SAFE FROM HER NOW, BUT I FEAR IT IS A TEMPORARY SECURITY.
"BEFORE SHE LEFT ATOMIA MADE A VOW..."
I'LL BE BACK, LADIES! I HAVE OTHER SOURCES OF POWER--SOURCES THAT DON'T RESIST QUITE AS EFFECTIVELY AS YOU!
BUT MARK MY WORDS: THE SUN JEWEL WILL BE MINE--GET USED TO THE IDEA!
WE SENT TASHIA, ONE OF OUR MOST DISTINGUISHED WARRIORS, IN OUR FASTEST MIRROR-SHIP, TO WARN YOU...
BUT FROM HER RADIOED MESSAGES, WE KNOW SHE ARRIVED TOO LATE TO WARN YOU, ALTHOUGH SOON ENOUGH TO GIVE AID.

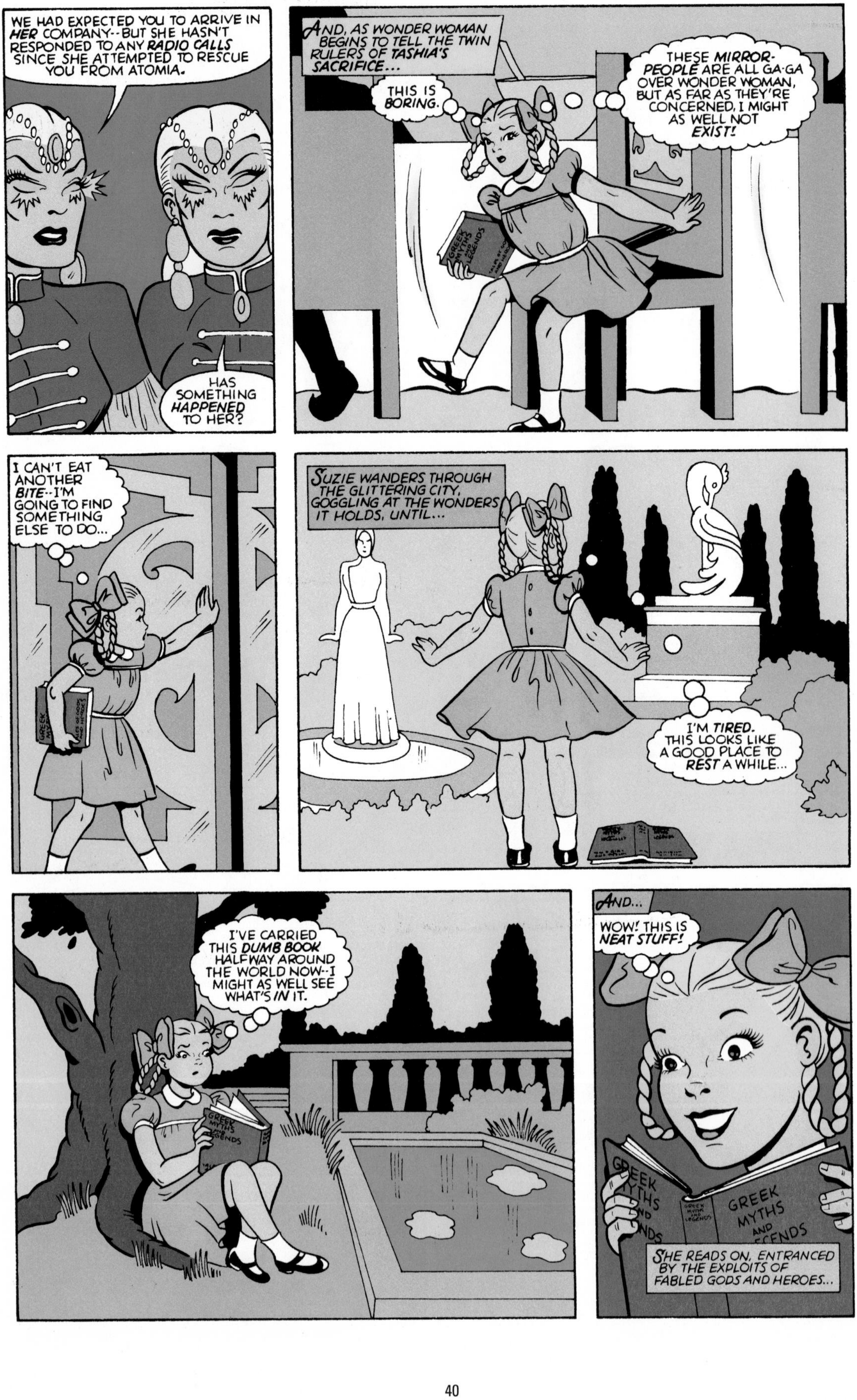
WE HAD EXPECTED YOU TO ARRIVE IN HER COMPANY--BUT SHE HASN'T RESPONDED TO ANY RADIO CALLS SINCE SHE ATTEMPTED TO RESCUE YOU FROM ATOMIA.
HAS SOMETHING HAPPENED TO HER?
AND, AS WONDER WOMAN BEGINS TO TELL THE TWIN RULERS OF TASHIA'S SACRIFICE...
THIS IS BORING.
THESE MIRROR-PEOPLE ARE ALL GA-GA OVER WONDER WOMAN, BUT AS FAR AS THEY'RE CONCERNED, I MIGHT AS WELL NOT EXIST!
I CAN'T EAT ANOTHER BITE--I'M GOING TO FIND SOMETHING ELSE TO DO...
SUZIE WANDERS THROUGH THE GLITTERING CITY, GOGGLING AT THE WONDERS IT HOLDS, UNTIL...
I'M TIRED. THIS LOOKS LIKE A GOOD PLACE TO REST A WHILE...
I'VE CARRIED THIS DUMB BOOK HALFWAY AROUND THE WORLD NOW--I MIGHT AS WELL SEE WHAT'S IN IT.
AND...
WOW! THIS IS NEAT STUFF!
GREEK MYTHS AND LEGENDS
SHE READS ON, ENTRANCED BY THE EXPLOITS OF FABLED GODS AND HEROES...

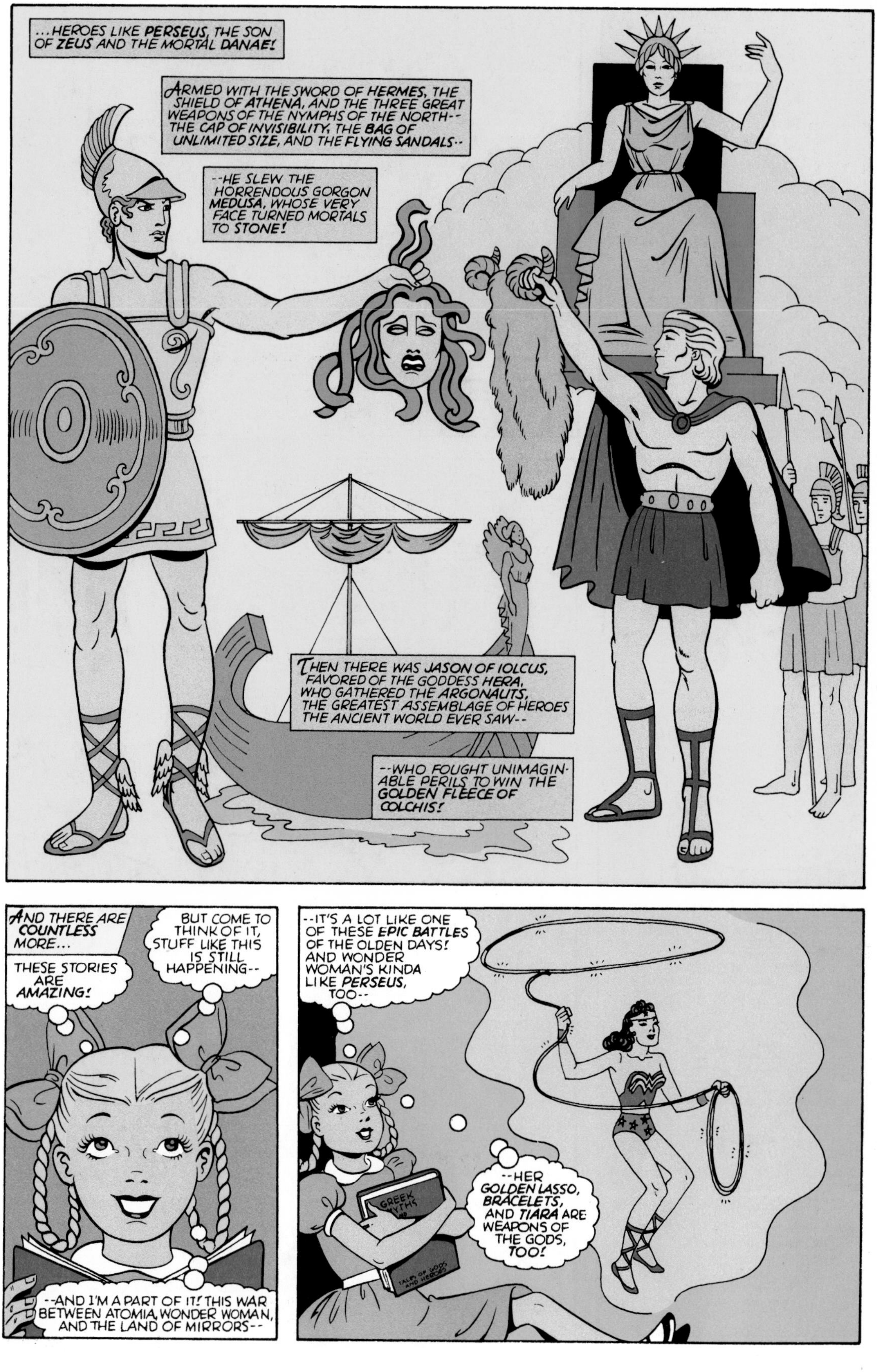
...HEROES LIKE PERSEUS, THE SON OF ZEUS AND THE MORTAL DANAE!
ARMED WITH THE SWORD OF HERMES, THE SHIELD OF ATHENA, AND THE THREE GREAT WEAPONS OF THE NYMPHS OF THE NORTH-- THE CAP OF INVISIBILITY, THE BAG OF UNLIMITED SIZE, AND THE FLYING SANDALS--
--HE SLEW THE HORRENDOUS GORGON MEDUSA, WHOSE VERY FACE TURNED MORTALS TO STONE!
THEN THERE WAS JASON OF IOLCUS, FAVORED OF THE GODDESS HERA, WHO GATHERED THE ARGONAUTS, THE GREATEST ASSEMBLAGE OF HEROES THE ANCIENT WORLD EVER SAW--
--WHO FOUGHT UNIMAGINABLE PERILS TO WIN THE GOLDEN FLEECE OF COLCHIS!
AND THERE ARE COUNTLESS MORE...
THESE STORIES ARE AMAZING!
BUT COME TO THINK OF IT, STUFF LIKE THIS IS STILL HAPPENING--
--AND I'M A PART OF IT! THIS WAR BETWEEN ATOMIA, WONDER WOMAN, AND THE LAND OF MIRRORS--
--IT'S A LOT LIKE ONE OF THESE EPIC BATTLES OF THE OLDEN DAYS! AND WONDER WOMAN'S KINDA LIKE PERSEUS, TOO--
--HER GOLDEN LASSO, BRACELETS, AND TIARA ARE WEAPONS OF THE GODS, TOO!
GREEK MYTHS
TALES OF GODS AND HEROES

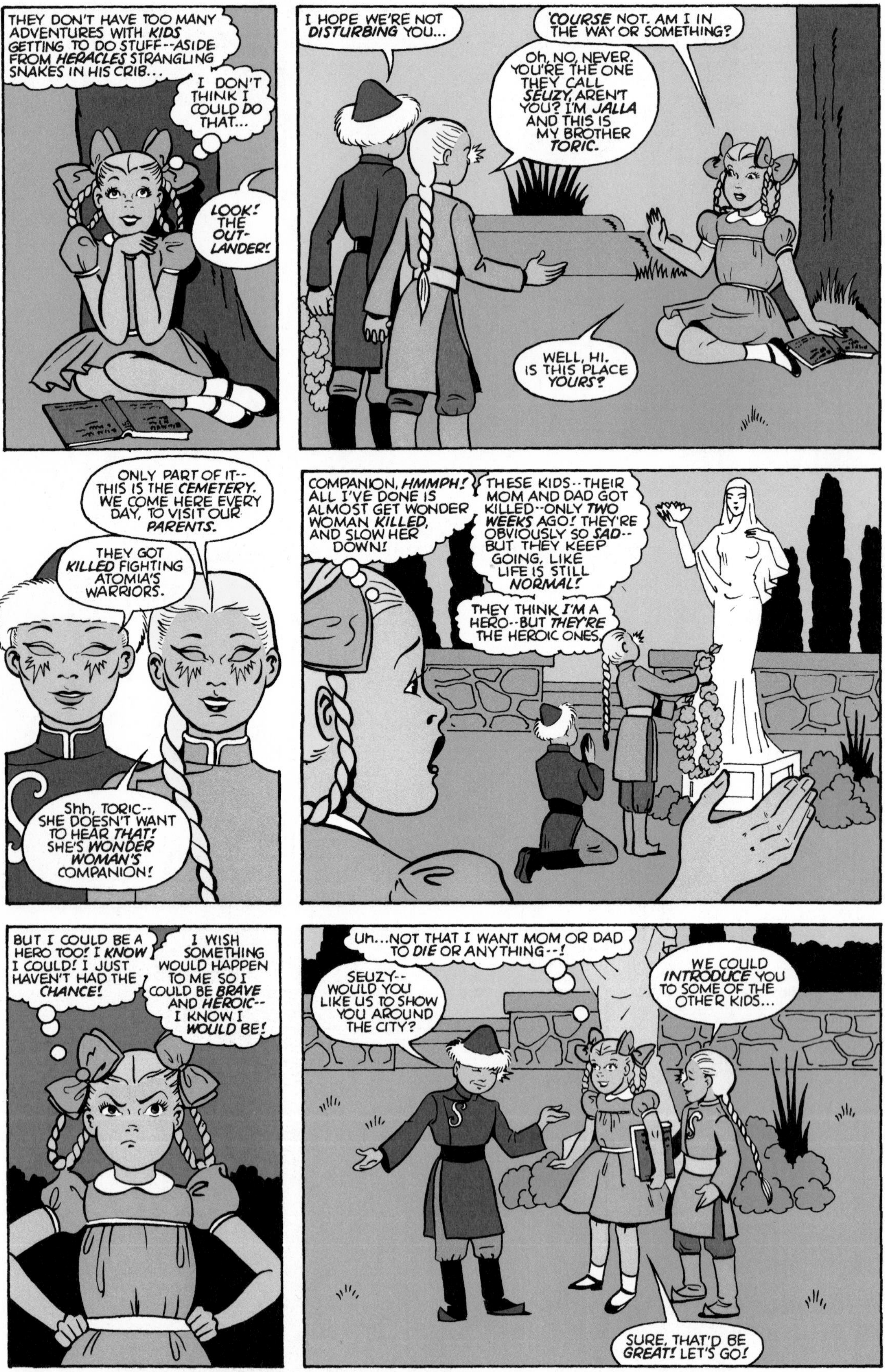
THEY DON'T HAVE TOO MANY ADVENTURES WITH KIDS GETTING TO DO STUFF--ASIDE FROM HERACLES STRANGLING SNAKES IN HIS CRIB...
I DON'T THINK I COULD DO THAT...
LOOK! THE OUT-LANDER!
I HOPE WE'RE NOT DISTURBING YOU...
'COURSE NOT. AM I IN THE WAY OR SOMETHING?
Oh, NO, NEVER. YOU'RE THE ONE THEY CALL SEUZY, AREN'T YOU? I'M JALLA AND THIS IS MY BROTHER TORIC.
WELL, HI. IS THIS PLACE YOURS?
ONLY PART OF IT--THIS IS THE CEMETERY. WE COME HERE EVERY DAY, TO VISIT OUR PARENTS.
THEY GOT KILLED FIGHTING ATOMIA'S WARRIORS.
Shh, TORIC--SHE DOESN'T WANT TO HEAR THAT! SHE'S WONDER WOMAN'S COMPANION!
COMPANION, HMMPH! ALL I'VE DONE IS ALMOST GET WONDER WOMAN KILLED, AND SLOW HER DOWN!
THESE KIDS--THEIR MOM AND DAD GOT KILLED--ONLY TWO WEEKS AGO! THEY'RE OBVIOUSLY SO SAD--BUT THEY KEEP GOING, LIKE LIFE IS STILL NORMAL!
THEY THINK I'M A HERO--BUT THEY'RE THE HEROIC ONES.
BUT I COULD BE A HERO TOO! I KNOW I COULD! I JUST HAVEN'T HAD THE CHANCE!
I WISH SOMETHING WOULD HAPPEN TO ME SO I COULD BE BRAVE AND HEROIC--I KNOW I WOULD BE!
Uh...NOT THAT I WANT MOM OR DAD TO DIE OR ANYTHING--!
SEUZY--WOULD YOU LIKE US TO SHOW YOU AROUND THE CITY?
WE COULD INTRODUCE YOU TO SOME OF THE OTHER KIDS...
SURE, THAT'D BE GREAT! LET'S GO!

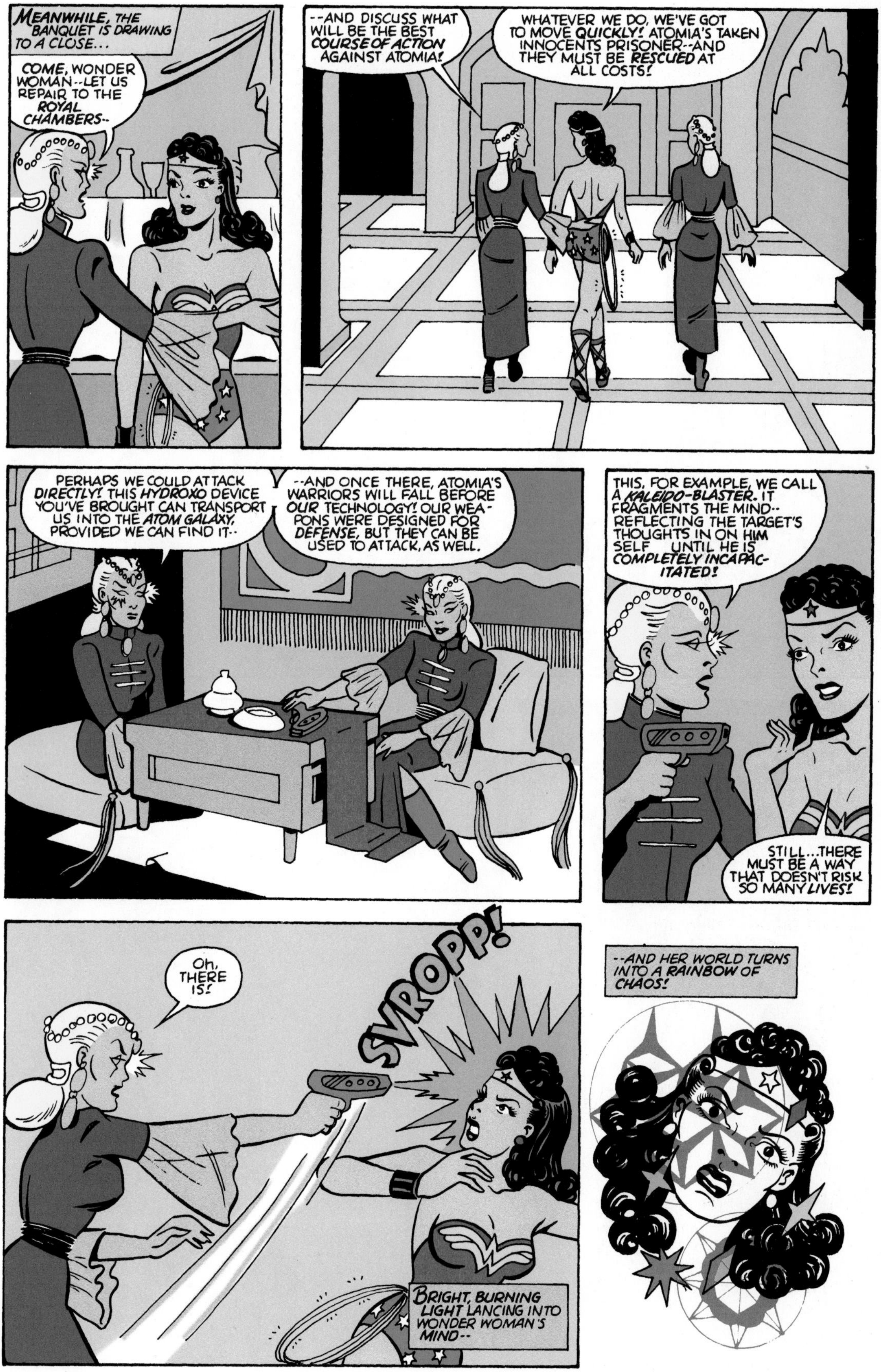

MEANWHILE, THE BANQUET IS DRAWING TO A CLOSE...
COME, WONDER WOMAN--LET US REPAIR TO THE ROYAL CHAMBERS--
--AND DISCUSS WHAT WILL BE THE BEST COURSE OF ACTION AGAINST ATOMIA!
WHATEVER WE DO, WE'VE GOT TO MOVE QUICKLY! ATOMIA'S TAKEN INNOCENTS PRISONER--AND THEY MUST BE RESCUED AT ALL COSTS!
PERHAPS WE COULD ATTACK DIRECTLY! THIS HYDROXO DEVICE YOU'VE BROUGHT CAN TRANSPORT US INTO THE ATOM GALAXY, PROVIDED WE CAN FIND IT--
--AND ONCE THERE, ATOMIA'S WARRIORS WILL FALL BEFORE OUR TECHNOLOGY! OUR WEAPONS WERE DESIGNED FOR DEFENSE, BUT THEY CAN BE USED TO ATTACK, AS WELL.
THIS, FOR EXAMPLE, WE CALL A KALEIDO-BLASTER. IT FRAGMENTS THE MIND--REFLECTING THE TARGET'S THOUGHTS IN ON HIMSELF UNTIL HE IS COMPLETELY INCAPACITATED!
STILL...THERE MUST BE A WAY THAT DOESN'T RISK SO MANY LIVES!
Oh, THERE IS!
SVROPP!
BRIGHT, BURNING LIGHT LANCING INTO WONDER WOMAN'S MIND--
--AND HER WORLD TURNS INTO A RAINBOW OF CHAOS!

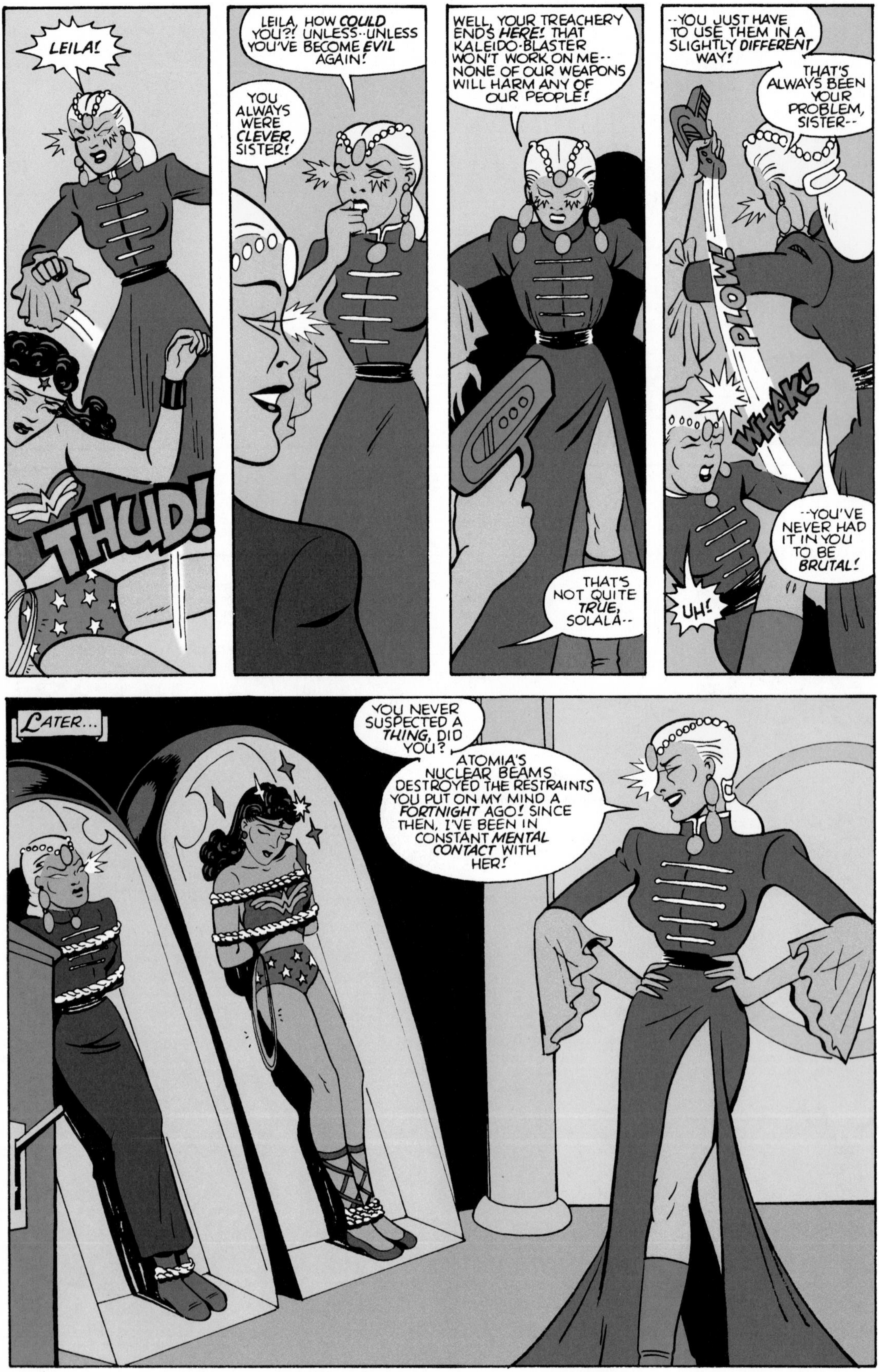
LEILA!
LEILA, HOW COULD YOU?! UNLESS--UNLESS YOU'VE BECOME EVIL AGAIN!
YOU ALWAYS WERE CLEVER, SISTER!
THUD!
WELL, YOUR TREACHERY ENDS HERE! THAT KALEIDO-BLASTER WON'T WORK ON ME-- NONE OF OUR WEAPONS WILL HARM ANY OF OUR PEOPLE!
THAT'S NOT QUITE TRUE, SOLALA--
--YOU JUST HAVE TO USE THEM IN A SLIGHTLY DIFFERENT WAY!
THAT'S ALWAYS BEEN YOUR PROBLEM, SISTER--
PLOW!
WHAK!
UH!
--YOU'VE NEVER HAD IT IN YOU TO BE BRUTAL!
LATER...
YOU NEVER SUSPECTED A THING, DID YOU?
ATOMIA'S NUCLEAR BEAMS DESTROYED THE RESTRAINTS YOU PUT ON MY MIND A FORTNIGHT AGO! SINCE THEN, I'VE BEEN IN CONSTANT MENTAL CONTACT WITH HER!

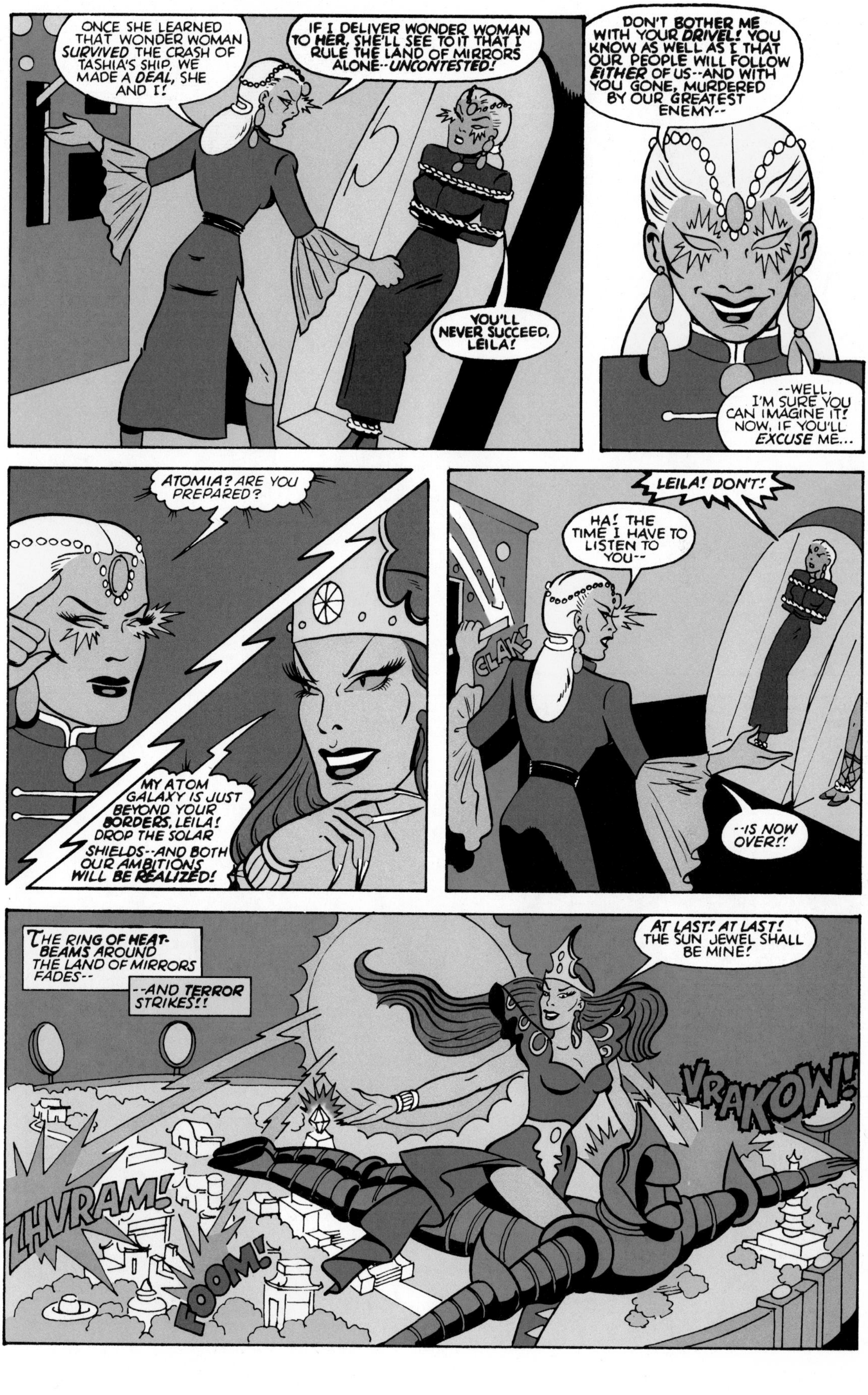
ONCE SHE LEARNED THAT WONDER WOMAN SURVIVED THE CRASH OF TASHIA'S SHIP, WE MADE A DEAL, SHE AND I!
IF I DELIVER WONDER WOMAN TO HER, SHE'LL SEE TO IT THAT I RULE THE LAND OF MIRRORS ALONE--UNCONTESTED!
YOU'LL NEVER SUCCEED, LEILA!
DON'T BOTHER ME WITH YOUR DRIVEL! YOU KNOW AS WELL AS I THAT OUR PEOPLE WILL FOLLOW EITHER OF US--AND WITH YOU GONE, MURDERED BY OUR GREATEST ENEMY--
--WELL, I'M SURE YOU CAN IMAGINE IT! NOW, IF YOU'LL EXCUSE ME...
ATOMIA? ARE YOU PREPARED?
MY ATOM GALAXY IS JUST BEYOND YOUR BORDERS, LEILA! DROP THE SOLAR SHIELDS--AND BOTH OUR AMBITIONS WILL BE REALIZED!
LEILA! DON'T!
HA! THE TIME I HAVE TO LISTEN TO YOU--
CLAK!
--IS NOW OVER!!
THE RING OF HEAT-BEAMS AROUND THE LAND OF MIRRORS FADES--
--AND TERROR STRIKES!!
AT LAST! AT LAST! THE SUN JEWEL SHALL BE MINE!
VRAKOW!
ZHVRAM!
FOOM!

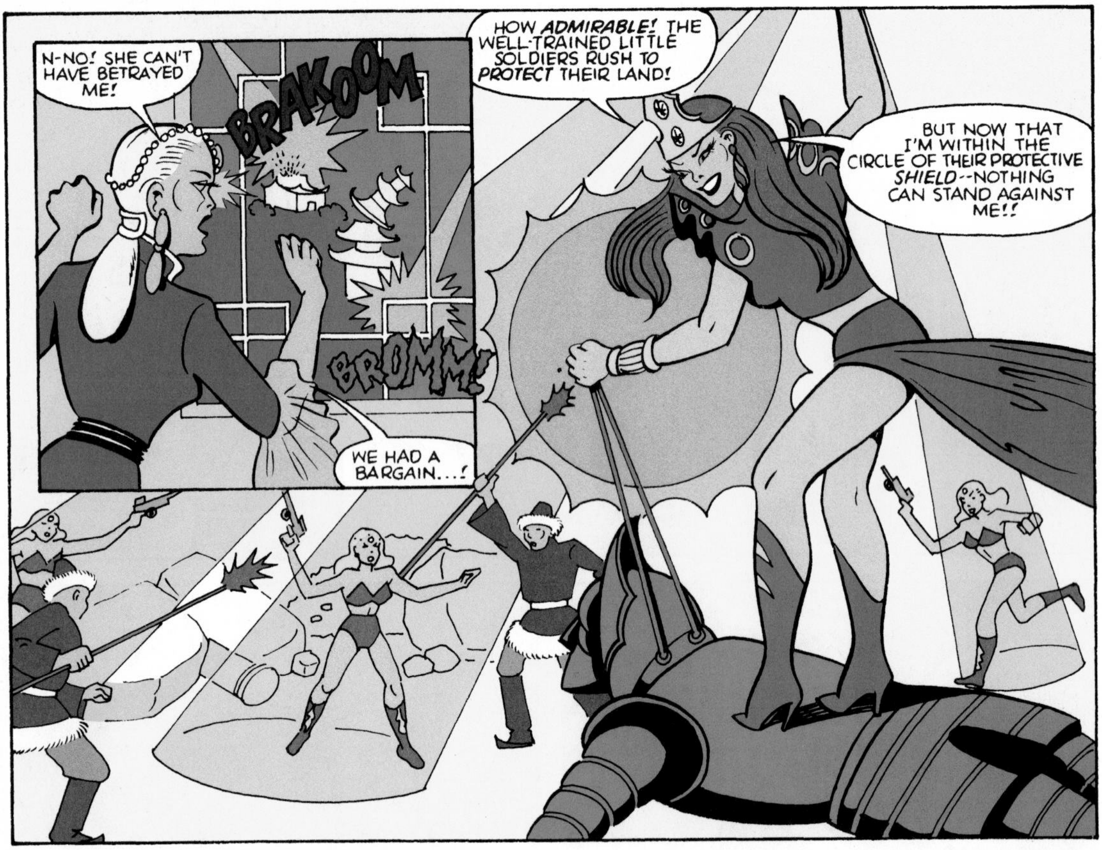
N-NO! SHE CAN'T HAVE BETRAYED ME!
BRAKOOM
BROMM!
WE HAD A BARGAIN...!
HOW ADMIRABLE! THE WELL-TRAINED LITTLE SOLDIERS RUSH TO PROTECT THEIR LAND!
BUT NOW THAT I'M WITHIN THE CIRCLE OF THEIR PROTECTIVE SHIELD--NOTHING CAN STAND AGAINST ME!!

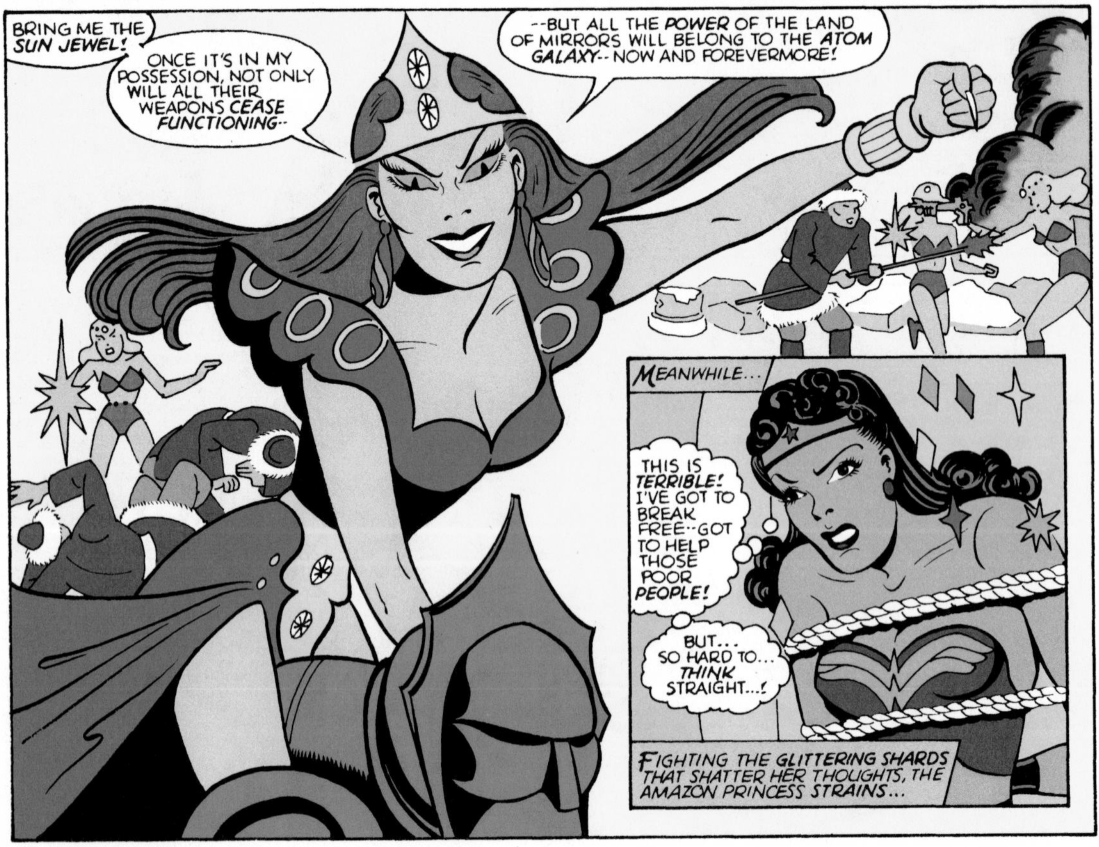
BRING ME THE SUN JEWEL!
ONCE IT'S IN MY POSSESSION, NOT ONLY WILL ALL THEIR WEAPONS CEASE FUNCTIONING--
--BUT ALL THE POWER OF THE LAND OF MIRRORS WILL BELONG TO THE ATOM GALAXY-- NOW AND FOREVERMORE!
MEANWHILE...
THIS IS TERRIBLE! I'VE GOT TO BREAK FREE--GOT TO HELP THOSE POOR PEOPLE!
BUT... SO HARD TO... THINK STRAIGHT...!
FIGHTING THE GLITTERING SHARDS THAT SHATTER HER THOUGHTS, THE AMAZON PRINCESS STRAINS...

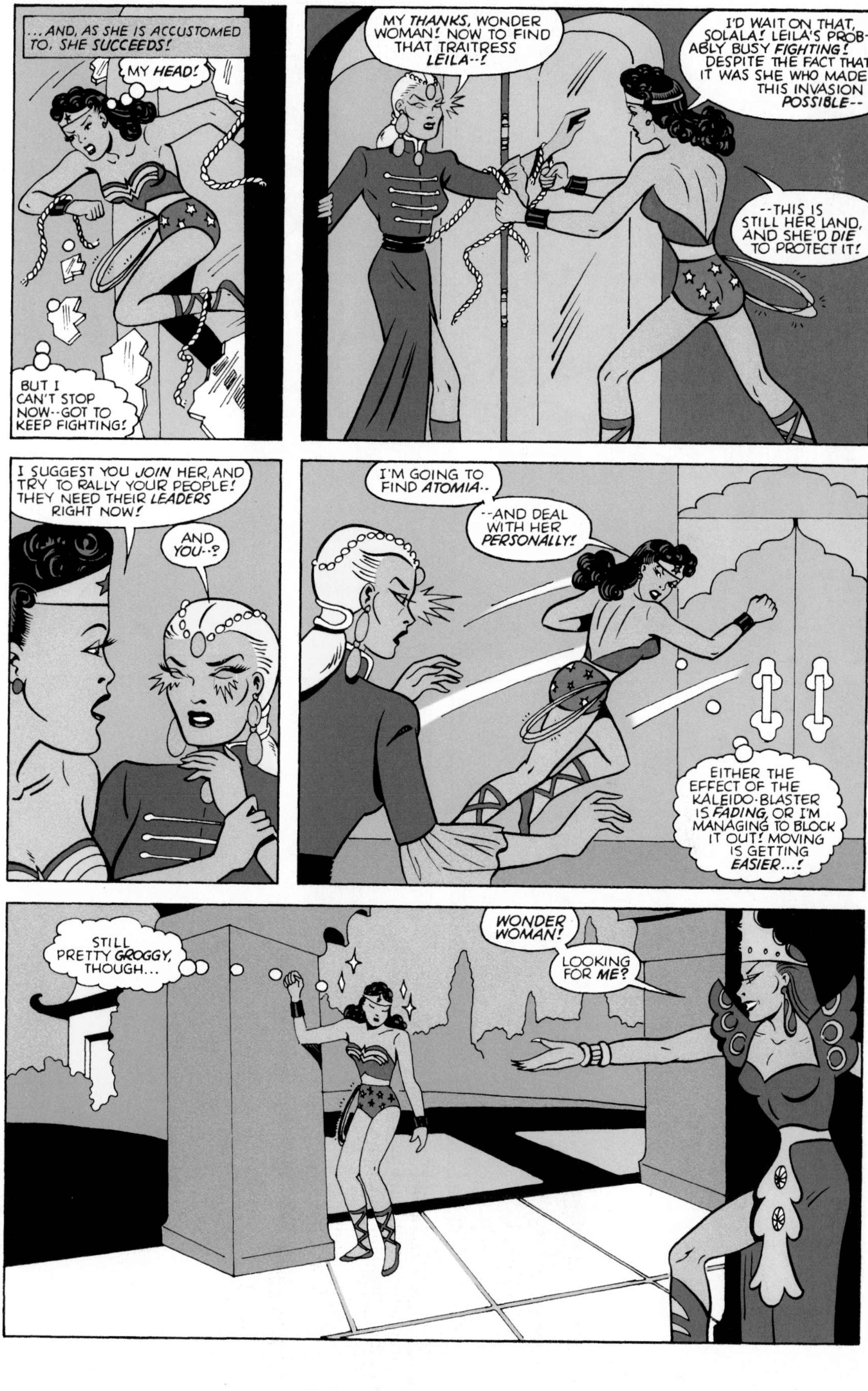

...AND, AS SHE IS ACCUSTOMED TO, SHE SUCCEEDS!
MY HEAD!
BUT I CAN'T STOP NOW--GOT TO KEEP FIGHTING!
MY THANKS, WONDER WOMAN! NOW TO FIND THAT TRAITRESS LEILA--!
I'D WAIT ON THAT, SOLALA! LEILA'S PROBABLY BUSY FIGHTING! DESPITE THE FACT THAT IT WAS SHE WHO MADE THIS INVASION POSSIBLE--
--THIS IS STILL HER LAND, AND SHE'D DIE TO PROTECT IT!
I SUGGEST YOU JOIN HER, AND TRY TO RALLY YOUR PEOPLE! THEY NEED THEIR LEADERS RIGHT NOW!
AND YOU--?
I'M GOING TO FIND ATOMIA--
--AND DEAL WITH HER PERSONALLY!
EITHER THE EFFECT OF THE KALEIDO-BLASTER IS FADING, OR I'M MANAGING TO BLOCK IT OUT! MOVING IS GETTING EASIER...!
STILL PRETTY GROGGY, THOUGH...
WONDER WOMAN!
LOOKING FOR ME?

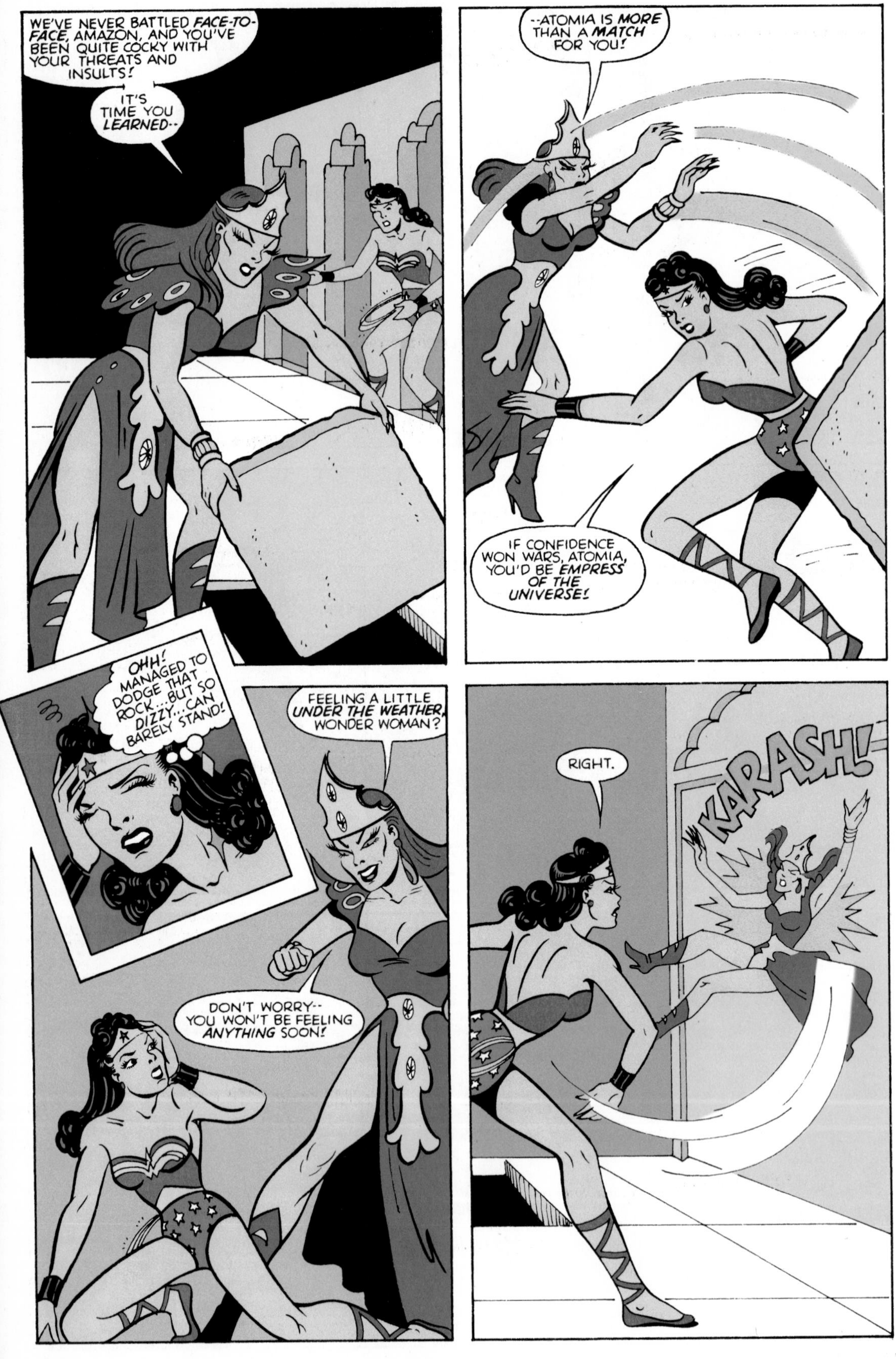
WE'VE NEVER BATTLED FACE-TO-FACE, AMAZON, AND YOU'VE BEEN QUITE COCKY WITH YOUR THREATS AND INSULTS!
IT'S TIME YOU LEARNED--
--ATOMIA IS MORE THAN A MATCH FOR YOU!
IF CONFIDENCE WON WARS, ATOMIA, YOU'D BE EMPRESS OF THE UNIVERSE!
OHH! MANAGED TO DODGE THAT ROCK...BUT SO DIZZY...CAN BARELY STAND!
FEELING A LITTLE UNDER THE WEATHER, WONDER WOMAN?
DON'T WORRY-- YOU WON'T BE FEELING ANYTHING SOON!
RIGHT.
KARASH!

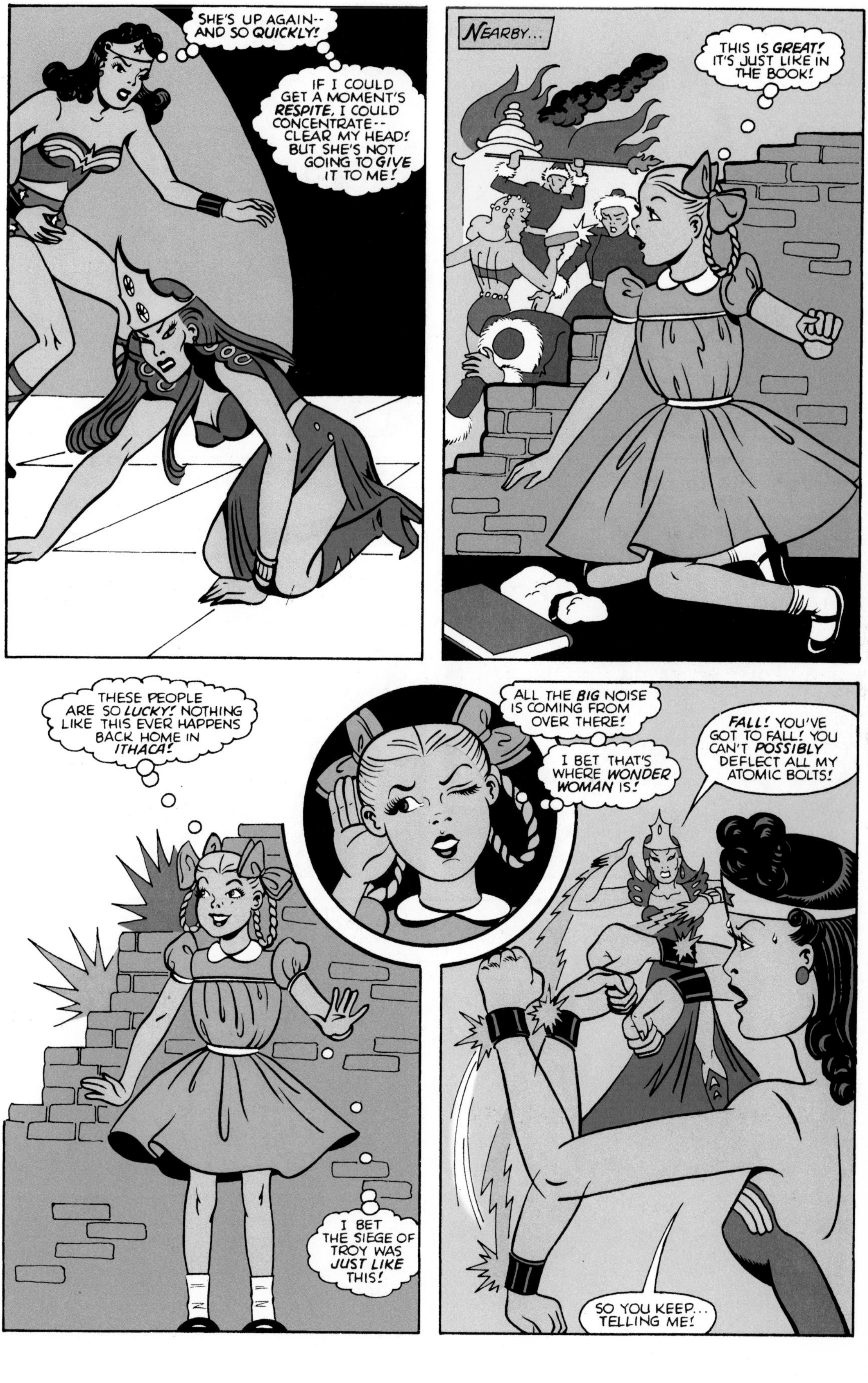
SHE'S UP AGAIN-- AND SO QUICKLY!
IF I COULD GET A MOMENT'S RESPITE, I COULD CONCENTRATE-- CLEAR MY HEAD! BUT SHE'S NOT GOING TO GIVE IT TO ME!
NEARBY...
THIS IS GREAT! IT'S JUST LIKE IN THE BOOK!
THESE PEOPLE ARE SO LUCKY! NOTHING LIKE THIS EVER HAPPENS BACK HOME IN ITHACA!
I BET THE SIEGE OF TROY WAS JUST LIKE THIS!
ALL THE BIG NOISE IS COMING FROM OVER THERE!
I BET THAT'S WHERE WONDER WOMAN IS!
FALL! YOU'VE GOT TO FALL! YOU CAN'T POSSIBLY DEFLECT ALL MY ATOMIC BOLTS!
SO YOU KEEP... TELLING ME!

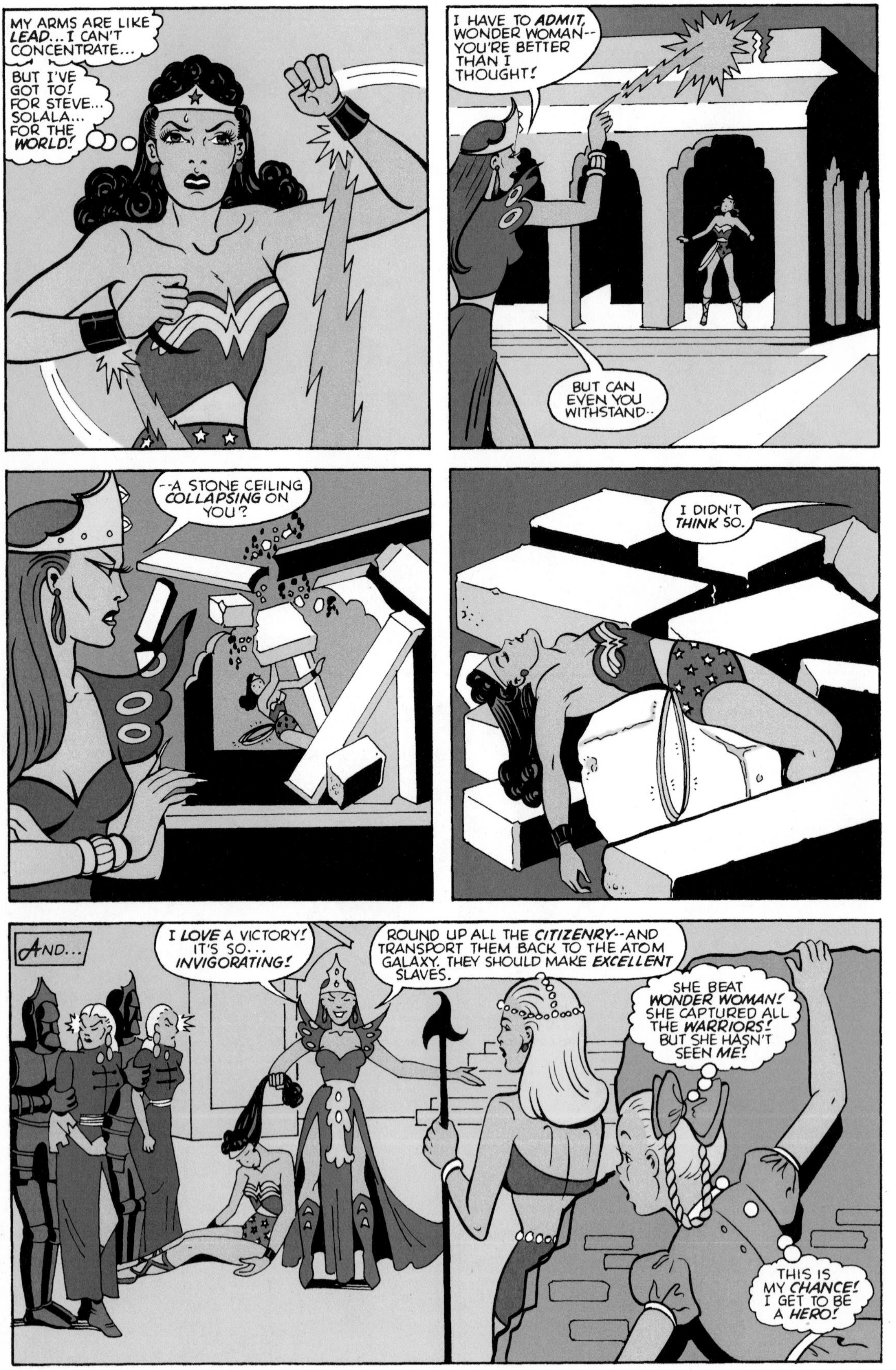

MY ARMS ARE LIKE LEAD... I CAN'T CONCENTRATE...
BUT I'VE GOT TO! FOR STEVE... SOLALA... FOR THE WORLD!
I HAVE TO ADMIT, WONDER WOMAN-- YOU'RE BETTER THAN I THOUGHT!
BUT CAN EVEN YOU WITHSTAND--
--A STONE CEILING COLLAPSING ON YOU?
I DIDN'T THINK SO.
AND...
I LOVE A VICTORY! IT'S SO... INVIGORATING!
ROUND UP ALL THE CITIZENRY--AND TRANSPORT THEM BACK TO THE ATOM GALAXY. THEY SHOULD MAKE EXCELLENT SLAVES.
SHE BEAT WONDER WOMAN! SHE CAPTURED ALL THE WARRIORS! BUT SHE HASN'T SEEN ME!
THIS IS MY CHANCE! I GET TO BE A HERO!

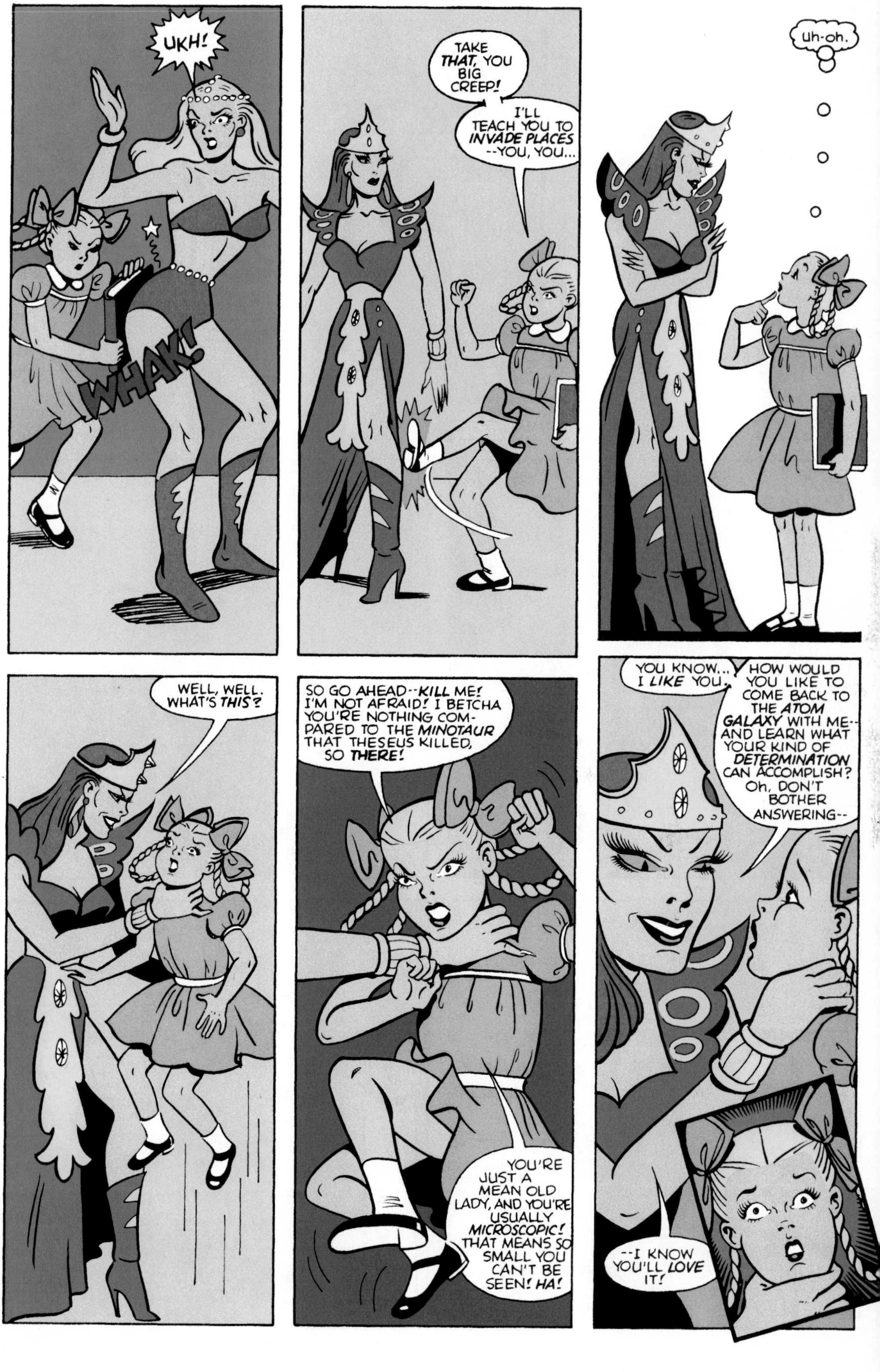
UKH!
WHAK!
TAKE THAT, YOU BIG CREEP!
I'LL TEACH YOU TO INVADE PLACES --YOU, YOU...
Uh-oh.
WELL, WELL. WHAT'S THIS?
SO GO AHEAD--KILL ME! I'M NOT AFRAID! I BETCHA YOU'RE NOTHING COMPARED TO THE MINOTAUR THAT THESEUS KILLED, SO THERE!
YOU'RE JUST A MEAN OLD LADY, AND YOU'RE USUALLY MICROSCOPIC! THAT MEANS SO SMALL YOU CAN'T BE SEEN! HA!
YOU KNOW... I LIKE YOU.
HOW WOULD YOU LIKE TO COME BACK TO THE ATOM GALAXY WITH ME--AND LEARN WHAT YOUR KIND OF DETERMINATION CAN ACCOMPLISH? Oh, DON'T BOTHER ANSWERING--
--I KNOW YOU'LL LOVE IT!

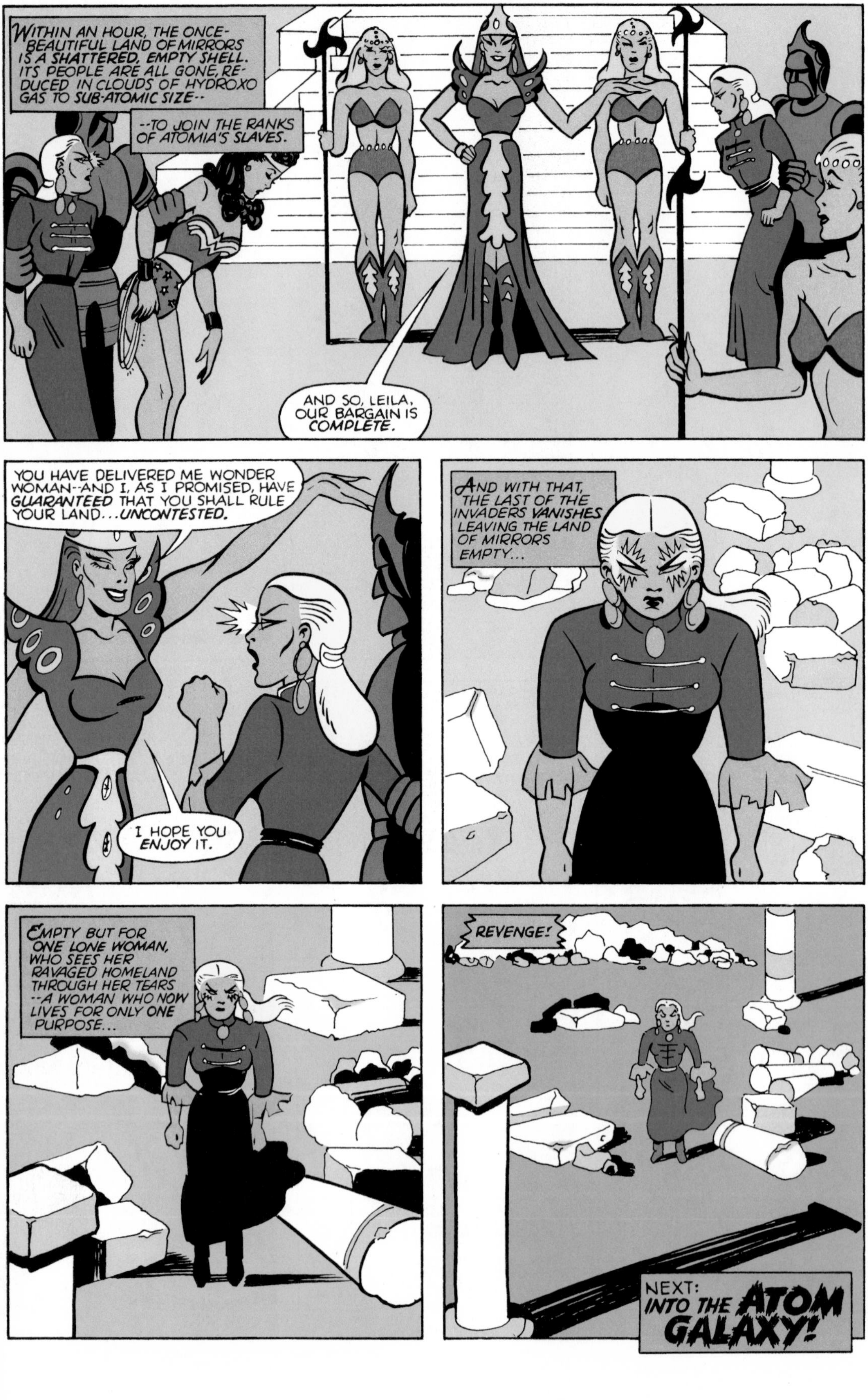
WITHIN AN HOUR, THE ONCE-BEAUTIFUL LAND OF MIRRORS IS A SHATTERED, EMPTY SHELL. ITS PEOPLE ARE ALL GONE, REDUCED IN CLOUDS OF HYDROXO GAS TO SUB-ATOMIC SIZE--
--TO JOIN THE RANKS OF ATOMIA'S SLAVES.
AND SO, LEILA, OUR BARGAIN IS COMPLETE.
YOU HAVE DELIVERED ME WONDER WOMAN--AND I, AS I PROMISED, HAVE GUARANTEED THAT YOU SHALL RULE YOUR LAND... UNCONTESTED.
I HOPE YOU ENJOY IT.
AND WITH THAT, THE LAST OF THE INVADERS VANISHES, LEAVING THE LAND OF MIRRORS EMPTY...
EMPTY BUT FOR ONE LONE WOMAN, WHO SEES HER RAVAGED HOMELAND THROUGH HER TEARS --A WOMAN WHO NOW LIVES FOR ONLY ONE PURPOSE...
REVENGE!
NEXT: INTO THE ATOM GALAXY!

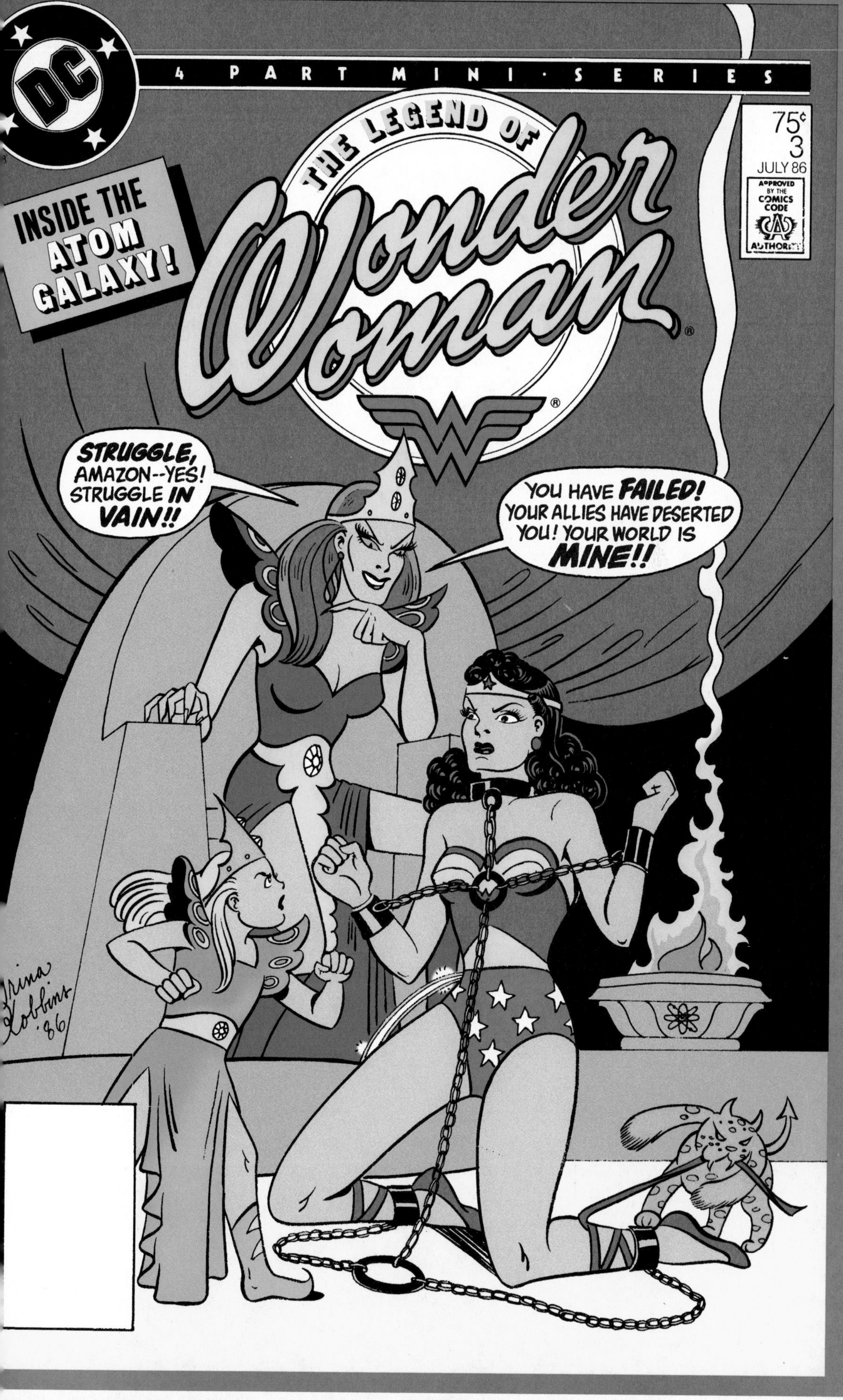

4 PART MINI·SERIES
THE LEGEND OF Wonder Woman
75¢
3
JULY 86
APPROVED BY THE COMICS CODE AUTHORITY
INSIDE THE ATOM GALAXY!
STRUGGLE, AMAZON--YES! STRUGGLE IN VAIN!!
YOU HAVE FAILED! YOUR ALLIES HAVE DESERTED YOU! YOUR WORLD IS MINE!!
Trina Robbins '86

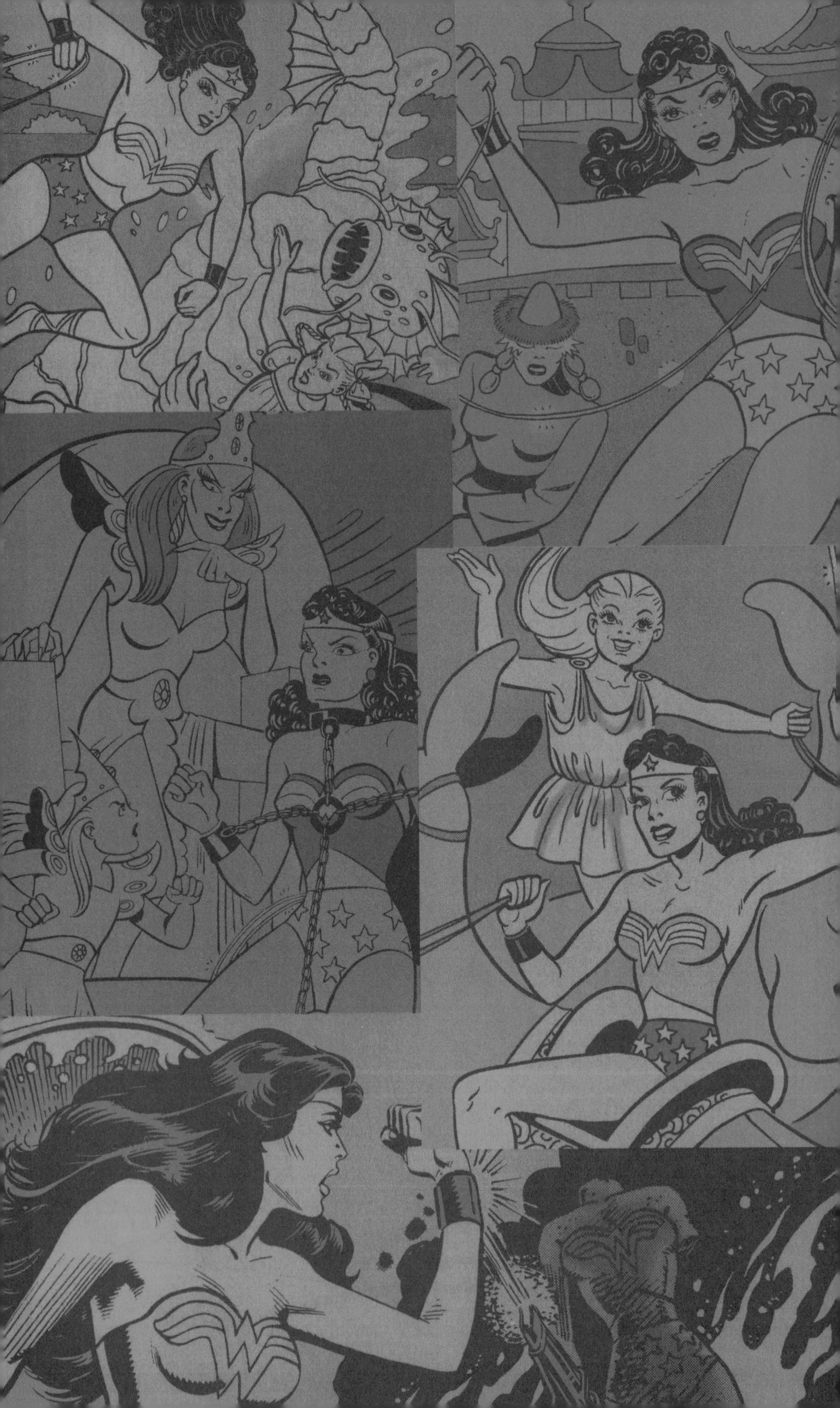

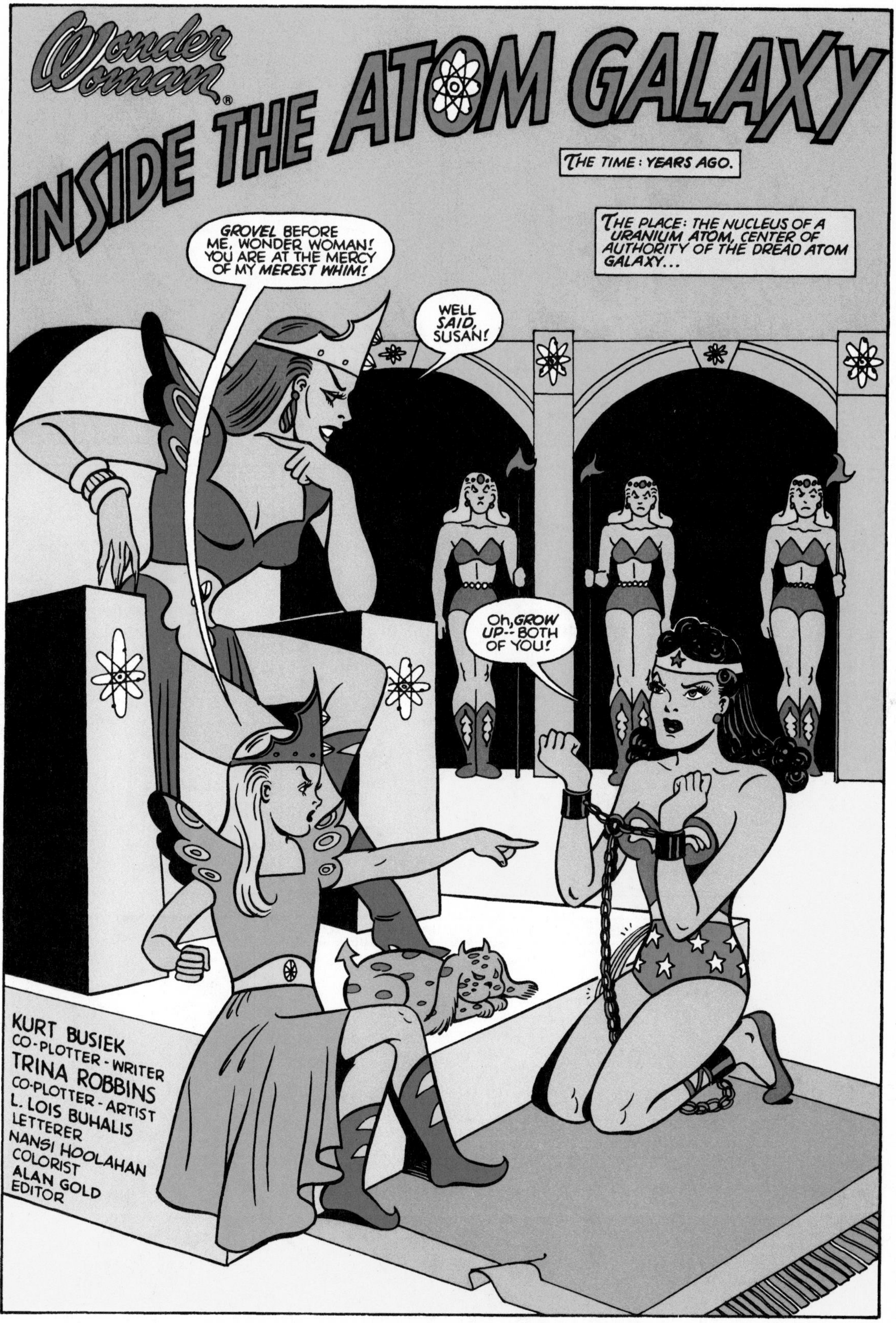

Wonder Woman®
INSIDE THE ATOM GALAXY
THE TIME: YEARS AGO.
THE PLACE: THE NUCLEUS OF A URANIUM ATOM, CENTER OF AUTHORITY OF THE DREAD ATOM GALAXY...
GROVEL BEFORE ME, WONDER WOMAN! YOU ARE AT THE MERCY OF MY MEREST WHIM!
WELL SAID, SUSAN!
Oh, GROW UP-- BOTH OF YOU!
KURT BUSIEK CO-PLOTTER - WRITER
TRINA ROBBINS CO-PLOTTER - ARTIST
L. LOIS BUHALIS LETTERER
NANSI HOOLAHAN COLORIST
ALAN GOLD EDITOR

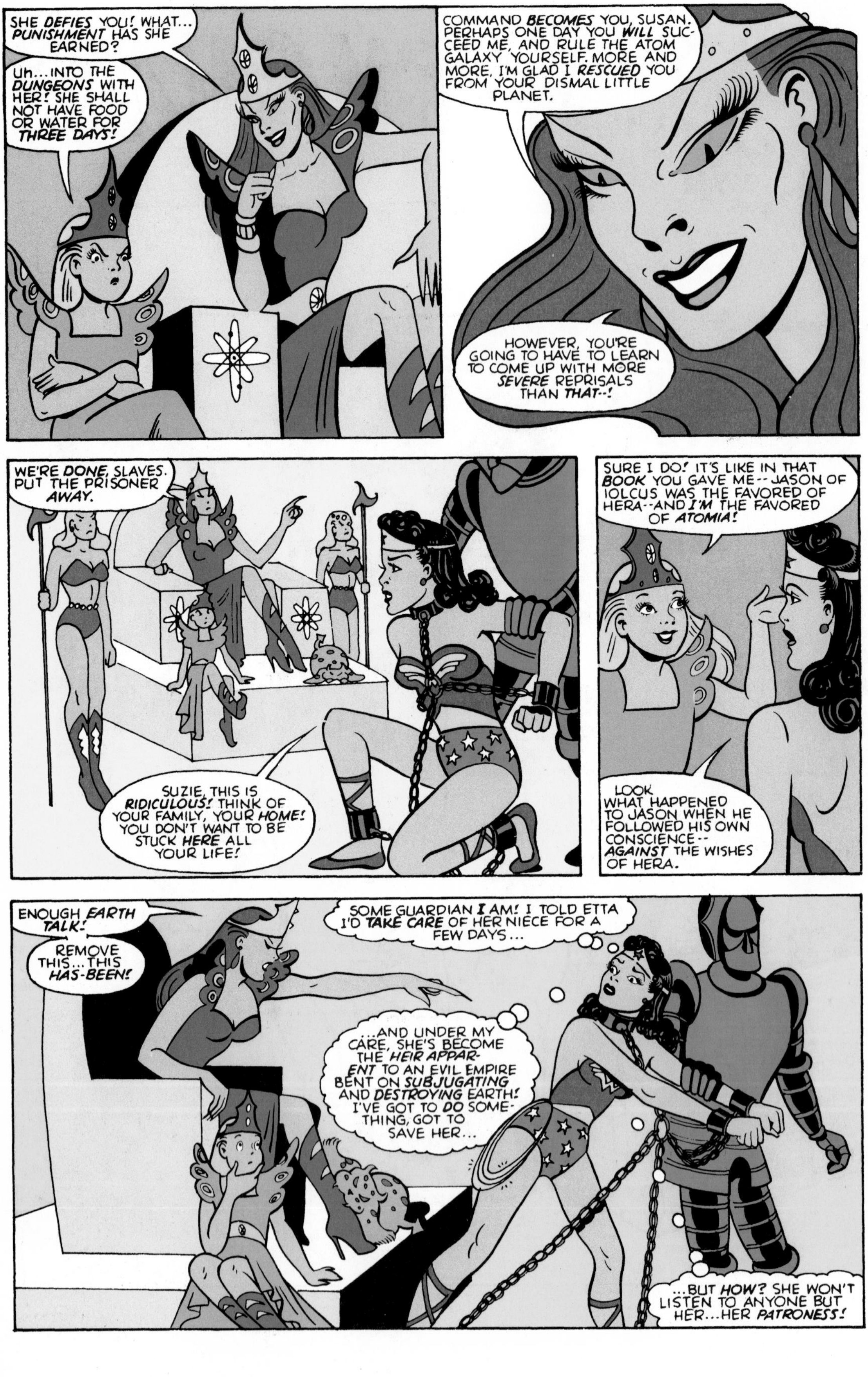
SHE DEFIES YOU! WHAT... PUNISHMENT HAS SHE EARNED?
Uh...INTO THE DUNGEONS WITH HER! SHE SHALL NOT HAVE FOOD OR WATER FOR THREE DAYS!
COMMAND BECOMES YOU, SUSAN. PERHAPS ONE DAY YOU WILL SUCCEED ME, AND RULE THE ATOM GALAXY YOURSELF. MORE AND MORE, I'M GLAD I RESCUED YOU FROM YOUR DISMAL LITTLE PLANET.
HOWEVER, YOU'RE GOING TO HAVE TO LEARN TO COME UP WITH MORE SEVERE REPRISALS THAN THAT--!
WE'RE DONE, SLAVES. PUT THE PRISONER AWAY.
SUZIE, THIS IS RIDICULOUS! THINK OF YOUR FAMILY, YOUR HOME! YOU DON'T WANT TO BE STUCK HERE ALL YOUR LIFE!
SURE I DO! IT'S LIKE IN THAT BOOK YOU GAVE ME--JASON OF IOLCUS WAS THE FAVORED OF HERA--AND I'M THE FAVORED OF ATOMIA!
LOOK WHAT HAPPENED TO JASON WHEN HE FOLLOWED HIS OWN CONSCIENCE--AGAINST THE WISHES OF HERA.
ENOUGH EARTH TALK!
REMOVE THIS...THIS HAS-BEEN!
SOME GUARDIAN I AM! I TOLD ETTA I'D TAKE CARE OF HER NIECE FOR A FEW DAYS...
...AND UNDER MY CARE, SHE'S BECOME THE HEIR APPARENT TO AN EVIL EMPIRE BENT ON SUBJUGATING AND DESTROYING EARTH! I'VE GOT TO DO SOMETHING, GOT TO SAVE HER...
...BUT HOW? SHE WON'T LISTEN TO ANYONE BUT HER...HER PATRONESS!

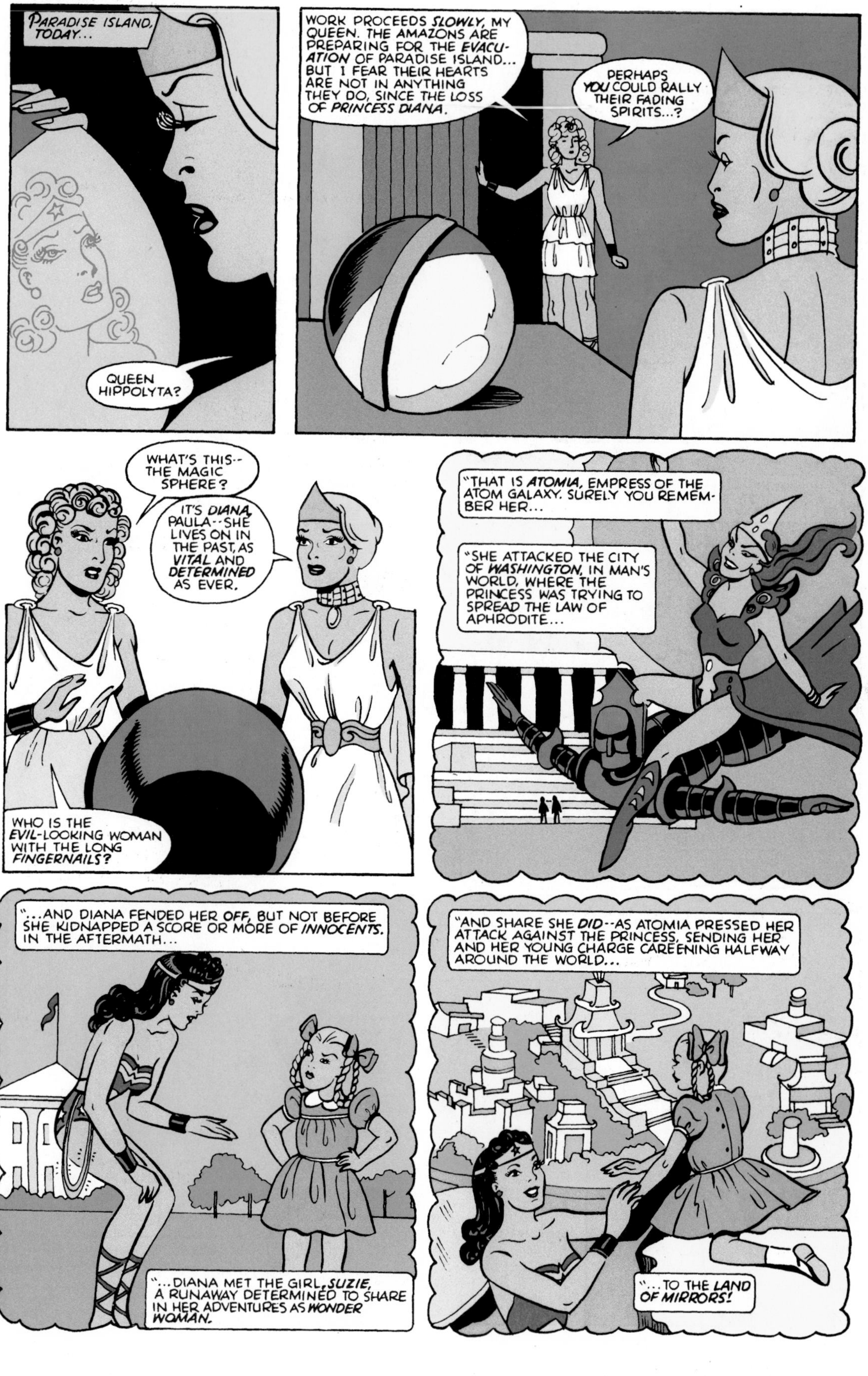

PARADISE ISLAND, TODAY...
QUEEN HIPPOLYTA?
WORK PROCEEDS SLOWLY, MY QUEEN. THE AMAZONS ARE PREPARING FOR THE EVACUATION OF PARADISE ISLAND... BUT I FEAR THEIR HEARTS ARE NOT IN ANYTHING THEY DO, SINCE THE LOSS OF PRINCESS DIANA.
PERHAPS YOU COULD RALLY THEIR FADING SPIRITS...?
WHAT'S THIS-- THE MAGIC SPHERE?
IT'S DIANA, PAULA--SHE LIVES ON IN THE PAST, AS VITAL AND DETERMINED AS EVER.
WHO IS THE EVIL-LOOKING WOMAN WITH THE LONG FINGERNAILS?
"THAT IS ATOMIA, EMPRESS OF THE ATOM GALAXY. SURELY YOU REMEMBER HER...
"SHE ATTACKED THE CITY OF WASHINGTON, IN MAN'S WORLD, WHERE THE PRINCESS WAS TRYING TO SPREAD THE LAW OF APHRODITE...
"...AND DIANA FENDED HER OFF, BUT NOT BEFORE SHE KIDNAPPED A SCORE OR MORE OF INNOCENTS. IN THE AFTERMATH...
"...DIANA MET THE GIRL, SUZIE, A RUNAWAY DETERMINED TO SHARE IN HER ADVENTURES AS WONDER WOMAN.
"AND SHARE SHE DID--AS ATOMIA PRESSED HER ATTACK AGAINST THE PRINCESS, SENDING HER AND HER YOUNG CHARGE CAREENING HALFWAY AROUND THE WORLD...
"...TO THE LAND OF MIRRORS!

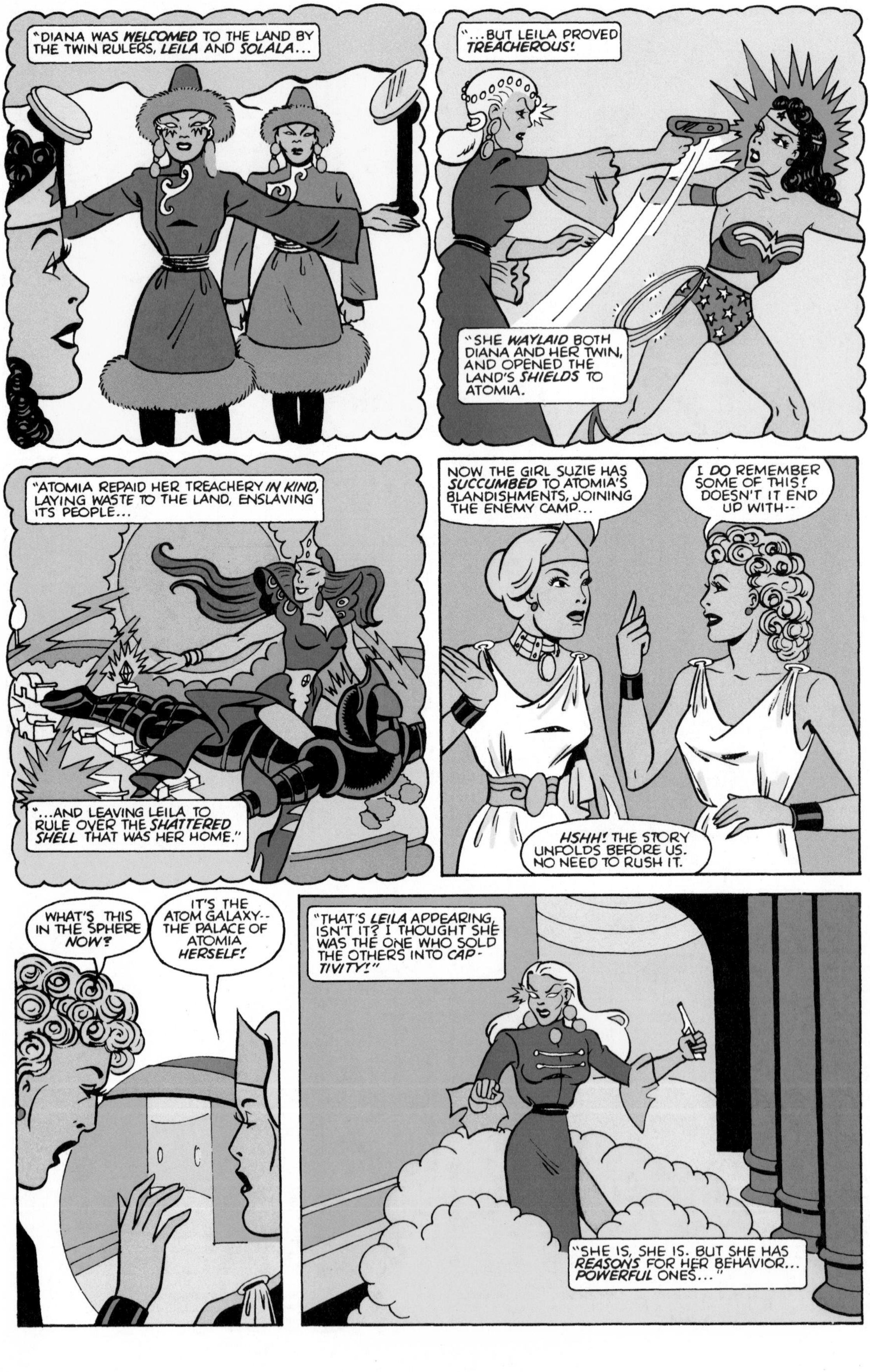
"DIANA WAS WELCOMED TO THE LAND BY THE TWIN RULERS, LEILA AND SOLALA...
"...BUT LEILA PROVED TREACHEROUS!
"SHE WAYLAID BOTH DIANA AND HER TWIN, AND OPENED THE LAND'S SHIELDS TO ATOMIA.
"ATOMIA REPAID HER TREACHERY IN KIND, LAYING WASTE TO THE LAND, ENSLAVING ITS PEOPLE...
"...AND LEAVING LEILA TO RULE OVER THE SHATTERED SHELL THAT WAS HER HOME."
NOW THE GIRL SUZIE HAS SUCCUMBED TO ATOMIA'S BLANDISHMENTS, JOINING THE ENEMY CAMP...
I DO REMEMBER SOME OF THIS! DOESN'T IT END UP WITH--
HSHH! THE STORY UNFOLDS BEFORE US. NO NEED TO RUSH IT.
WHAT'S THIS IN THE SPHERE NOW?
IT'S THE ATOM GALAXY-- THE PALACE OF ATOMIA HERSELF!
"THAT'S LEILA APPEARING, ISN'T IT? I THOUGHT SHE WAS THE ONE WHO SOLD THE OTHERS INTO CAPTIVITY!"
"SHE IS, SHE IS. BUT SHE HAS REASONS FOR HER BEHAVIOR... POWERFUL ONES..."

WHAT DID WONDER WOMAN CALL THIS? A *HYDROXO SYNTHESIZER?*

WHATEVER IT IS-- I'M SORRY NOW THAT I *AMBUSHED* HER, BUT I'M *GLAD* THAT I *CONFISCATED* SOME OF HER WEAPONS WHEN I DID--

--BECAUSE NOW IT AFFORDS ME *ENTRANCE* INTO THIS PLACE-- WHERE I CAN RESCUE MY SISTER--

--AND *REVENGE* MYSELF ON OUR *ENEMY!!*

MMMMMF!

MMMMMMMMMMFF!

EASY, SOLALA, WE'RE *GOOD GUYS!* I'M STEVE TREVOR, A FRIEND OF *WONDER WOMAN'S*-- AND THESE ARE SOME OF THE OTHER PRISONERS.

HOW DID YOU BUST OUT OF YOUR *CELL?*

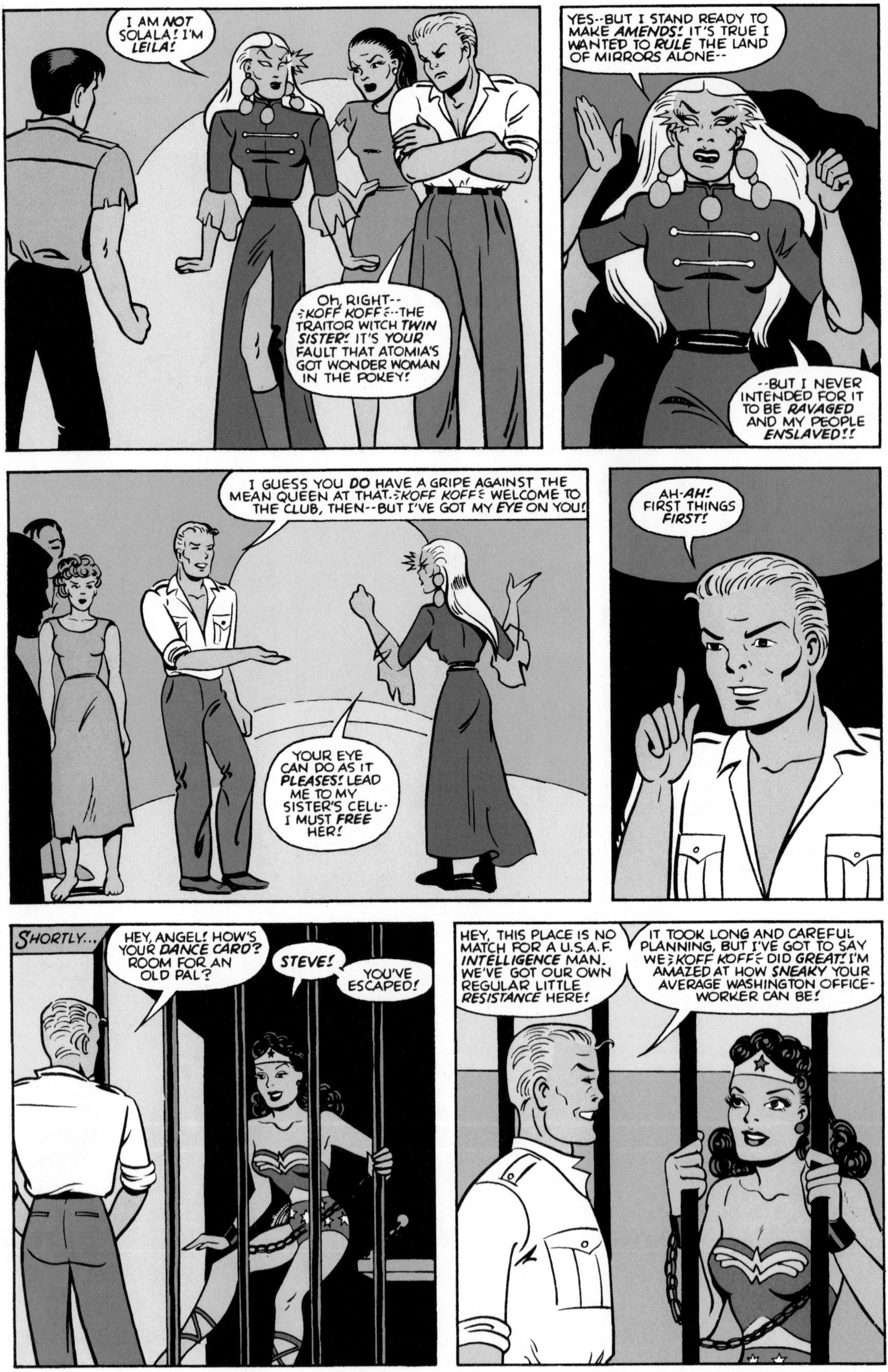
I AM NOT SOLALA! I'M LEILA!
Oh, RIGHT-- =KOFF KOFF=--THE TRAITOR WITCH TWIN SISTER! IT'S YOUR FAULT THAT ATOMIA'S GOT WONDER WOMAN IN THE POKEY!
YES--BUT I STAND READY TO MAKE AMENDS! IT'S TRUE I WANTED TO RULE THE LAND OF MIRRORS ALONE--
--BUT I NEVER INTENDED FOR IT TO BE RAVAGED AND MY PEOPLE ENSLAVED!!
I GUESS YOU DO HAVE A GRIPE AGAINST THE MEAN QUEEN AT THAT. =KOFF KOFF= WELCOME TO THE CLUB, THEN--BUT I'VE GOT MY EYE ON YOU!
YOUR EYE CAN DO AS IT PLEASES! LEAD ME TO MY SISTER'S CELL-- I MUST FREE HER!
AH-AH! FIRST THINGS FIRST!
SHORTLY...
HEY, ANGEL! HOW'S YOUR DANCE CARD? ROOM FOR AN OLD PAL?
STEVE!
YOU'VE ESCAPED!
HEY, THIS PLACE IS NO MATCH FOR A U.S.A.F. INTELLIGENCE MAN. WE'VE GOT OUR OWN REGULAR LITTLE RESISTANCE HERE!
IT TOOK LONG AND CAREFUL PLANNING, BUT I'VE GOT TO SAY WE =KOFF KOFF= DID GREAT! I'M AMAZED AT HOW SNEAKY YOUR AVERAGE WASHINGTON OFFICE-WORKER CAN BE!

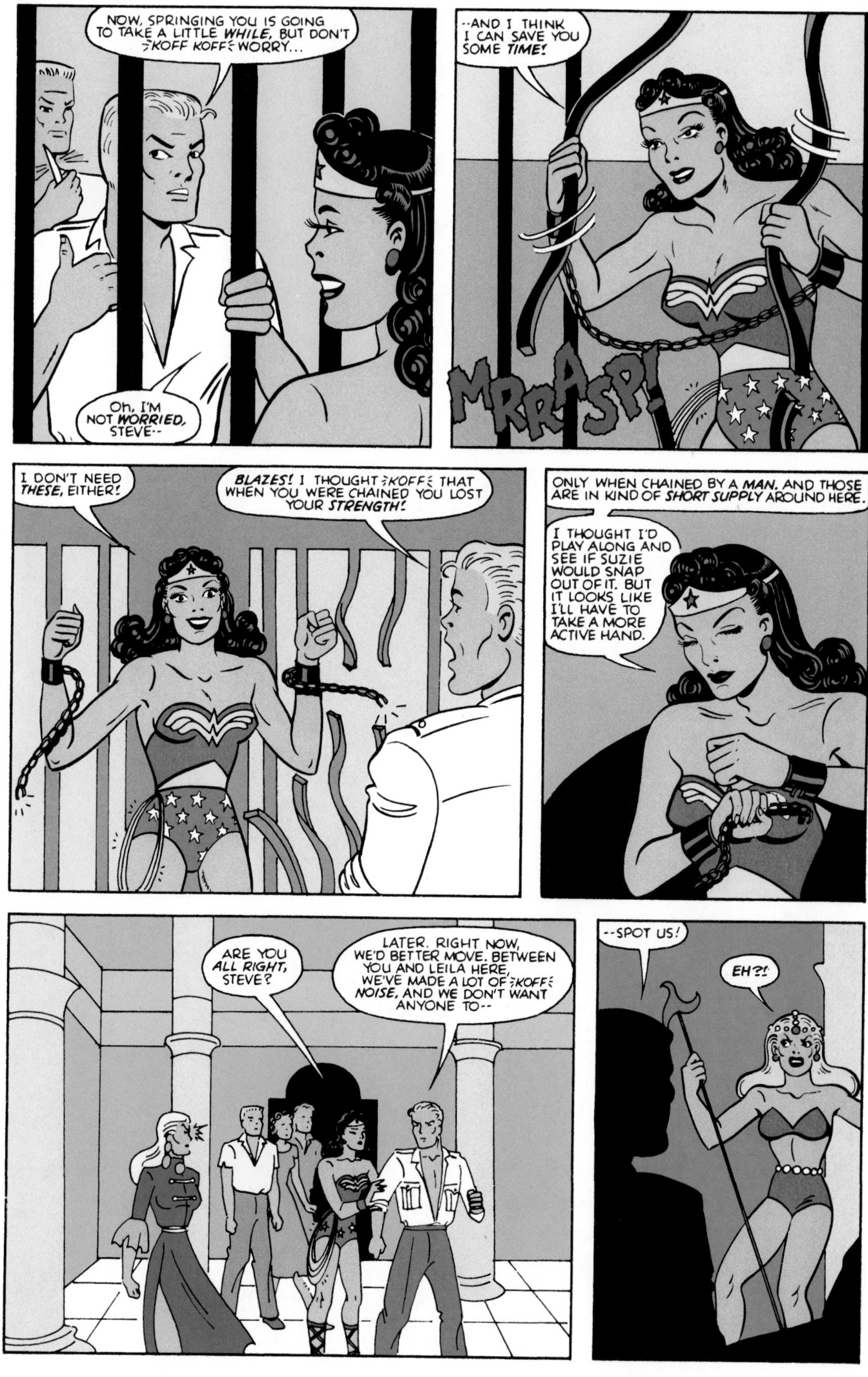
NOW, SPRINGING YOU IS GOING TO TAKE A LITTLE WHILE, BUT DON'T *KOFF KOFF* WORRY...
Oh, I'M NOT WORRIED, STEVE--
--AND I THINK I CAN SAVE YOU SOME TIME!
MRRASP!
I DON'T NEED THESE, EITHER!
BLAZES! I THOUGHT *KOFF* THAT WHEN YOU WERE CHAINED YOU LOST YOUR STRENGTH!
ONLY WHEN CHAINED BY A MAN. AND THOSE ARE IN KIND OF SHORT SUPPLY AROUND HERE.
I THOUGHT I'D PLAY ALONG AND SEE IF SUZIE WOULD SNAP OUT OF IT. BUT IT LOOKS LIKE I'LL HAVE TO TAKE A MORE ACTIVE HAND.
ARE YOU ALL RIGHT, STEVE?
LATER. RIGHT NOW, WE'D BETTER MOVE. BETWEEN YOU AND LEILA HERE, WE'VE MADE A LOT OF *KOFF* NOISE, AND WE DON'T WANT ANYONE TO--
--SPOT US!
EH?!

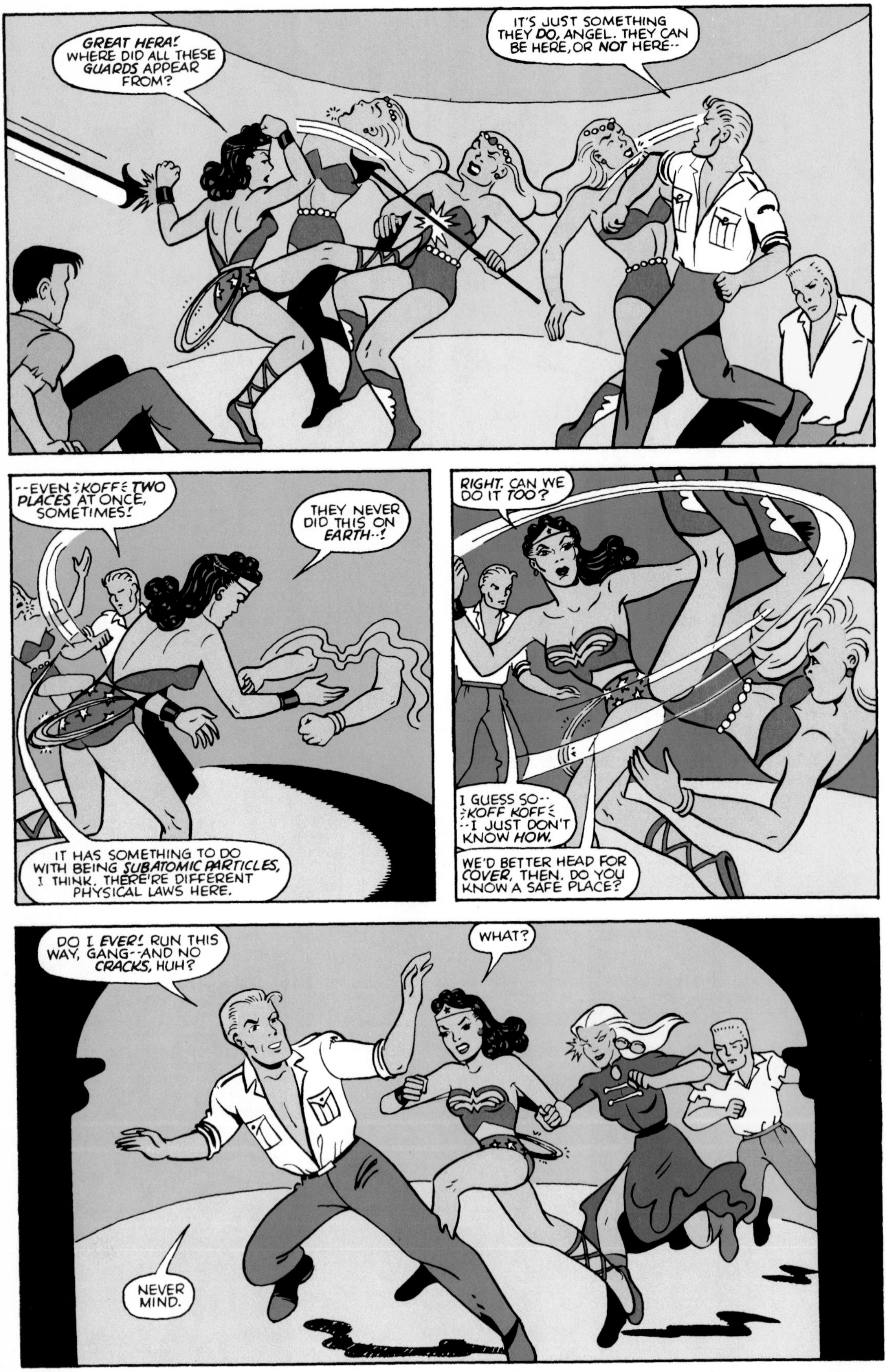
GREAT HERA! WHERE DID ALL THESE GUARDS APPEAR FROM?
IT'S JUST SOMETHING THEY DO, ANGEL. THEY CAN BE HERE, OR NOT HERE--
--EVEN ⸗KOFF⸗ TWO PLACES AT ONCE, SOMETIMES!
THEY NEVER DID THIS ON EARTH--!
IT HAS SOMETHING TO DO WITH BEING SUBATOMIC PARTICLES, I THINK. THERE'RE DIFFERENT PHYSICAL LAWS HERE.
RIGHT. CAN WE DO IT TOO?
I GUESS SO-- ⸗KOFF KOFF⸗ --I JUST DON'T KNOW HOW.
WE'D BETTER HEAD FOR COVER, THEN. DO YOU KNOW A SAFE PLACE?
DO I EVER! RUN THIS WAY, GANG--AND NO CRACKS, HUH?
WHAT?
NEVER MIND.

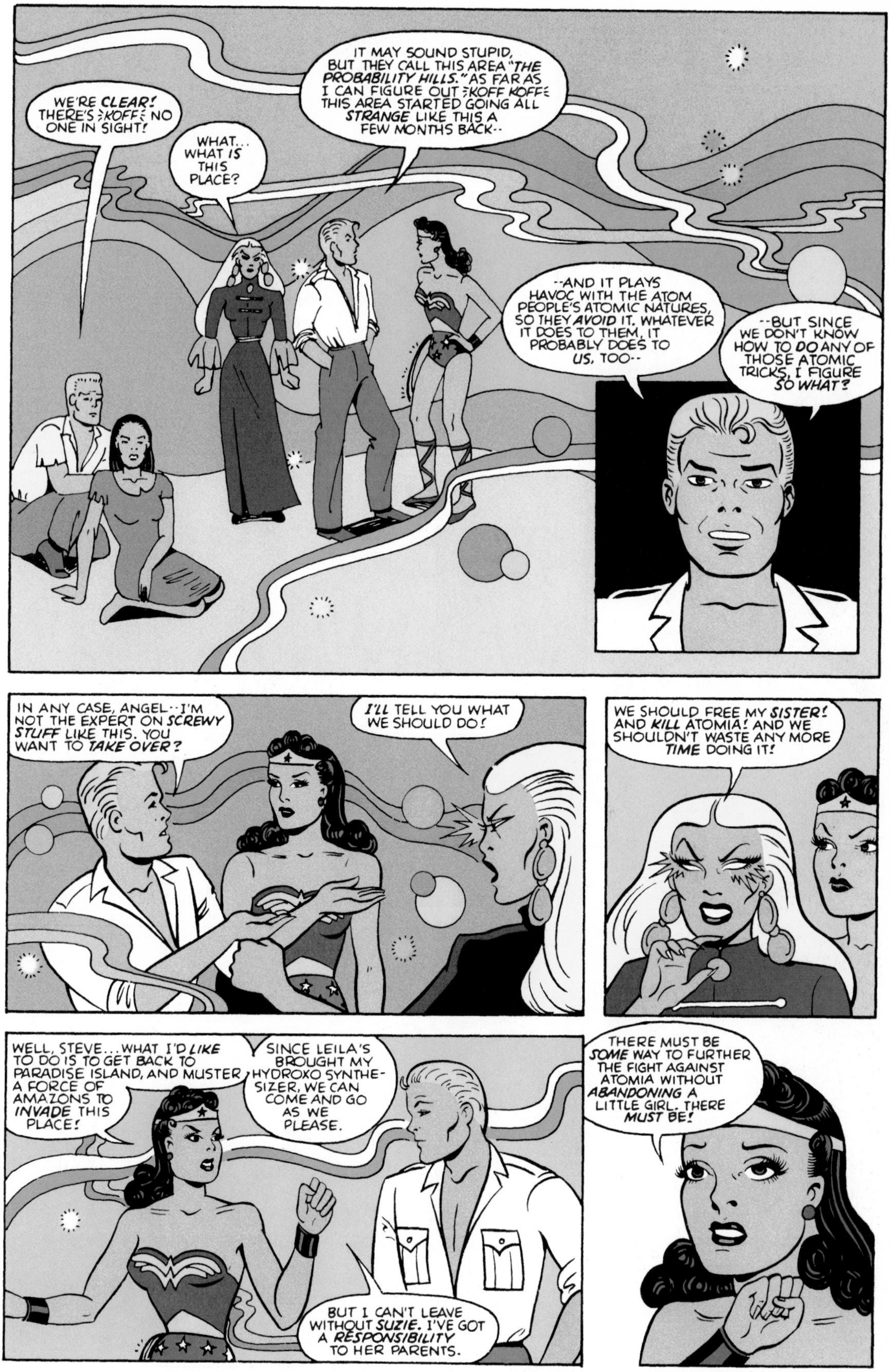

WE'RE CLEAR! THERE'S KOFF NO ONE IN SIGHT!
WHAT... WHAT IS THIS PLACE?
IT MAY SOUND STUPID, BUT THEY CALL THIS AREA "THE PROBABILITY HILLS." AS FAR AS I CAN FIGURE OUT KOFF KOFF THIS AREA STARTED GOING ALL STRANGE LIKE THIS A FEW MONTHS BACK--
--AND IT PLAYS HAVOC WITH THE ATOM PEOPLE'S ATOMIC NATURES, SO THEY AVOID IT. WHATEVER IT DOES TO THEM, IT PROBABLY DOES TO US, TOO--
--BUT SINCE WE DON'T KNOW HOW TO DO ANY OF THOSE ATOMIC TRICKS, I FIGURE SO WHAT?
IN ANY CASE, ANGEL--I'M NOT THE EXPERT ON SCREWY STUFF LIKE THIS. YOU WANT TO TAKE OVER?
I'LL TELL YOU WHAT WE SHOULD DO!
WE SHOULD FREE MY SISTER! AND KILL ATOMIA! AND WE SHOULDN'T WASTE ANY MORE TIME DOING IT!
WELL, STEVE... WHAT I'D LIKE TO DO IS TO GET BACK TO PARADISE ISLAND, AND MUSTER A FORCE OF AMAZONS TO INVADE THIS PLACE!
SINCE LEILA'S BROUGHT MY HYDROXO SYNTHESIZER, WE CAN COME AND GO AS WE PLEASE.
BUT I CAN'T LEAVE WITHOUT SUZIE. I'VE GOT A RESPONSIBILITY TO HER PARENTS.
THERE MUST BE SOME WAY TO FURTHER THE FIGHT AGAINST ATOMIA WITHOUT ABANDONING A LITTLE GIRL. THERE MUST BE!

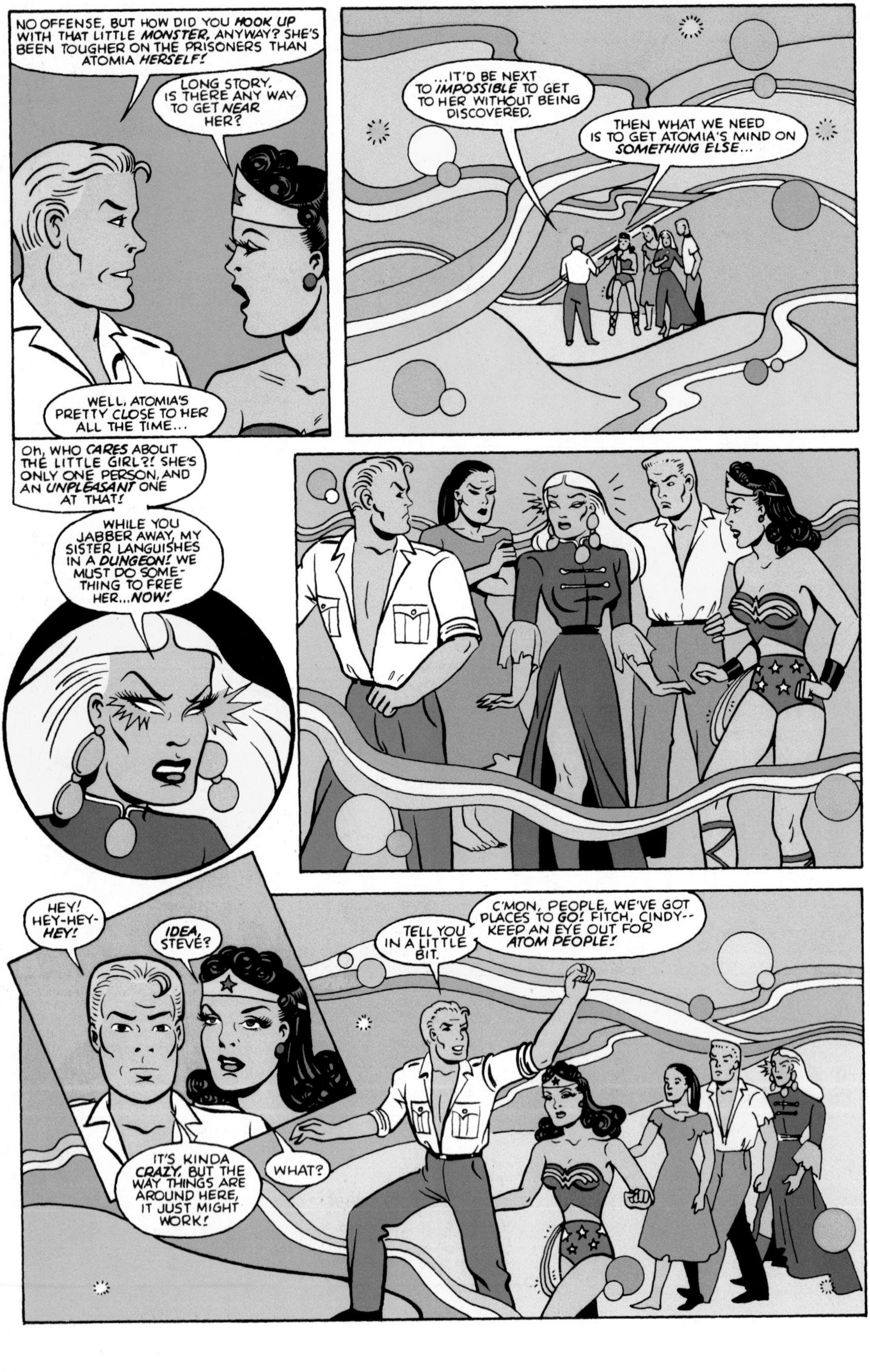
NO OFFENSE, BUT HOW DID YOU HOOK UP WITH THAT LITTLE MONSTER, ANYWAY? SHE'S BEEN TOUGHER ON THE PRISONERS THAN ATOMIA HERSELF!
LONG STORY. IS THERE ANY WAY TO GET NEAR HER?
WELL, ATOMIA'S PRETTY CLOSE TO HER ALL THE TIME...
...IT'D BE NEXT TO IMPOSSIBLE TO GET TO HER WITHOUT BEING DISCOVERED.
THEN WHAT WE NEED IS TO GET ATOMIA'S MIND ON SOMETHING ELSE...
Oh, WHO CARES ABOUT THE LITTLE GIRL?! SHE'S ONLY ONE PERSON, AND AN UNPLEASANT ONE AT THAT!
WHILE YOU JABBER AWAY, MY SISTER LANGUISHES IN A DUNGEON! WE MUST DO SOME-THING TO FREE HER...NOW!
HEY! HEY-HEY-HEY!
IDEA, STEVE?
IT'S KINDA CRAZY, BUT THE WAY THINGS ARE AROUND HERE, IT JUST MIGHT WORK!
WHAT?
TELL YOU IN A LITTLE BIT.
C'MON, PEOPLE, WE'VE GOT PLACES TO GO! FITCH, CINDY--KEEP AN EYE OUT FOR ATOM PEOPLE!

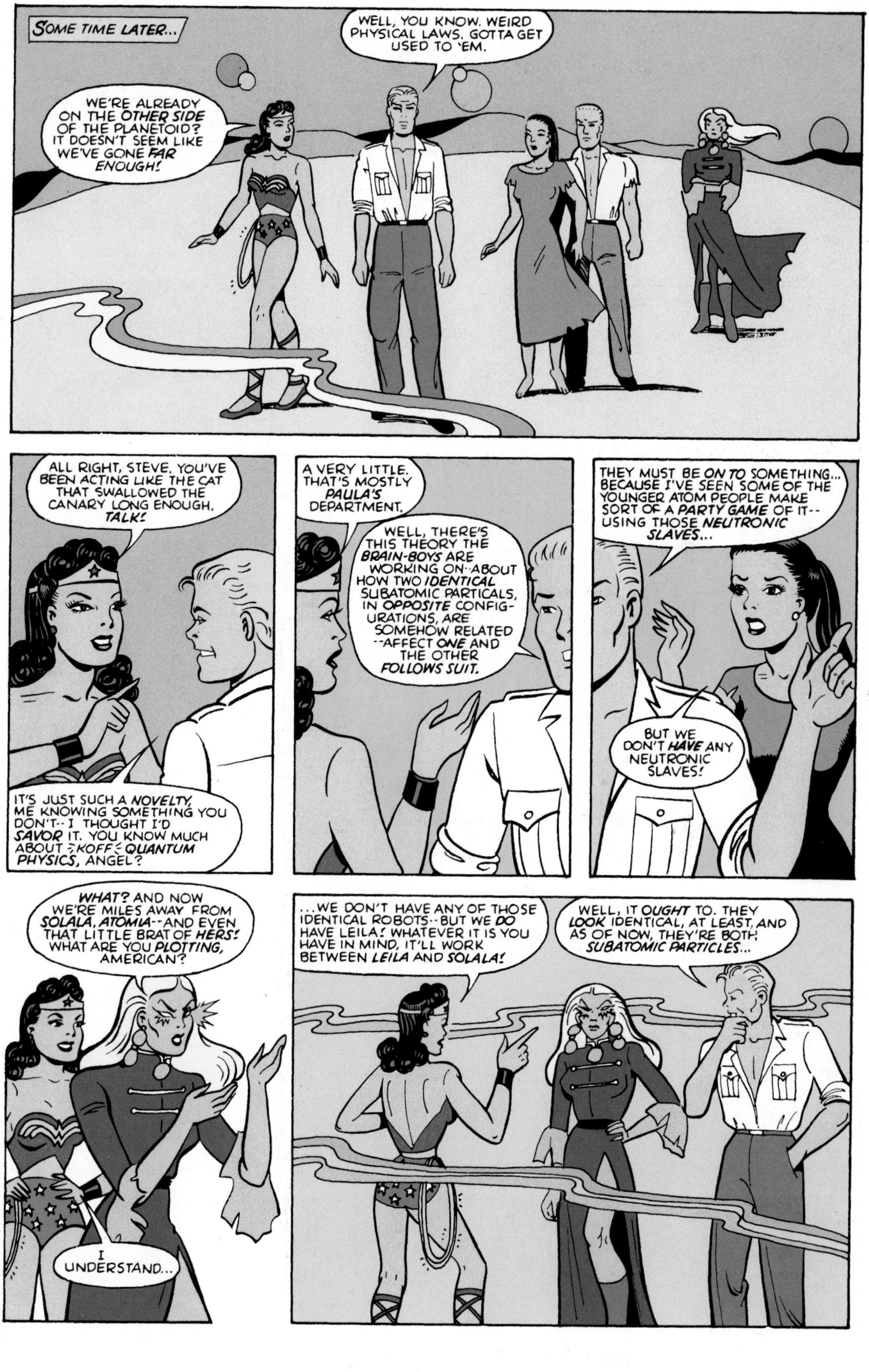
SOME TIME LATER...
WELL, YOU KNOW. WEIRD PHYSICAL LAWS. GOTTA GET USED TO 'EM.
WE'RE ALREADY ON THE OTHER SIDE OF THE PLANETOID? IT DOESN'T SEEM LIKE WE'VE GONE FAR ENOUGH!
ALL RIGHT, STEVE. YOU'VE BEEN ACTING LIKE THE CAT THAT SWALLOWED THE CANARY LONG ENOUGH. TALK!
IT'S JUST SUCH A NOVELTY, ME KNOWING SOMETHING YOU DON'T-- I THOUGHT I'D SAVOR IT. YOU KNOW MUCH ABOUT ≷KOFF≶ QUANTUM PHYSICS, ANGEL?
A VERY LITTLE. THAT'S MOSTLY PAULA'S DEPARTMENT.
WELL, THERE'S THIS THEORY THE BRAIN-BOYS ARE WORKING ON--ABOUT HOW TWO IDENTICAL SUBATOMIC PARTICALS, IN OPPOSITE CONFIG-URATIONS, ARE SOMEHOW RELATED --AFFECT ONE AND THE OTHER FOLLOWS SUIT.
THEY MUST BE ON TO SOMETHING... BECAUSE I'VE SEEN SOME OF THE YOUNGER ATOM PEOPLE MAKE SORT OF A PARTY GAME OF IT-- USING THOSE NEUTRONIC SLAVES...
BUT WE DON'T HAVE ANY NEUTRONIC SLAVES!
WHAT? AND NOW WE'RE MILES AWAY FROM SOLALA, ATOMIA--AND EVEN THAT LITTLE BRAT OF HERS! WHAT ARE YOU PLOTTING, AMERICAN?
I UNDERSTAND...
...WE DON'T HAVE ANY OF THOSE IDENTICAL ROBOTS--BUT WE DO HAVE LEILA! WHATEVER IT IS YOU HAVE IN MIND, IT'LL WORK BETWEEN LEILA AND SOLALA!
WELL, IT OUGHT TO. THEY LOOK IDENTICAL, AT LEAST, AND AS OF NOW, THEY'RE BOTH SUBATOMIC PARTICLES...

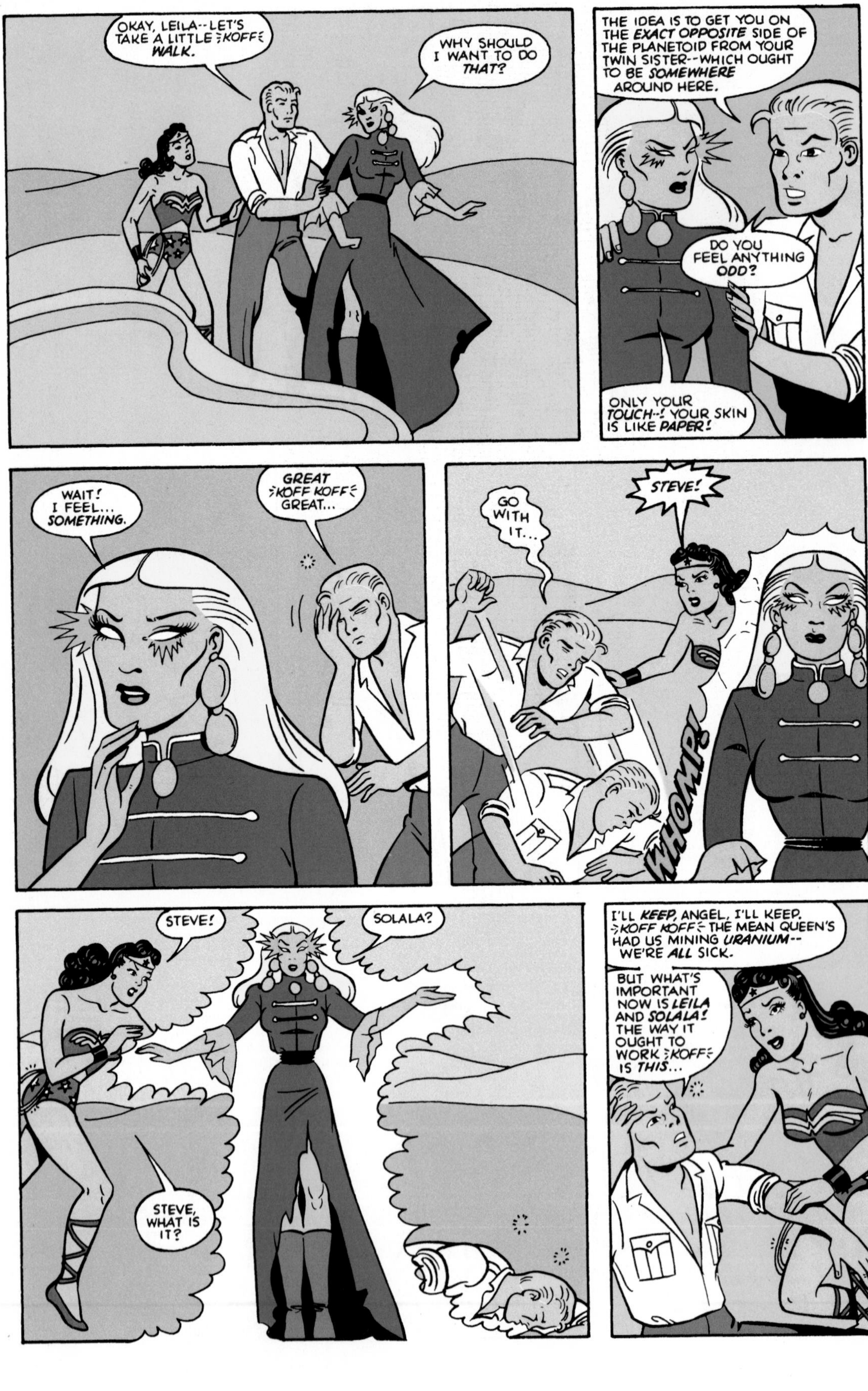

OKAY, LEILA--LET'S TAKE A LITTLE KOFF WALK.
WHY SHOULD I WANT TO DO THAT?
THE IDEA IS TO GET YOU ON THE EXACT OPPOSITE SIDE OF THE PLANETOID FROM YOUR TWIN SISTER--WHICH OUGHT TO BE SOMEWHERE AROUND HERE.
DO YOU FEEL ANYTHING ODD?
ONLY YOUR TOUCH--! YOUR SKIN IS LIKE PAPER!
WAIT! I FEEL... SOMETHING.
GREAT KOFF KOFF GREAT...
GO WITH IT...
STEVE!
WHOMP!
STEVE!
SOLALA?
STEVE, WHAT IS IT?
I'LL KEEP, ANGEL, I'LL KEEP. KOFF KOFF THE MEAN QUEEN'S HAD US MINING URANIUM-- WE'RE ALL SICK.
BUT WHAT'S IMPORTANT NOW IS LEILA AND SOLALA! THE WAY IT OUGHT TO WORK KOFF IS THIS...

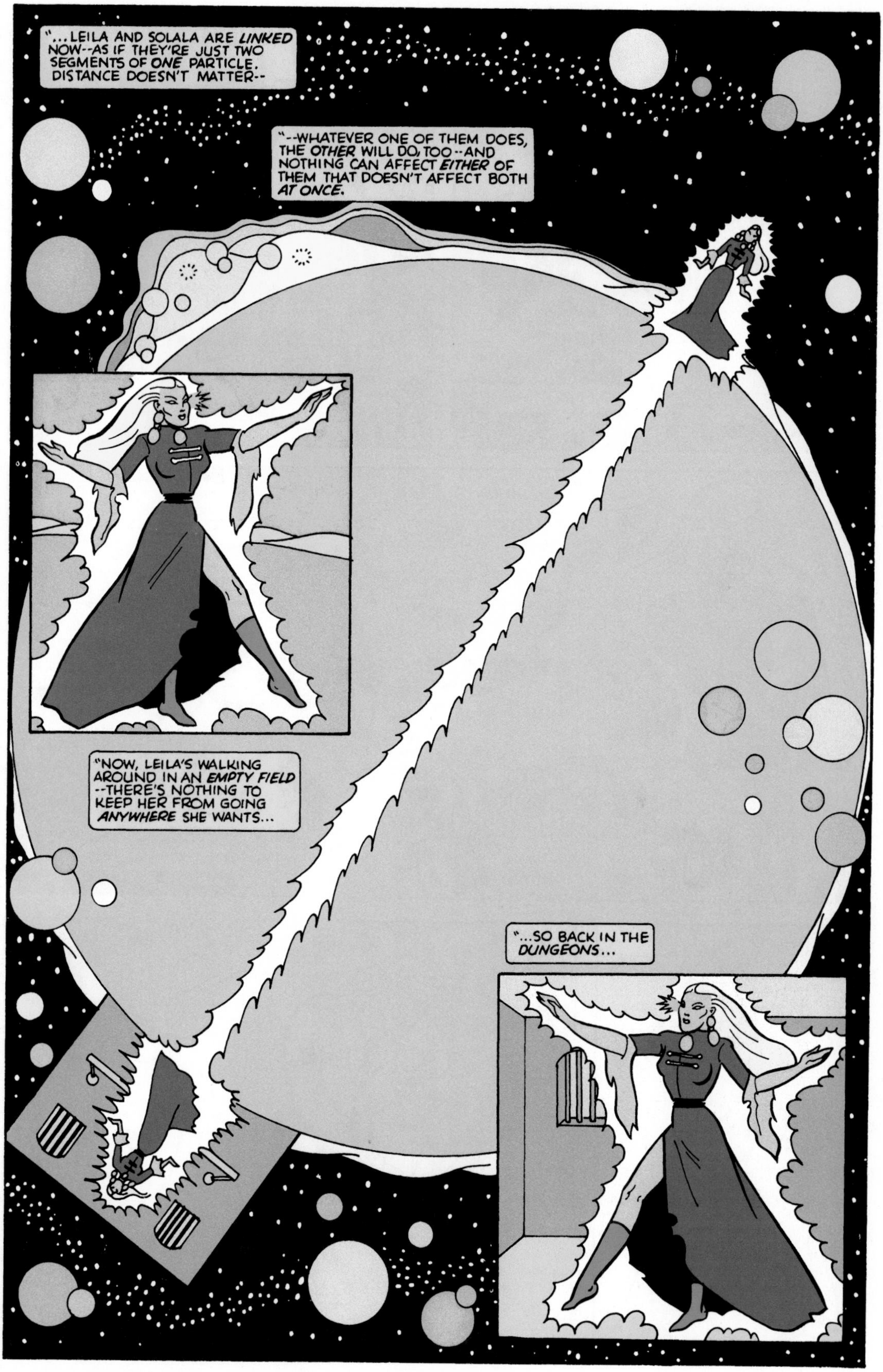
"...LEILA AND SOLALA ARE LINKED NOW--AS IF THEY'RE JUST TWO SEGMENTS OF ONE PARTICLE. DISTANCE DOESN'T MATTER--
"--WHATEVER ONE OF THEM DOES, THE OTHER WILL DO, TOO--AND NOTHING CAN AFFECT EITHER OF THEM THAT DOESN'T AFFECT BOTH AT ONCE.
"NOW, LEILA'S WALKING AROUND IN AN EMPTY FIELD --THERE'S NOTHING TO KEEP HER FROM GOING ANYWHERE SHE WANTS...
"...SO BACK IN THE DUNGEONS...

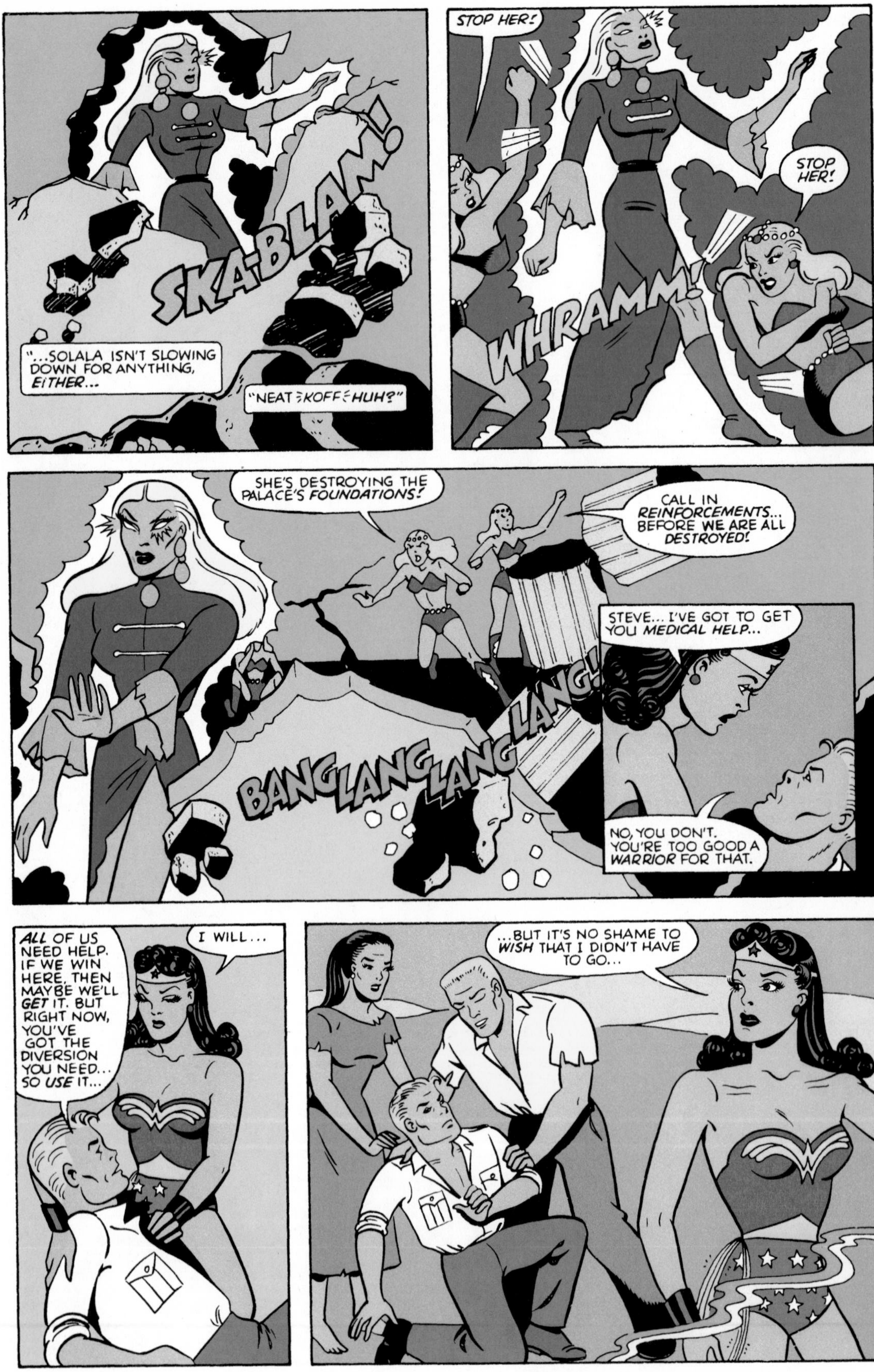

SKA-BLAM!
"...SOLALA ISN'T SLOWING DOWN FOR ANYTHING, EITHER...
"NEAT KOFF HUH?"
STOP HER!
STOP HER!
WHRAMM!
SHE'S DESTROYING THE PALACE'S FOUNDATIONS!
CALL IN REINFORCEMENTS... BEFORE WE ARE ALL DESTROYED!
BANG LANG LANG LANG LANG!
STEVE... I'VE GOT TO GET YOU MEDICAL HELP...
NO, YOU DON'T. YOU'RE TOO GOOD A WARRIOR FOR THAT.
ALL OF US NEED HELP. IF WE WIN HERE, THEN MAYBE WE'LL GET IT. BUT RIGHT NOW, YOU'VE GOT THE DIVERSION YOU NEED... SO USE IT...
I WILL...
...BUT IT'S NO SHAME TO WISH THAT I DIDN'T HAVE TO GO...

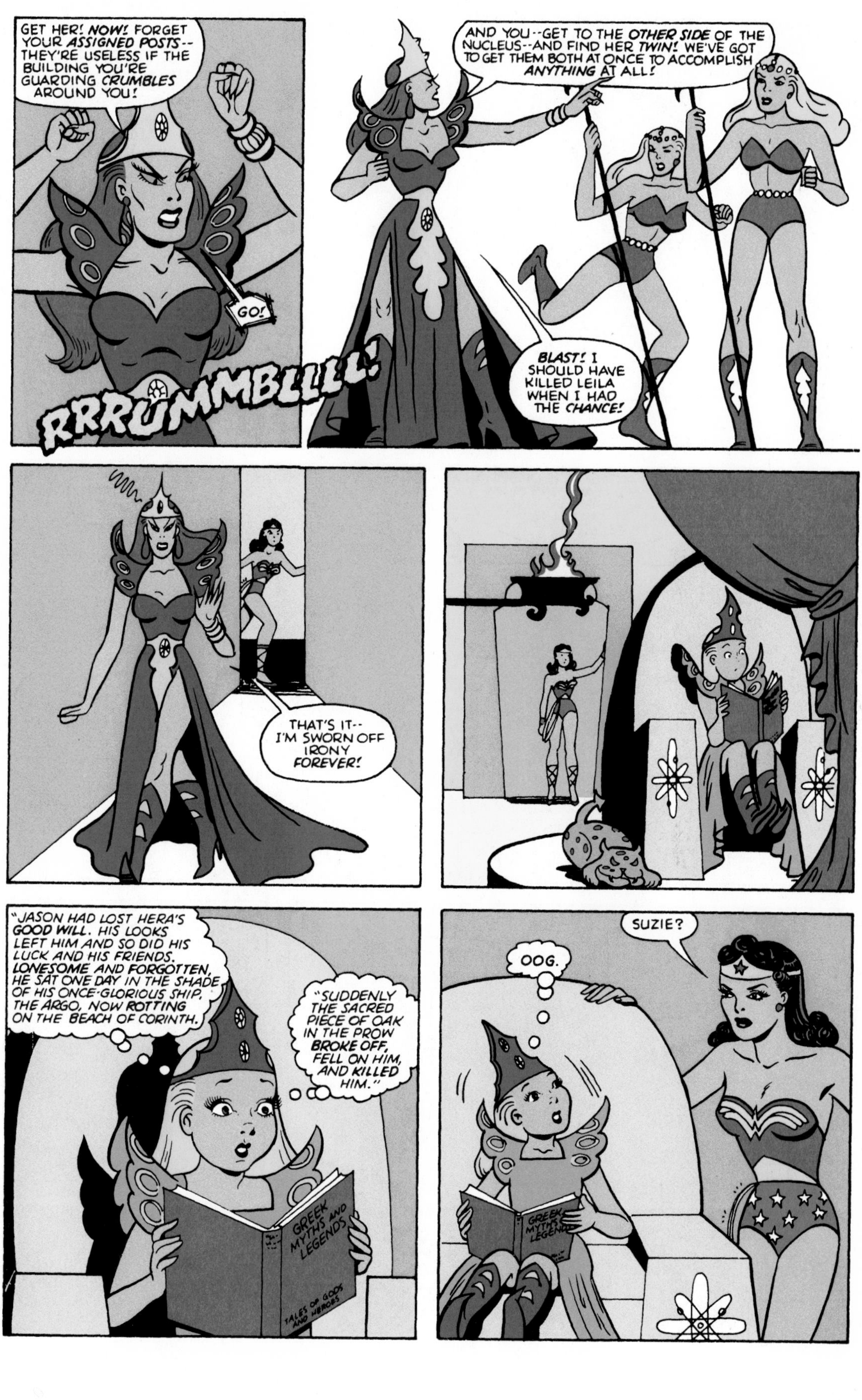
GET HER! NOW! FORGET YOUR ASSIGNED POSTS--THEY'RE USELESS IF THE BUILDING YOU'RE GUARDING CRUMBLES AROUND YOU!
GO!
RRRUMMBLLLL!
AND YOU--GET TO THE OTHER SIDE OF THE NUCLEUS--AND FIND HER TWIN! WE'VE GOT TO GET THEM BOTH AT ONCE TO ACCOMPLISH ANYTHING AT ALL!
BLAST! I SHOULD HAVE KILLED LEILA WHEN I HAD THE CHANCE!
THAT'S IT--I'M SWORN OFF IRONY FOREVER!
"JASON HAD LOST HERA'S GOOD WILL. HIS LOOKS LEFT HIM AND SO DID HIS LUCK AND HIS FRIENDS. LONESOME AND FORGOTTEN, HE SAT ONE DAY IN THE SHADE OF HIS ONCE-GLORIOUS SHIP, THE ARGO, NOW ROTTING ON THE BEACH OF CORINTH.
"SUDDENLY THE SACRED PIECE OF OAK IN THE PROW BROKE OFF, FELL ON HIM, AND KILLED HIM."
GREEK MYTHS AND LEGENDS
TALES OF GODS AND HEROES
SUZIE?
OOG.
GREEK MYTHS AND LEGENDS

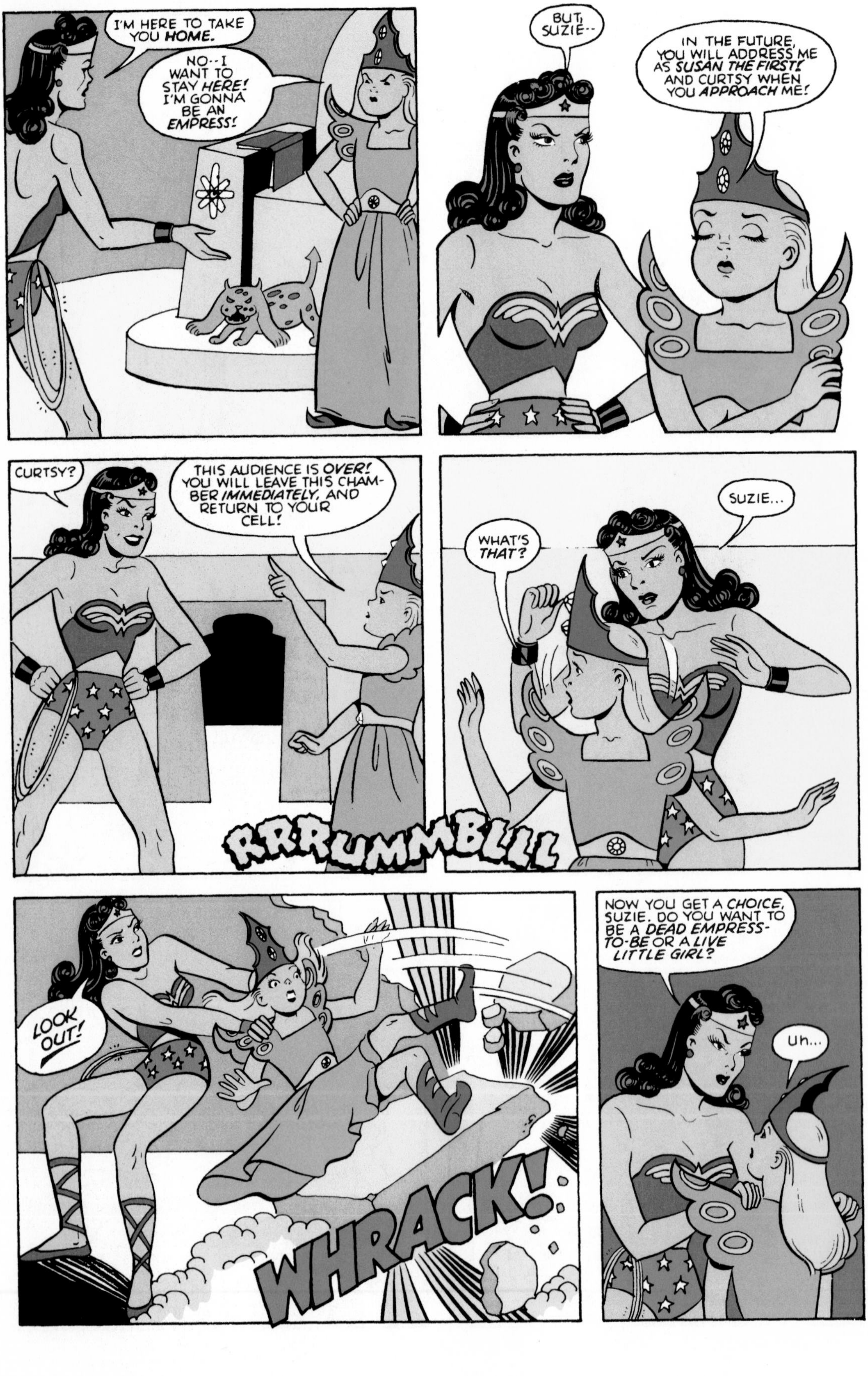

I'M HERE TO TAKE YOU **HOME.**
NO--I WANT TO STAY *HERE!* I'M GONNA BE AN *EMPRESS!*
BUT, SUZIE--
IN THE FUTURE, YOU WILL ADDRESS ME AS *SUSAN THE FIRST!* AND CURTSY WHEN YOU *APPROACH* ME!
CURTSY?
THIS AUDIENCE IS *OVER!* YOU WILL LEAVE THIS CHAMBER *IMMEDIATELY,* AND RETURN TO YOUR CELL!
SUZIE...
WHAT'S *THAT?*
RRRUMMBLLL
LOOK OUT!
WHRACK!
NOW YOU GET A *CHOICE,* SUZIE. DO YOU WANT TO BE A *DEAD EMPRESS-TO-BE* OR A *LIVE LITTLE GIRL?*
Uh...

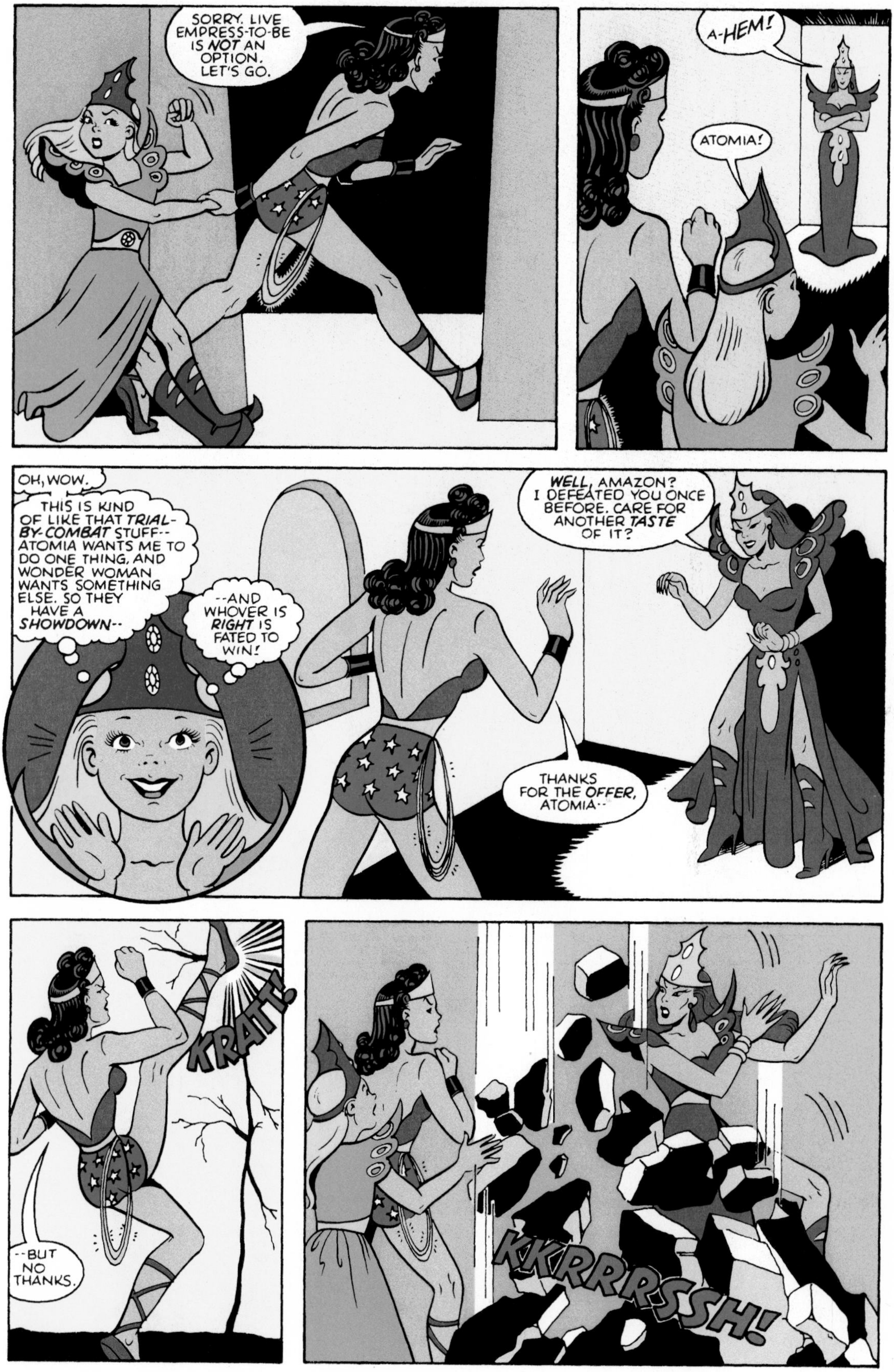

SORRY. LIVE EMPRESS-TO-BE IS *NOT* AN OPTION. LET'S GO.
A-HEM!
ATOMIA!
OH, WOW.
THIS IS KIND OF LIKE THAT *TRIAL-BY-COMBAT* STUFF-- ATOMIA WANTS ME TO DO ONE THING, AND WONDER WOMAN WANTS SOMETHING ELSE. SO THEY HAVE A *SHOWDOWN*--
--AND WHOVER IS *RIGHT* IS FATED TO WIN!
WELL, AMAZON? I DEFEATED YOU ONCE BEFORE. CARE FOR ANOTHER *TASTE* OF IT?
THANKS FOR THE *OFFER*, ATOMIA--
KRATT!
--BUT NO THANKS.
KKRRRRSSH!

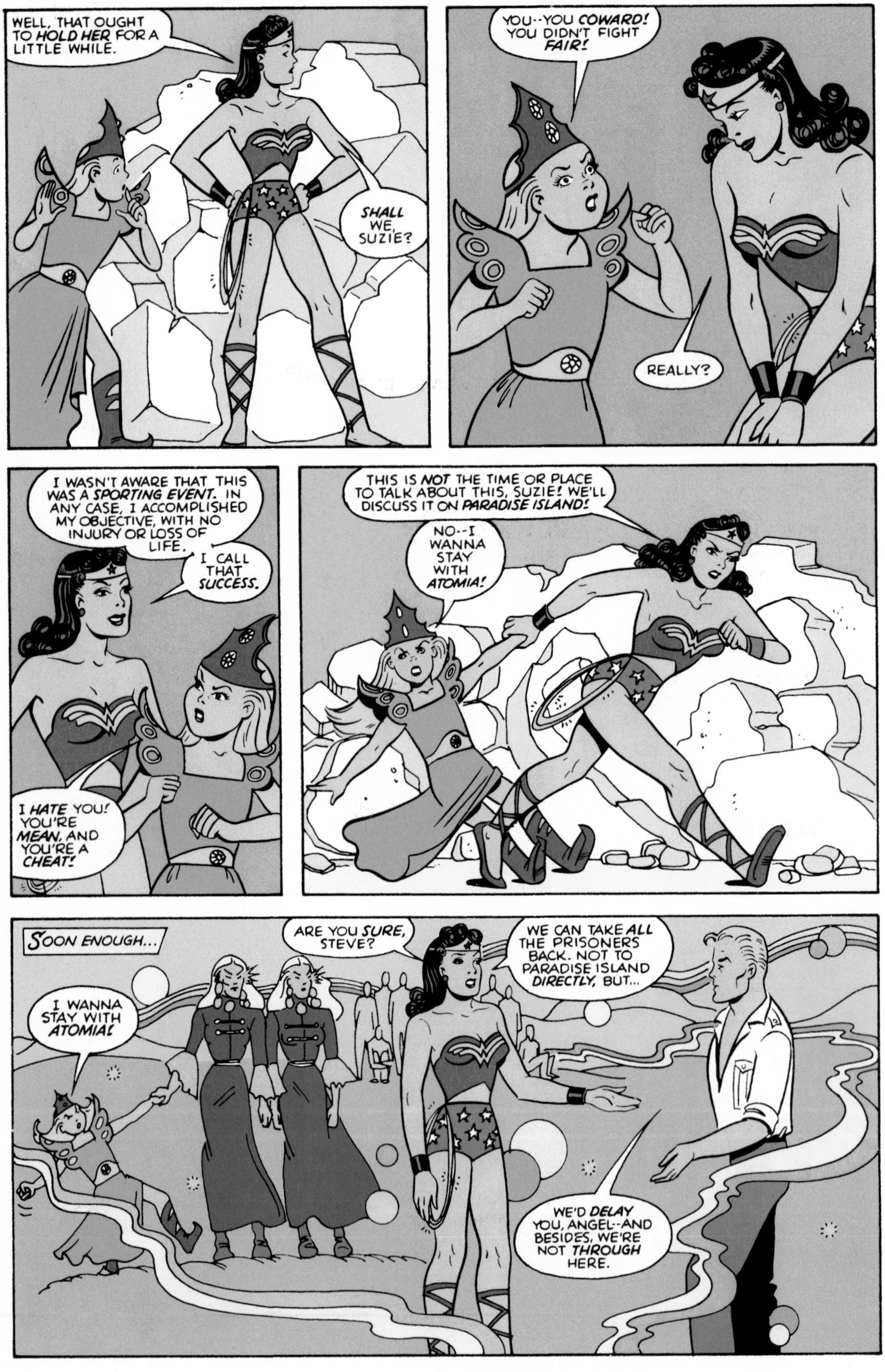

WELL, THAT OUGHT TO HOLD HER FOR A LITTLE WHILE.
SHALL WE, SUZIE?
YOU--YOU COWARD! YOU DIDN'T FIGHT FAIR!
REALLY?
I WASN'T AWARE THAT THIS WAS A SPORTING EVENT. IN ANY CASE, I ACCOMPLISHED MY OBJECTIVE, WITH NO INJURY OR LOSS OF LIFE.
I CALL THAT SUCCESS.
I HATE YOU! YOU'RE MEAN, AND YOU'RE A CHEAT!
THIS IS NOT THE TIME OR PLACE TO TALK ABOUT THIS, SUZIE! WE'LL DISCUSS IT ON PARADISE ISLAND!
NO--I WANNA STAY WITH ATOMIA!
SOON ENOUGH...
I WANNA STAY WITH ATOMIA!
ARE YOU SURE, STEVE?
WE CAN TAKE ALL THE PRISONERS BACK. NOT TO PARADISE ISLAND DIRECTLY, BUT...
WE'D DELAY YOU, ANGEL--AND BESIDES, WE'RE NOT THROUGH HERE.

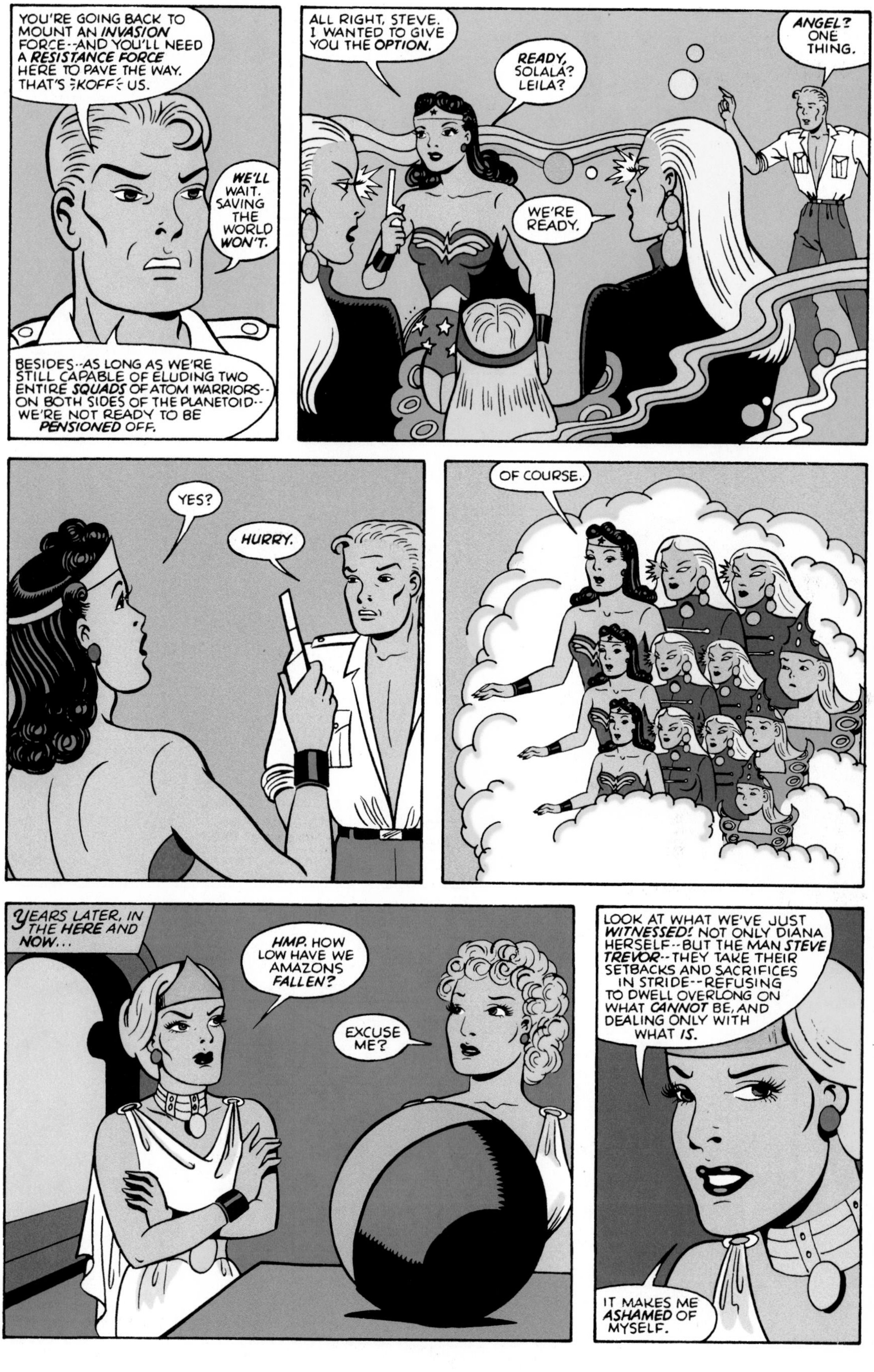

YOU'RE GOING BACK TO MOUNT AN INVASION FORCE--AND YOU'LL NEED A RESISTANCE FORCE HERE TO PAVE THE WAY. THAT'S *KOFF* US.
WE'LL WAIT. SAVING THE WORLD WON'T.
BESIDES--AS LONG AS WE'RE STILL CAPABLE OF ELUDING TWO ENTIRE SQUADS OF ATOM WARRIORS--ON BOTH SIDES OF THE PLANETOID--WE'RE NOT READY TO BE PENSIONED OFF.
ALL RIGHT, STEVE. I WANTED TO GIVE YOU THE OPTION.
READY, SOLALA? LEILA?
WE'RE READY.
ANGEL? ONE THING.
YES?
HURRY.
OF COURSE.
YEARS LATER, IN THE HERE AND NOW...
HMP. HOW LOW HAVE WE AMAZONS FALLEN?
EXCUSE ME?
LOOK AT WHAT WE'VE JUST WITNESSED! NOT ONLY DIANA HERSELF--BUT THE MAN STEVE TREVOR--THEY TAKE THEIR SETBACKS AND SACRIFICES IN STRIDE--REFUSING TO DWELL OVERLONG ON WHAT CANNOT BE, AND DEALING ONLY WITH WHAT IS.
IT MAKES ME ASHAMED OF MYSELF.

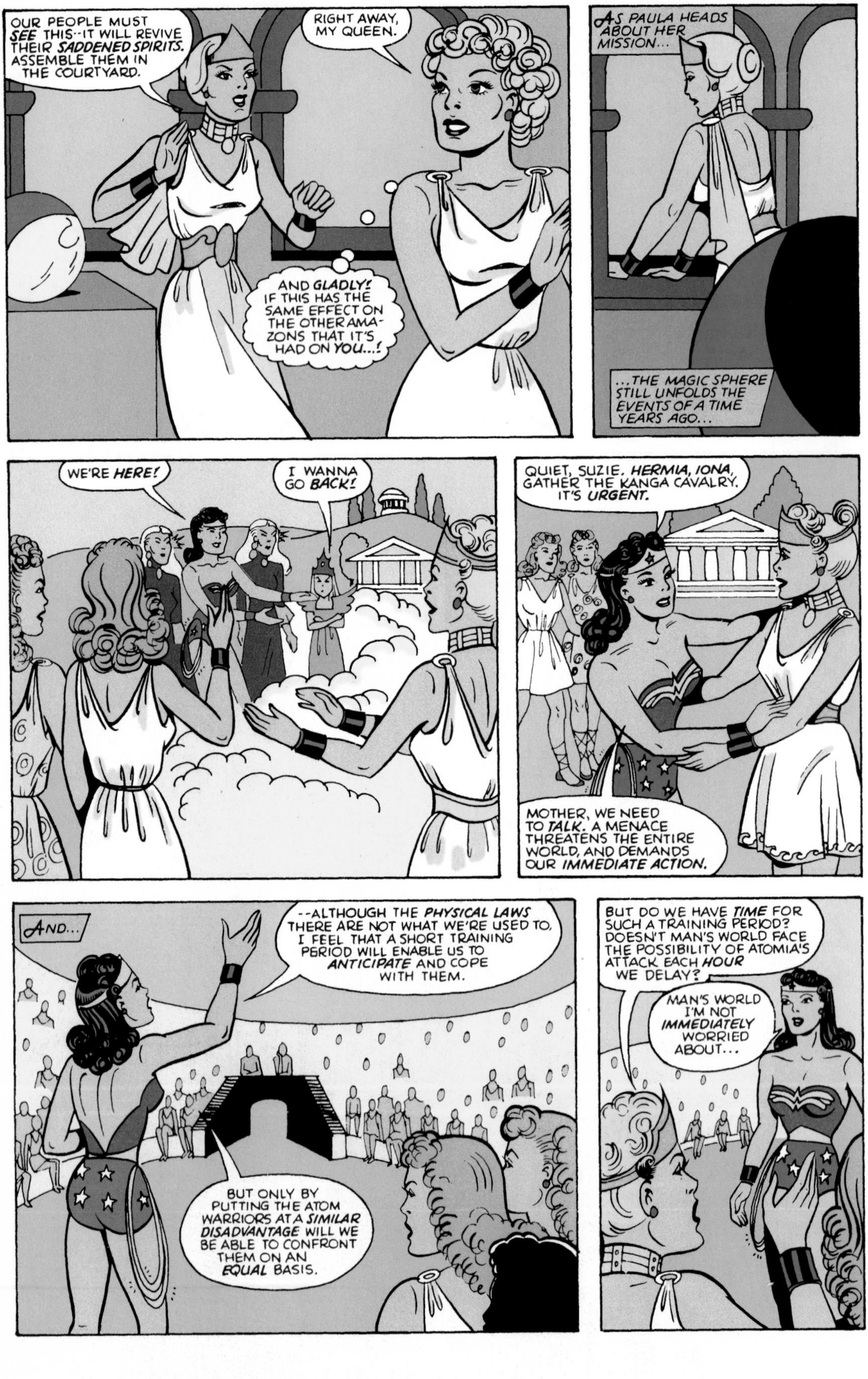
OUR PEOPLE MUST SEE THIS--IT WILL REVIVE THEIR SADDENED SPIRITS. ASSEMBLE THEM IN THE COURTYARD.
RIGHT AWAY, MY QUEEN.
AND GLADLY! IF THIS HAS THE SAME EFFECT ON THE OTHER AMAZONS THAT IT'S HAD ON YOU...!
AS PAULA HEADS ABOUT HER MISSION...
...THE MAGIC SPHERE STILL UNFOLDS THE EVENTS OF A TIME YEARS AGO...
WE'RE HERE!
I WANNA GO BACK!
QUIET, SUZIE. HERMIA, IONA, GATHER THE KANGA CAVALRY. IT'S URGENT.
MOTHER, WE NEED TO TALK. A MENACE THREATENS THE ENTIRE WORLD, AND DEMANDS OUR IMMEDIATE ACTION.
AND...
--ALTHOUGH THE PHYSICAL LAWS THERE ARE NOT WHAT WE'RE USED TO, I FEEL THAT A SHORT TRAINING PERIOD WILL ENABLE US TO ANTICIPATE AND COPE WITH THEM.
BUT ONLY BY PUTTING THE ATOM WARRIORS AT A SIMILAR DISADVANTAGE WILL WE BE ABLE TO CONFRONT THEM ON AN EQUAL BASIS.
BUT DO WE HAVE TIME FOR SUCH A TRAINING PERIOD? DOESN'T MAN'S WORLD FACE THE POSSIBILITY OF ATOMIA'S ATTACK EACH HOUR WE DELAY?
MAN'S WORLD I'M NOT IMMEDIATELY WORRIED ABOUT...

...I THINK SHE'S MAD ENOUGH AT *US* SO THAT SHE WON'T HAVE MUCH ELSE ON HER *MIND* FOR AWHILE...

WHERE ARE THEY?!

BLAST IT, WHERE *ARE* THEY?!!

I'VE BEEN ON THEIR *INCONSEQUENTIAL LITTLE ISLAND* BEFORE-- I WAS THERE *SEVERAL TIMES,* WHEN WONDER WOMAN AND I FIRST CLASHED!

I KNOW IT WAS IN THIS AREA!! IT'S GOT TO BE HERE!

I'LL FIND IT!

AND WHEN I DO--

BLAM!

SHRACK!

SSSSSS SSSSSS

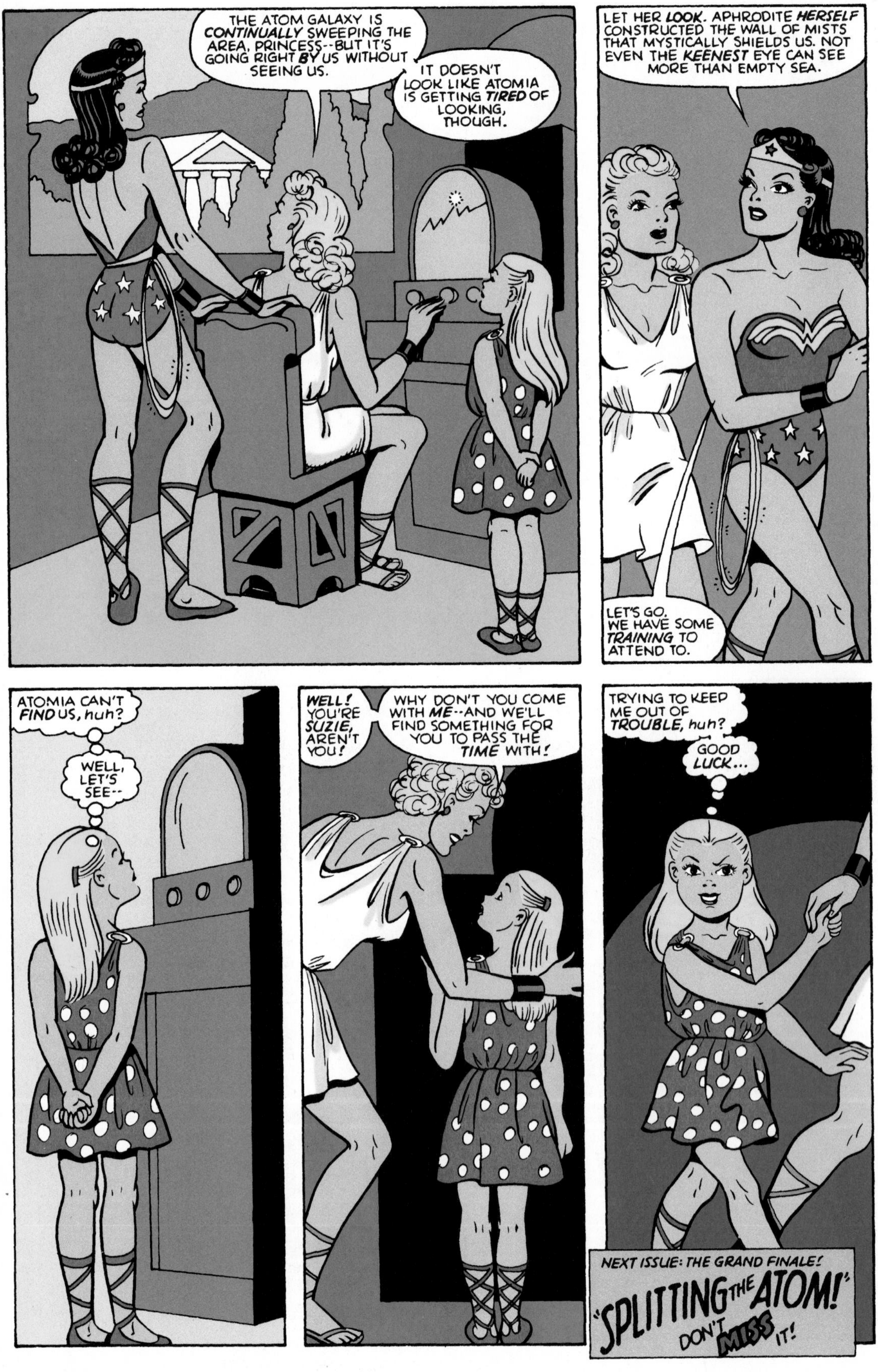
THE ATOM GALAXY IS CONTINUALLY SWEEPING THE AREA, PRINCESS--BUT IT'S GOING RIGHT BY US WITHOUT SEEING US.
IT DOESN'T LOOK LIKE ATOMIA IS GETTING TIRED OF LOOKING, THOUGH.
LET HER LOOK. APHRODITE HERSELF CONSTRUCTED THE WALL OF MISTS THAT MYSTICALLY SHIELDS US. NOT EVEN THE KEENEST EYE CAN SEE MORE THAN EMPTY SEA.
LET'S GO. WE HAVE SOME TRAINING TO ATTEND TO.
ATOMIA CAN'T FIND US, huh?
WELL, LET'S SEE--
WELL! YOU'RE SUZIE, AREN'T YOU!
WHY DON'T YOU COME WITH ME--AND WE'LL FIND SOMETHING FOR YOU TO PASS THE TIME WITH!
TRYING TO KEEP ME OUT OF TROUBLE, huh?
GOOD LUCK...
NEXT ISSUE: THE GRAND FINALE!
"SPLITTING THE ATOM!"
DON'T MISS IT!

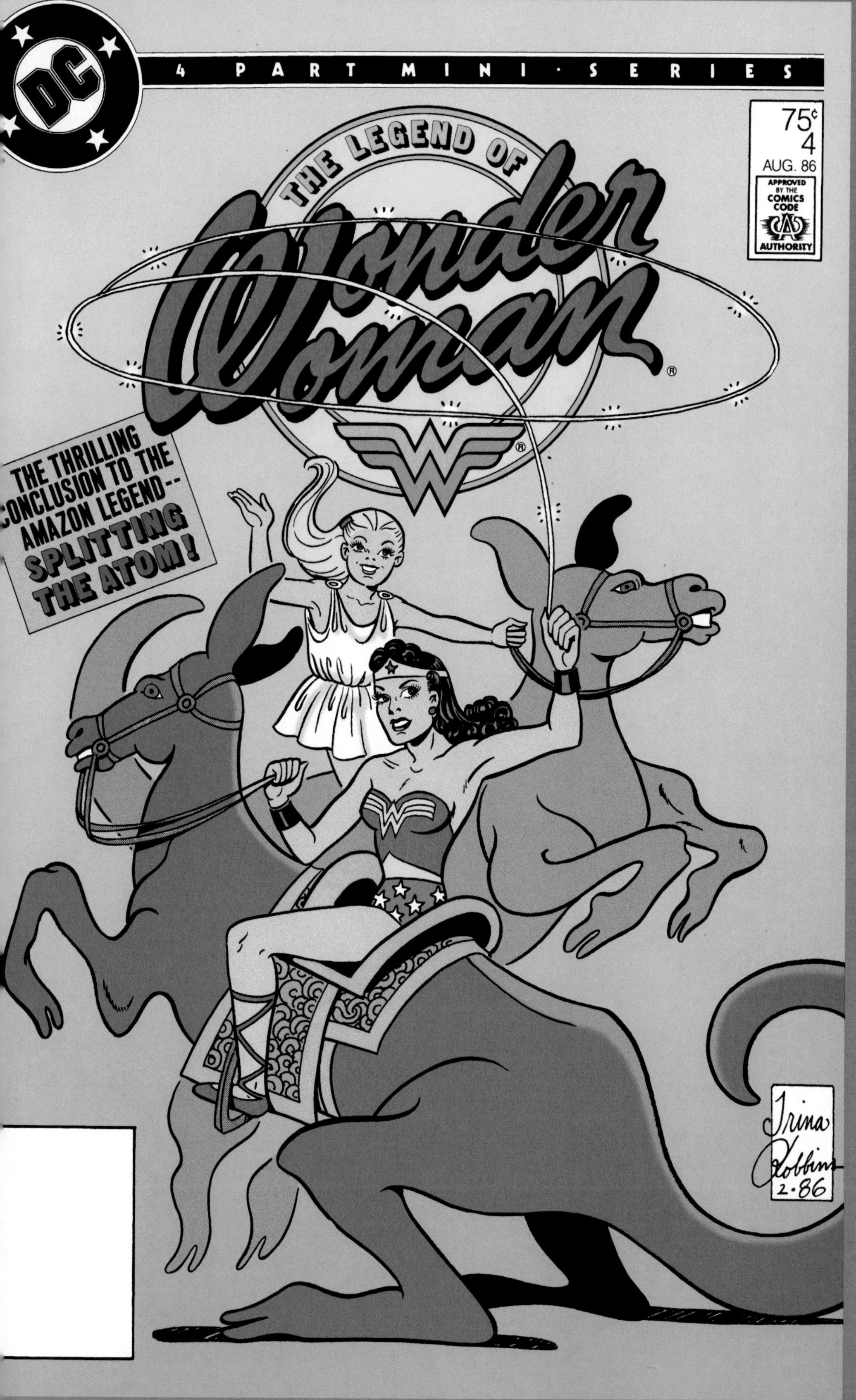

DC
4 PART MINI-SERIES
75¢
4
AUG. 86
APPROVED BY THE COMICS CODE AUTHORITY
THE LEGEND OF
Wonder Woman®
THE THRILLING CONCLUSION TO THE AMAZON LEGEND--
SPLITTING THE ATOM!
Trina Robbins 2-86

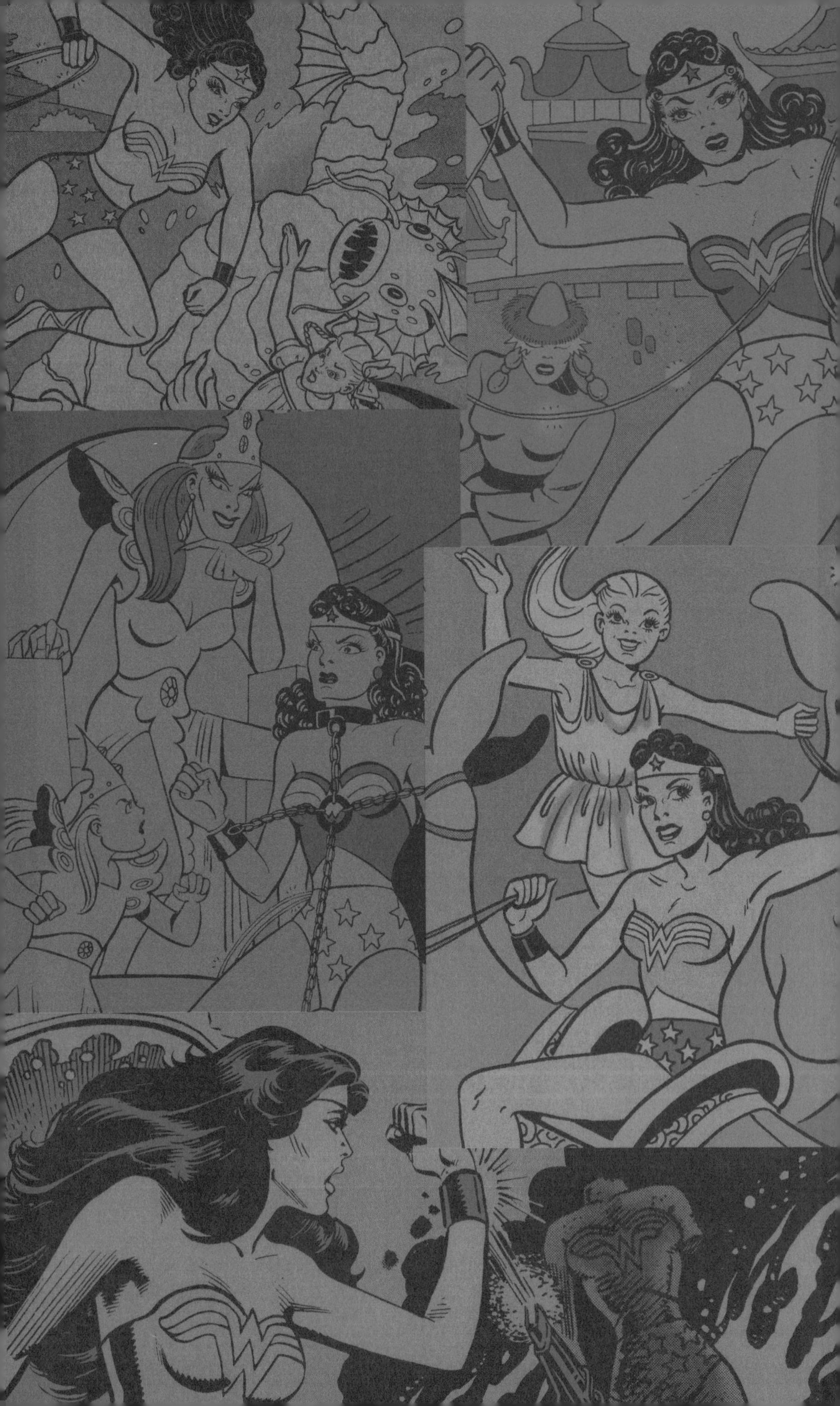

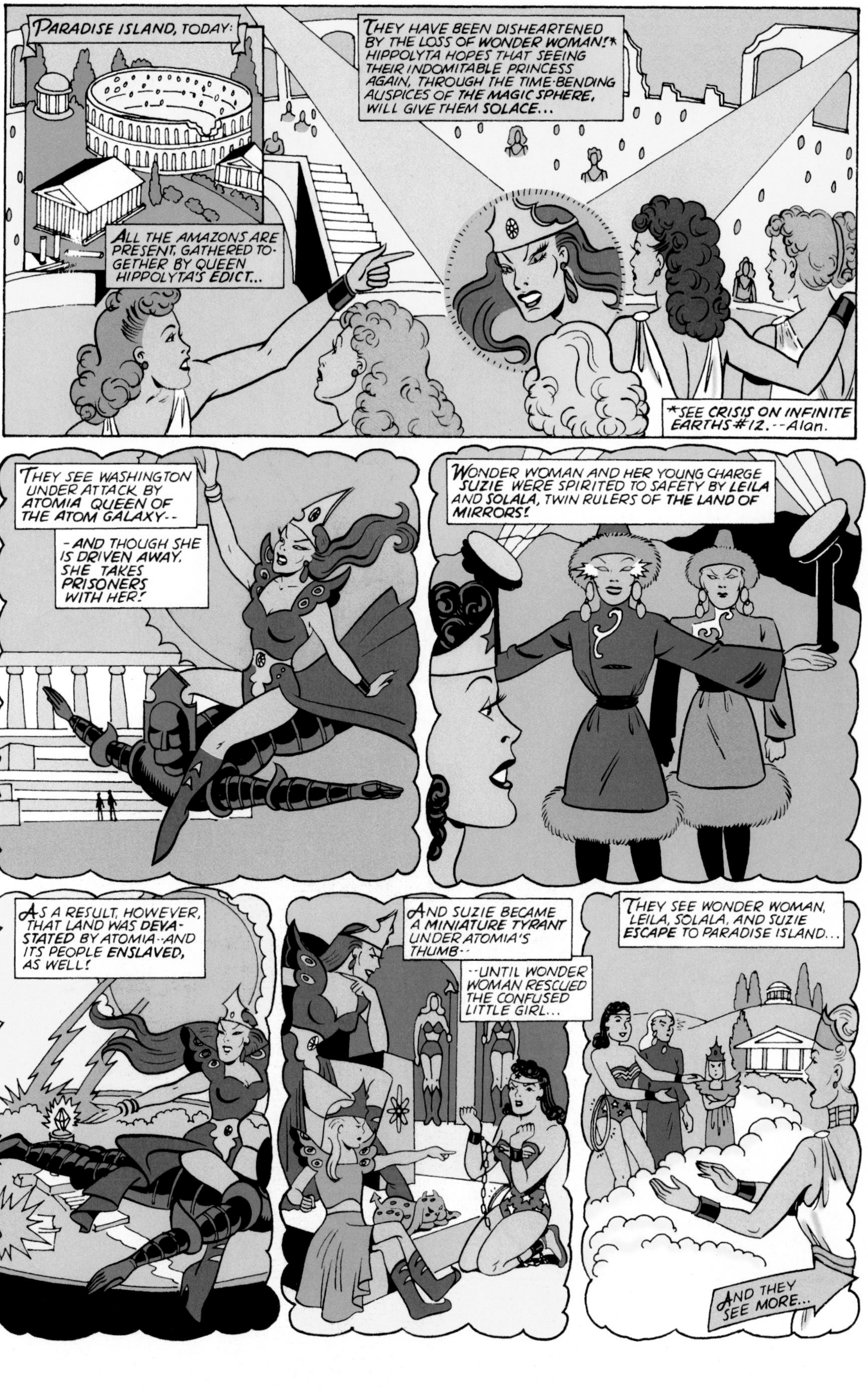
PARADISE ISLAND, TODAY:
THEY HAVE BEEN DISHEARTENED BY THE LOSS OF WONDER WOMAN!* HIPPOLYTA HOPES THAT SEEING THEIR INDOMITABLE PRINCESS AGAIN, THROUGH THE TIME-BENDING AUSPICES OF THE MAGIC SPHERE, WILL GIVE THEM SOLACE...
ALL THE AMAZONS ARE PRESENT, GATHERED TOGETHER BY QUEEN HIPPOLYTA'S EDICT...
*SEE CRISIS ON INFINITE EARTHS #12. --Alan.
THEY SEE WASHINGTON UNDER ATTACK BY ATOMIA QUEEN OF THE ATOM GALAXY--
-AND THOUGH SHE IS DRIVEN AWAY, SHE TAKES PRISONERS WITH HER!
WONDER WOMAN AND HER YOUNG CHARGE SUZIE WERE SPIRITED TO SAFETY BY LEILA AND SOLALA, TWIN RULERS OF THE LAND OF MIRRORS!
AS A RESULT, HOWEVER, THAT LAND WAS DEVASTATED BY ATOMIA--AND ITS PEOPLE ENSLAVED, AS WELL!
AND SUZIE BECAME A MINIATURE TYRANT UNDER ATOMIA'S THUMB--
--UNTIL WONDER WOMAN RESCUED THE CONFUSED LITTLE GIRL...
THEY SEE WONDER WOMAN, LEILA, SOLALA, AND SUZIE ESCAPE TO PARADISE ISLAND...
AND THEY SEE MORE...

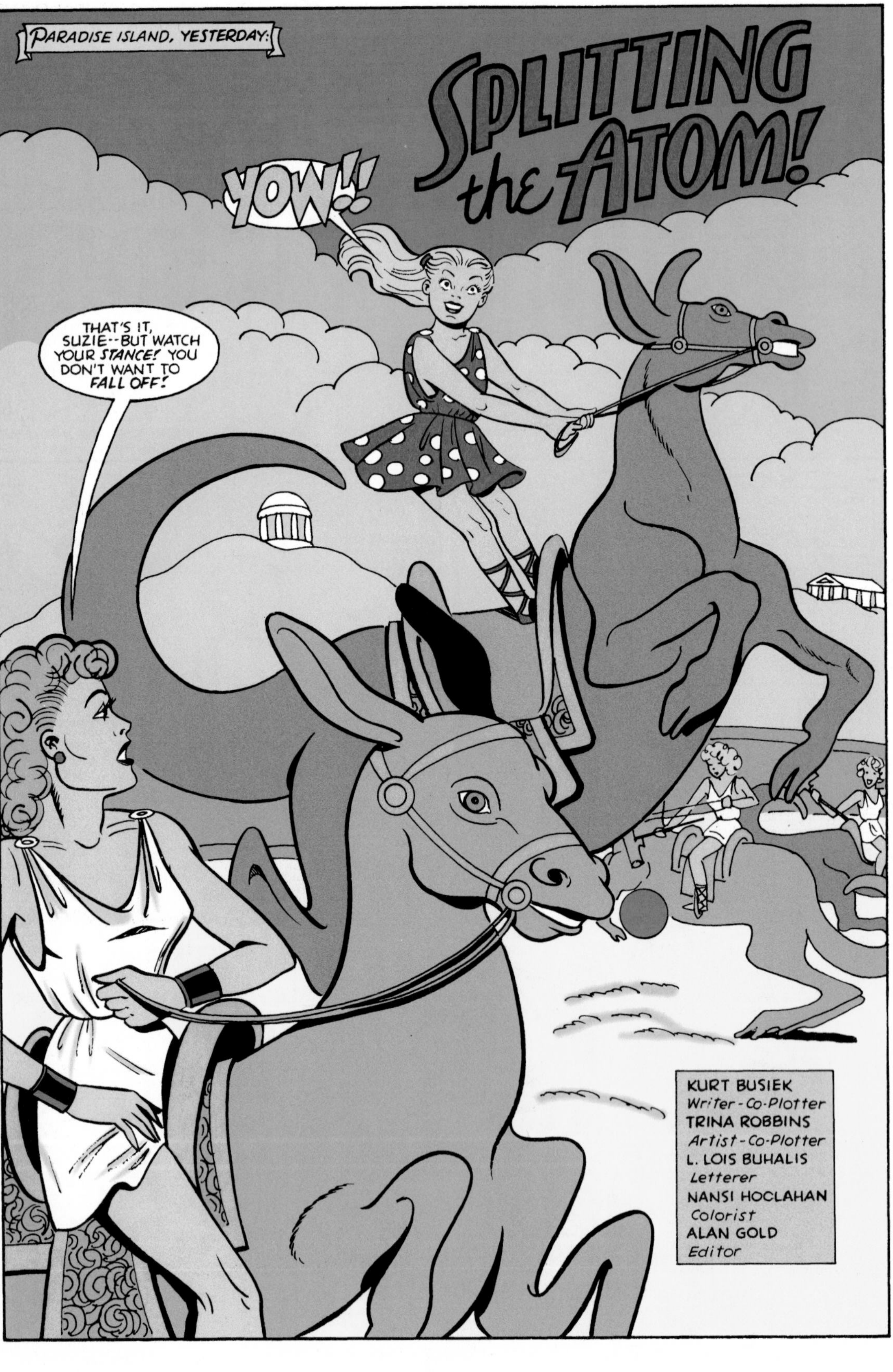
PARADISE ISLAND, YESTERDAY:
SPLITTING the ATOM!
YOW!!
THAT'S IT, SUZIE--BUT WATCH YOUR STANCE! YOU DON'T WANT TO FALL OFF!
KURT BUSIEK Writer-Co-Plotter
TRINA ROBBINS Artist-Co-Plotter
L. LOIS BUHALIS Letterer
NANSI HOCLAHAN Colorist
ALAN GOLD Editor

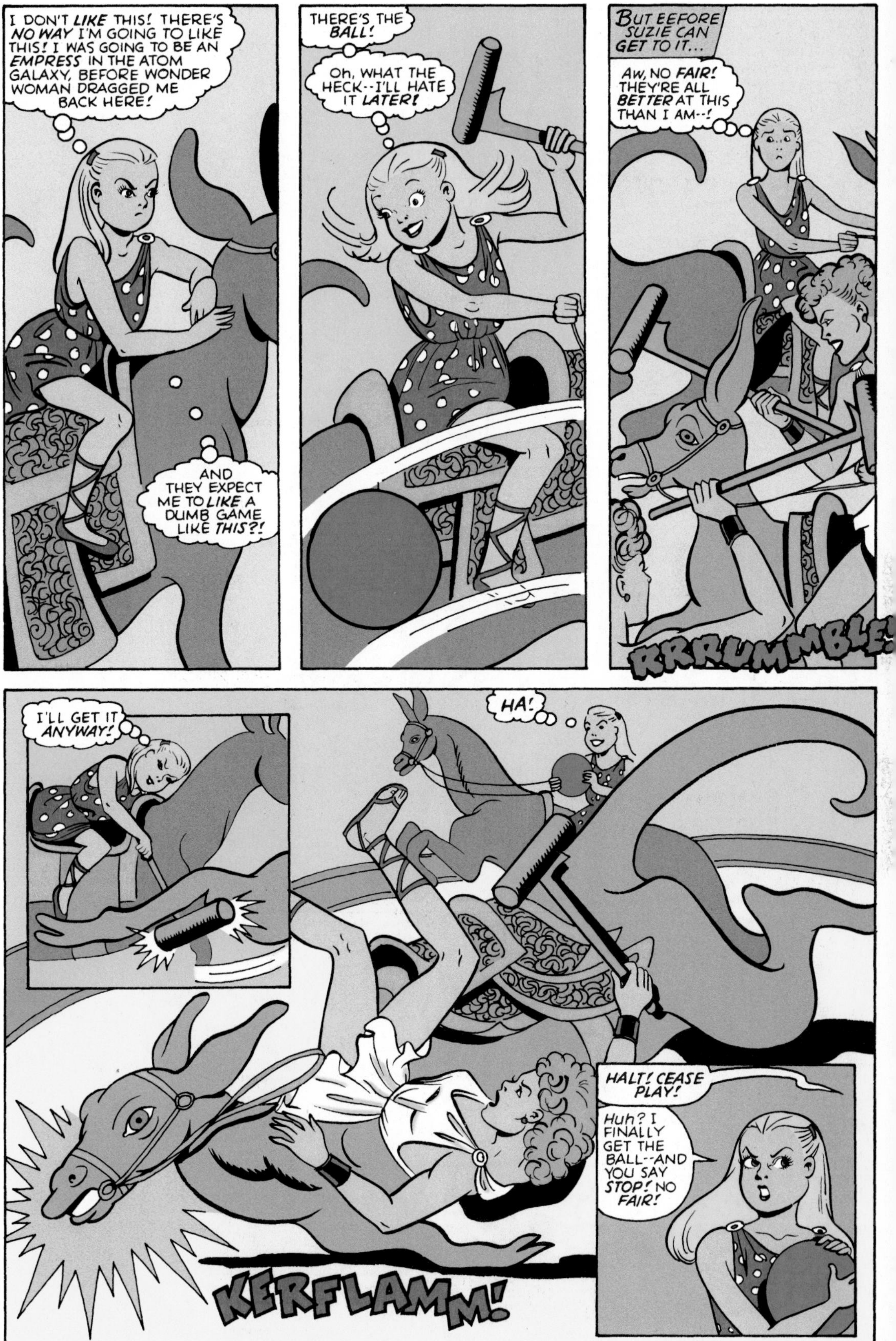
I DON'T LIKE THIS! THERE'S NO WAY I'M GOING TO LIKE THIS! I WAS GOING TO BE AN EMPRESS IN THE ATOM GALAXY, BEFORE WONDER WOMAN DRAGGED ME BACK HERE!
AND THEY EXPECT ME TO LIKE A DUMB GAME LIKE THIS?!
THERE'S THE BALL!
Oh, WHAT THE HECK--I'LL HATE IT LATER!
BUT EEFORE SUZIE CAN GET TO IT...
Aw, NO FAIR! THEY'RE ALL BETTER AT THIS THAN I AM--!
KRRUMMBLE!
I'LL GET IT ANYWAY!
HA!
KERFLAMM!
HALT! CEASE PLAY!
Huh? I FINALLY GET THE BALL--AND YOU SAY STOP! NO FAIR!

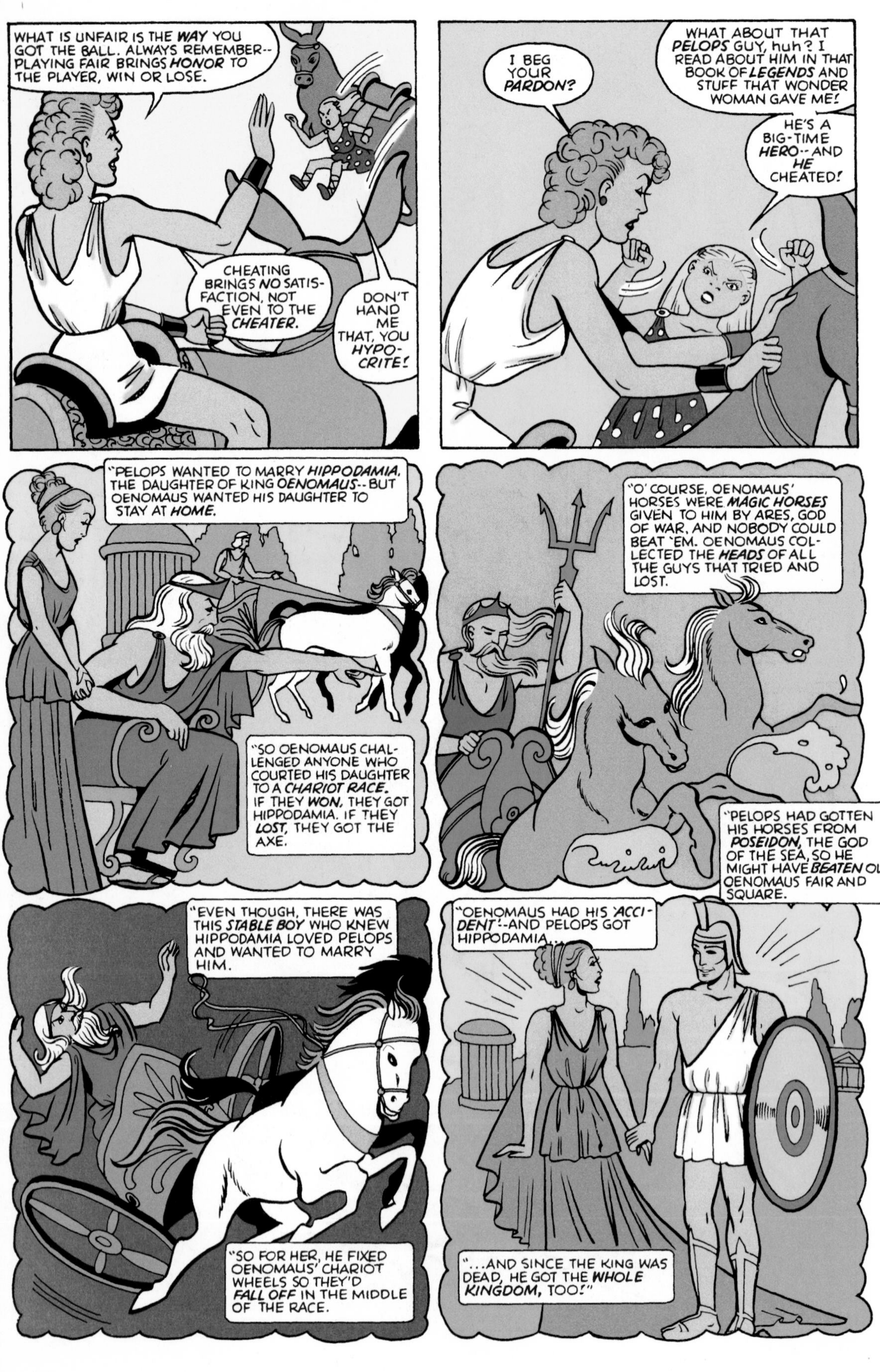

WHAT IS UNFAIR IS THE WAY YOU GOT THE BALL. ALWAYS REMEMBER-- PLAYING FAIR BRINGS HONOR TO THE PLAYER, WIN OR LOSE.
CHEATING BRINGS NO SATISFACTION, NOT EVEN TO THE CHEATER.
DON'T HAND ME THAT, YOU HYPOCRITE!
I BEG YOUR PARDON?
WHAT ABOUT THAT PELOPS GUY, huh? I READ ABOUT HIM IN THAT BOOK OF LEGENDS AND STUFF THAT WONDER WOMAN GAVE ME!
HE'S A BIG-TIME HERO--AND HE CHEATED!
"PELOPS WANTED TO MARRY HIPPODAMIA, THE DAUGHTER OF KING OENOMAUS--BUT OENOMAUS WANTED HIS DAUGHTER TO STAY AT HOME.
"SO OENOMAUS CHALLENGED ANYONE WHO COURTED HIS DAUGHTER TO A CHARIOT RACE. IF THEY WON, THEY GOT HIPPODAMIA. IF THEY LOST, THEY GOT THE AXE.
"O' COURSE, OENOMAUS' HORSES WERE MAGIC HORSES GIVEN TO HIM BY ARES, GOD OF WAR, AND NOBODY COULD BEAT 'EM. OENOMAUS COLLECTED THE HEADS OF ALL THE GUYS THAT TRIED AND LOST.
"PELOPS HAD GOTTEN HIS HORSES FROM POSEIDON, THE GOD OF THE SEA, SO HE MIGHT HAVE BEATEN OL' OENOMAUS FAIR AND SQUARE.
"EVEN THOUGH, THERE WAS THIS STABLE BOY WHO KNEW HIPPODAMIA LOVED PELOPS AND WANTED TO MARRY HIM.
"SO FOR HER, HE FIXED OENOMAUS' CHARIOT WHEELS SO THEY'D FALL OFF IN THE MIDDLE OF THE RACE.
"OENOMAUS HAD HIS 'ACCIDENT'--AND PELOPS GOT HIPPODAMIA...
"...AND SINCE THE KING WAS DEAD, HE GOT THE WHOLE KINGDOM, TOO!"

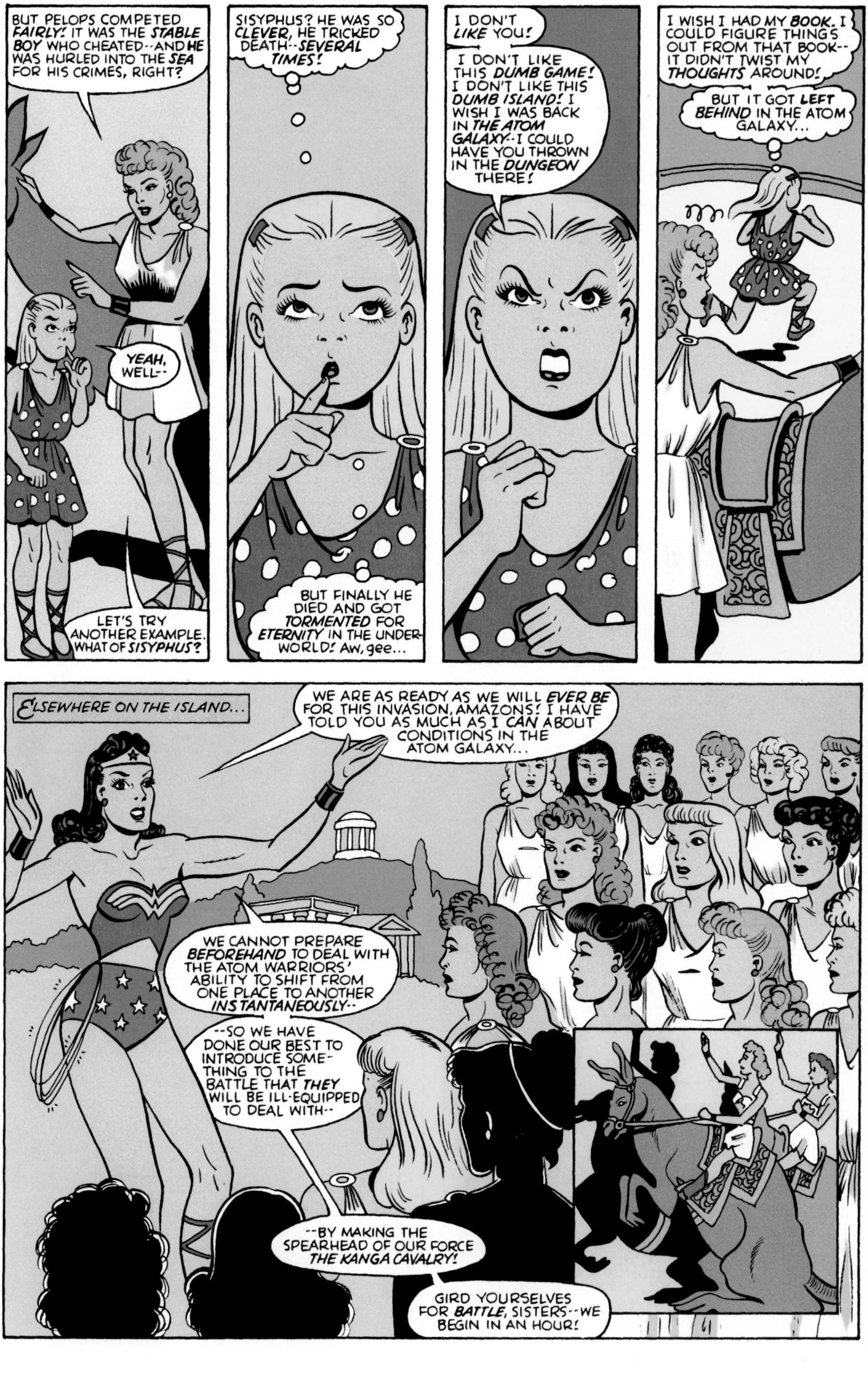
BUT PELOPS COMPETED FAIRLY! IT WAS THE STABLE BOY WHO CHEATED--AND HE WAS HURLED INTO THE SEA FOR HIS CRIMES, RIGHT?
YEAH, WELL--
LET'S TRY ANOTHER EXAMPLE. WHAT OF SISYPHUS?
SISYPHUS? HE WAS SO CLEVER, HE TRICKED DEATH--SEVERAL TIMES!
BUT FINALLY HE DIED AND GOT TORMENTED FOR ETERNITY IN THE UNDER-WORLD! Aw, gee...
I DON'T LIKE YOU!
I DON'T LIKE THIS DUMB GAME! I DON'T LIKE THIS DUMB ISLAND! I WISH I WAS BACK IN THE ATOM GALAXY--I COULD HAVE YOU THROWN IN THE DUNGEON THERE!
I WISH I HAD MY BOOK. I COULD FIGURE THINGS OUT FROM THAT BOOK--IT DIDN'T TWIST MY THOUGHTS AROUND!
BUT IT GOT LEFT BEHIND IN THE ATOM GALAXY...
ELSEWHERE ON THE ISLAND...
WE ARE AS READY AS WE WILL EVER BE FOR THIS INVASION, AMAZONS! I HAVE TOLD YOU AS MUCH AS I CAN ABOUT CONDITIONS IN THE ATOM GALAXY...
WE CANNOT PREPARE BEFOREHAND TO DEAL WITH THE ATOM WARRIORS' ABILITY TO SHIFT FROM ONE PLACE TO ANOTHER INSTANTANEOUSLY--
--SO WE HAVE DONE OUR BEST TO INTRODUCE SOME-THING TO THE BATTLE THAT THEY WILL BE ILL-EQUIPPED TO DEAL WITH--
--BY MAKING THE SPEARHEAD OF OUR FORCE THE KANGA CAVALRY!
GIRD YOURSELVES FOR BATTLE, SISTERS--WE BEGIN IN AN HOUR!

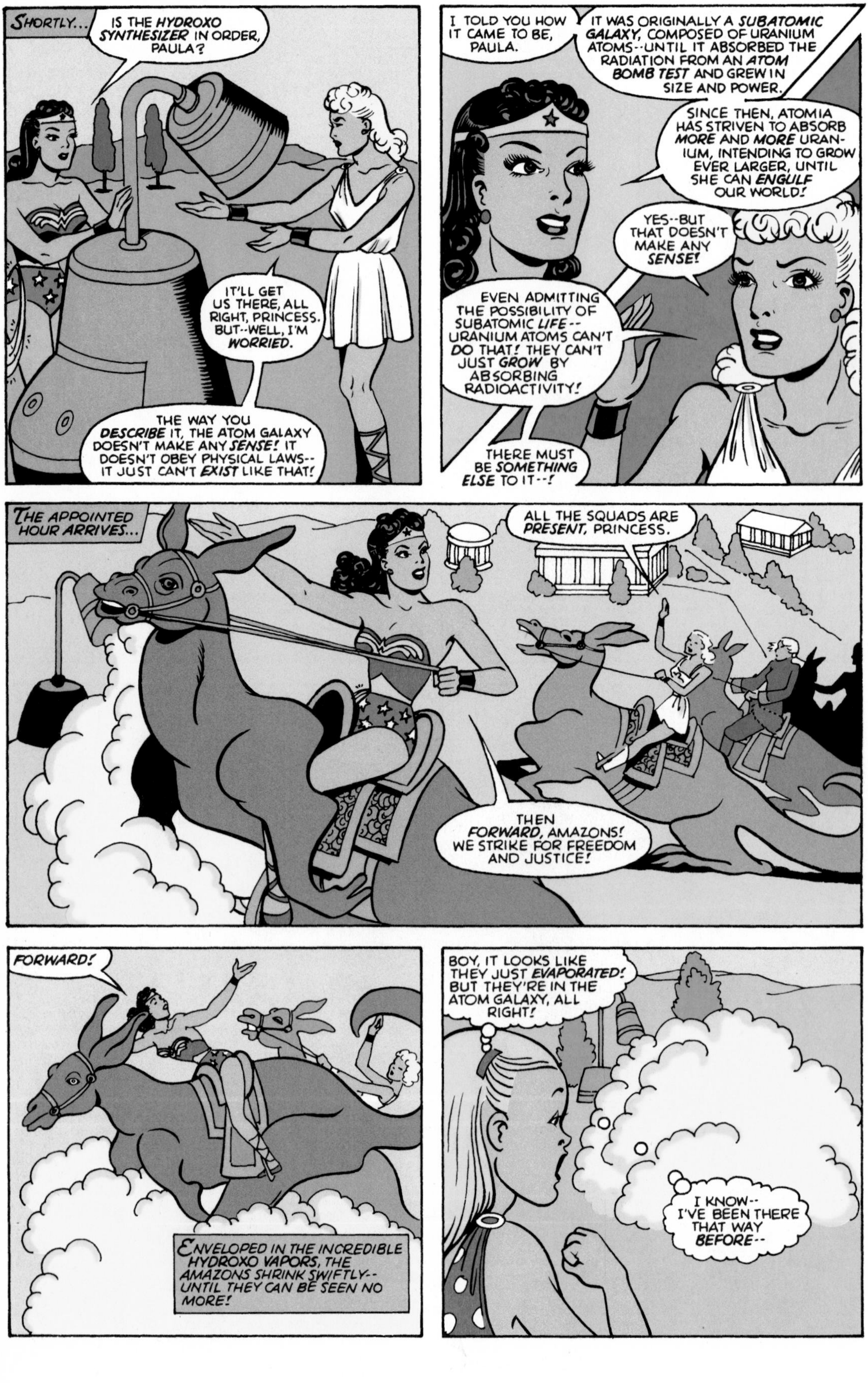

SHORTLY...
IS THE HYDROXO SYNTHESIZER IN ORDER, PAULA?
IT'LL GET US THERE, ALL RIGHT, PRINCESS. BUT--WELL, I'M WORRIED.
THE WAY YOU DESCRIBE IT, THE ATOM GALAXY DOESN'T MAKE ANY SENSE! IT DOESN'T OBEY PHYSICAL LAWS-- IT JUST CAN'T EXIST LIKE THAT!
I TOLD YOU HOW IT CAME TO BE, PAULA.
IT WAS ORIGINALLY A SUBATOMIC GALAXY, COMPOSED OF URANIUM ATOMS--UNTIL IT ABSORBED THE RADIATION FROM AN ATOM BOMB TEST AND GREW IN SIZE AND POWER.
SINCE THEN, ATOMIA HAS STRIVEN TO ABSORB MORE AND MORE URANIUM, INTENDING TO GROW EVER LARGER, UNTIL SHE CAN ENGULF OUR WORLD!
YES--BUT THAT DOESN'T MAKE ANY SENSE!
EVEN ADMITTING THE POSSIBILITY OF SUBATOMIC LIFE-- URANIUM ATOMS CAN'T DO THAT! THEY CAN'T JUST GROW BY ABSORBING RADIOACTIVITY!
THERE MUST BE SOMETHING ELSE TO IT--!
THE APPOINTED HOUR ARRIVES...
ALL THE SQUADS ARE PRESENT, PRINCESS.
THEN FORWARD, AMAZONS! WE STRIKE FOR FREEDOM AND JUSTICE!
FORWARD!
ENVELOPED IN THE INCREDIBLE HYDROXO VAPORS, THE AMAZONS SHRINK SWIFTLY-- UNTIL THEY CAN BE SEEN NO MORE!
BOY, IT LOOKS LIKE THEY JUST EVAPORATED! BUT THEY'RE IN THE ATOM GALAXY, ALL RIGHT!
I KNOW-- I'VE BEEN THERE THAT WAY BEFORE--

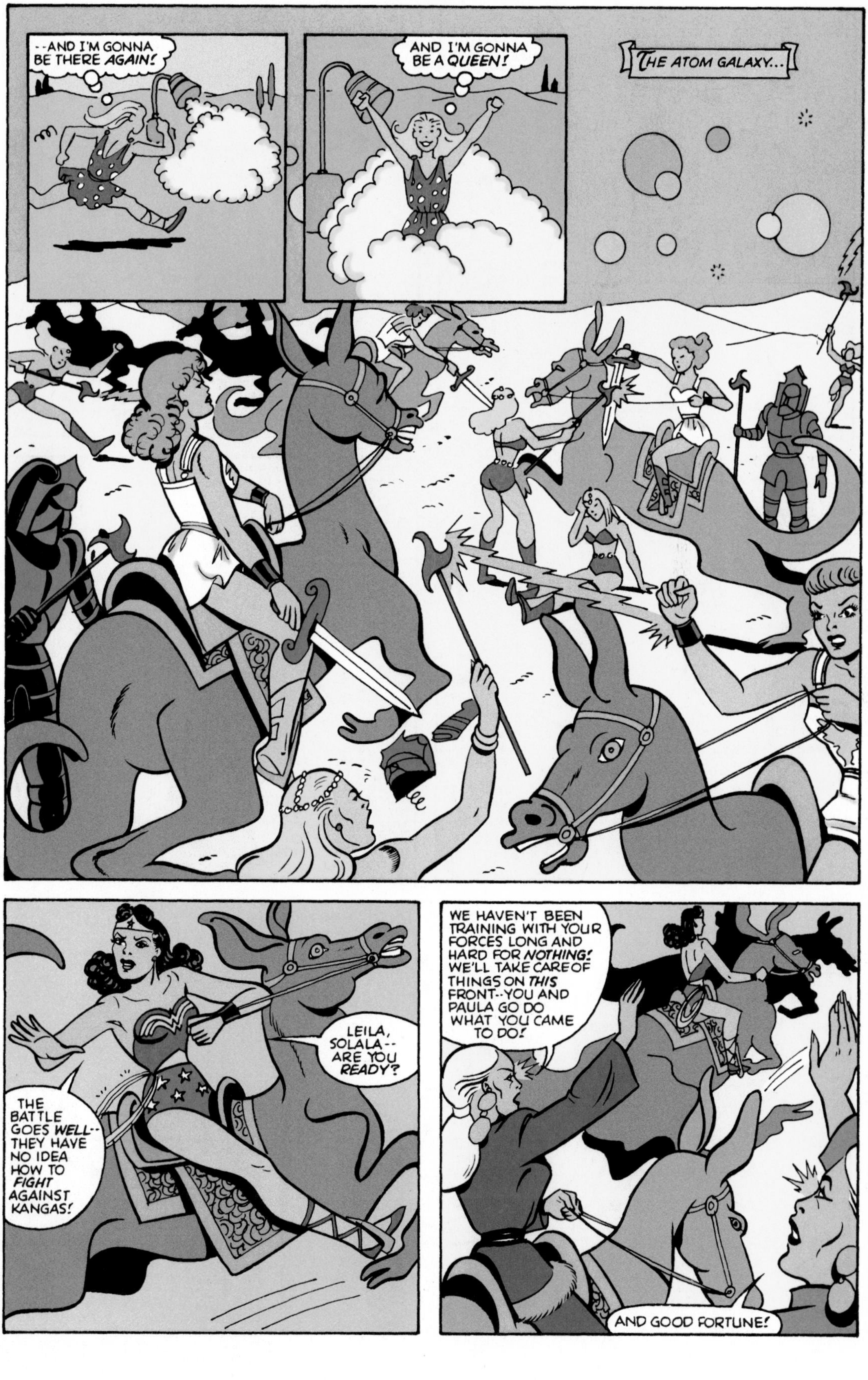
--AND I'M GONNA BE THERE AGAIN!
AND I'M GONNA BE A QUEEN!
THE ATOM GALAXY...
LEILA, SOLALA--ARE YOU READY?
THE BATTLE GOES WELL--THEY HAVE NO IDEA HOW TO FIGHT AGAINST KANGAS!
WE HAVEN'T BEEN TRAINING WITH YOUR FORCES LONG AND HARD FOR NOTHING! WE'LL TAKE CARE OF THINGS ON THIS FRONT--YOU AND PAULA GO DO WHAT YOU CAME TO DO!
AND GOOD FORTUNE!

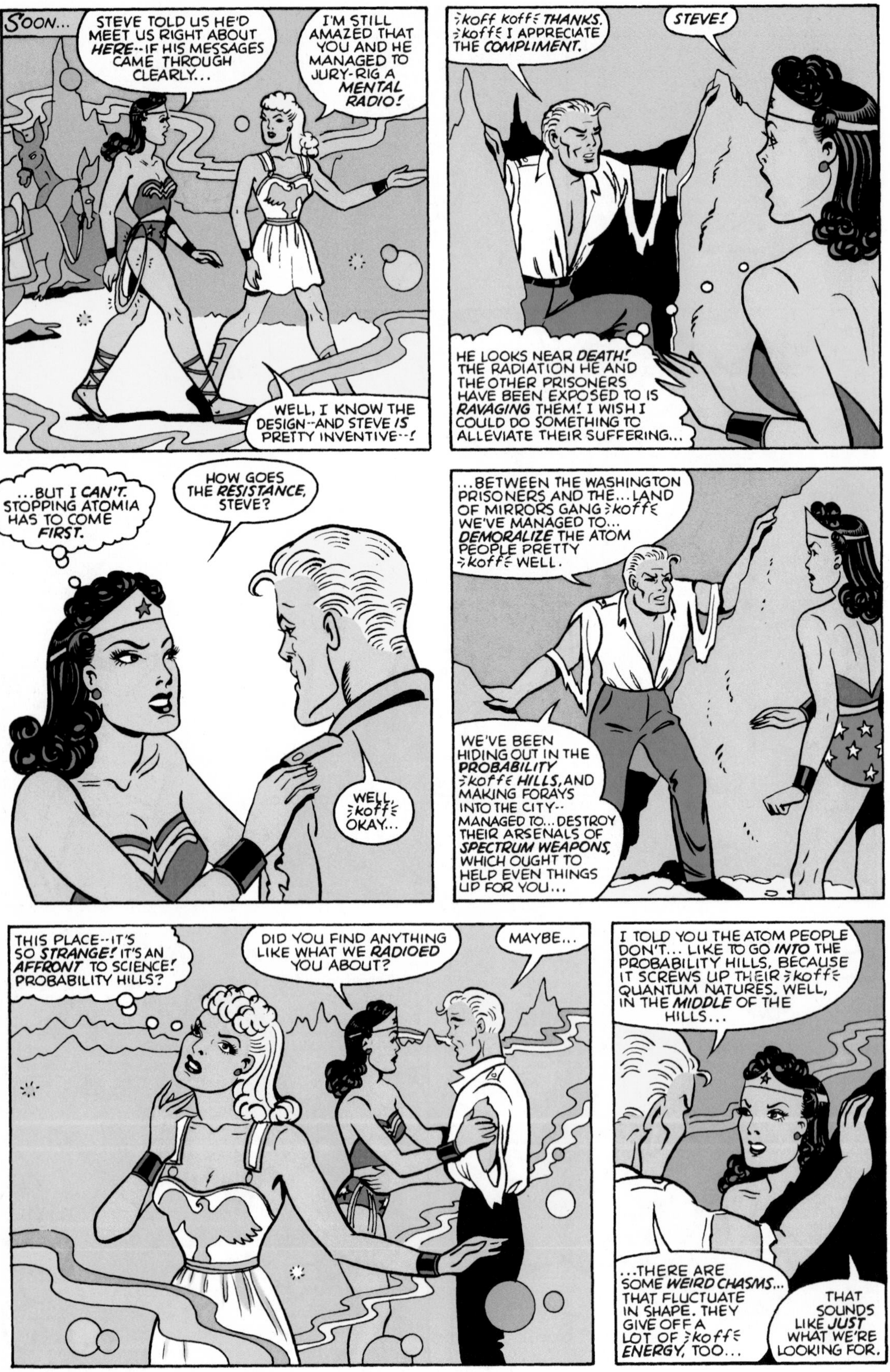
SOON...
STEVE TOLD US HE'D MEET US RIGHT ABOUT HERE--IF HIS MESSAGES CAME THROUGH CLEARLY...
I'M STILL AMAZED THAT YOU AND HE MANAGED TO JURY-RIG A MENTAL RADIO!
WELL, I KNOW THE DESIGN--AND STEVE IS PRETTY INVENTIVE--!
≷koff koff≷ THANKS. ≷koff≷ I APPRECIATE THE COMPLIMENT.
STEVE!
HE LOOKS NEAR DEATH! THE RADIATION HE AND THE OTHER PRISONERS HAVE BEEN EXPOSED TO IS RAVAGING THEM! I WISH I COULD DO SOMETHING TO ALLEVIATE THEIR SUFFERING...
...BUT I CAN'T. STOPPING ATOMIA HAS TO COME FIRST.
HOW GOES THE RESISTANCE, STEVE?
WELL, ≷koff≷ OKAY...
...BETWEEN THE WASHINGTON PRISONERS AND THE...LAND OF MIRRORS GANG ≷koff≷ WE'VE MANAGED TO... DEMORALIZE THE ATOM PEOPLE PRETTY ≷koff≷ WELL.
WE'VE BEEN HIDING OUT IN THE PROBABILITY ≷koff≷ HILLS, AND MAKING FORAYS INTO THE CITY-- MANAGED TO...DESTROY THEIR ARSENALS OF SPECTRUM WEAPONS, WHICH OUGHT TO HELP EVEN THINGS UP FOR YOU...
THIS PLACE--IT'S SO STRANGE! IT'S AN AFFRONT TO SCIENCE! PROBABILITY HILLS?
DID YOU FIND ANYTHING LIKE WHAT WE RADIOED YOU ABOUT?
MAYBE...
I TOLD YOU THE ATOM PEOPLE DON'T... LIKE TO GO INTO THE PROBABILITY HILLS, BECAUSE IT SCREWS UP THEIR ≷koff≷ QUANTUM NATURES. WELL, IN THE MIDDLE OF THE HILLS...
...THERE ARE SOME WEIRD CHASMS... THAT FLUCTUATE IN SHAPE. THEY GIVE OFF A LOT OF ≷koff≷ ENERGY, TOO...
THAT SOUNDS LIKE JUST WHAT WE'RE LOOKING FOR.

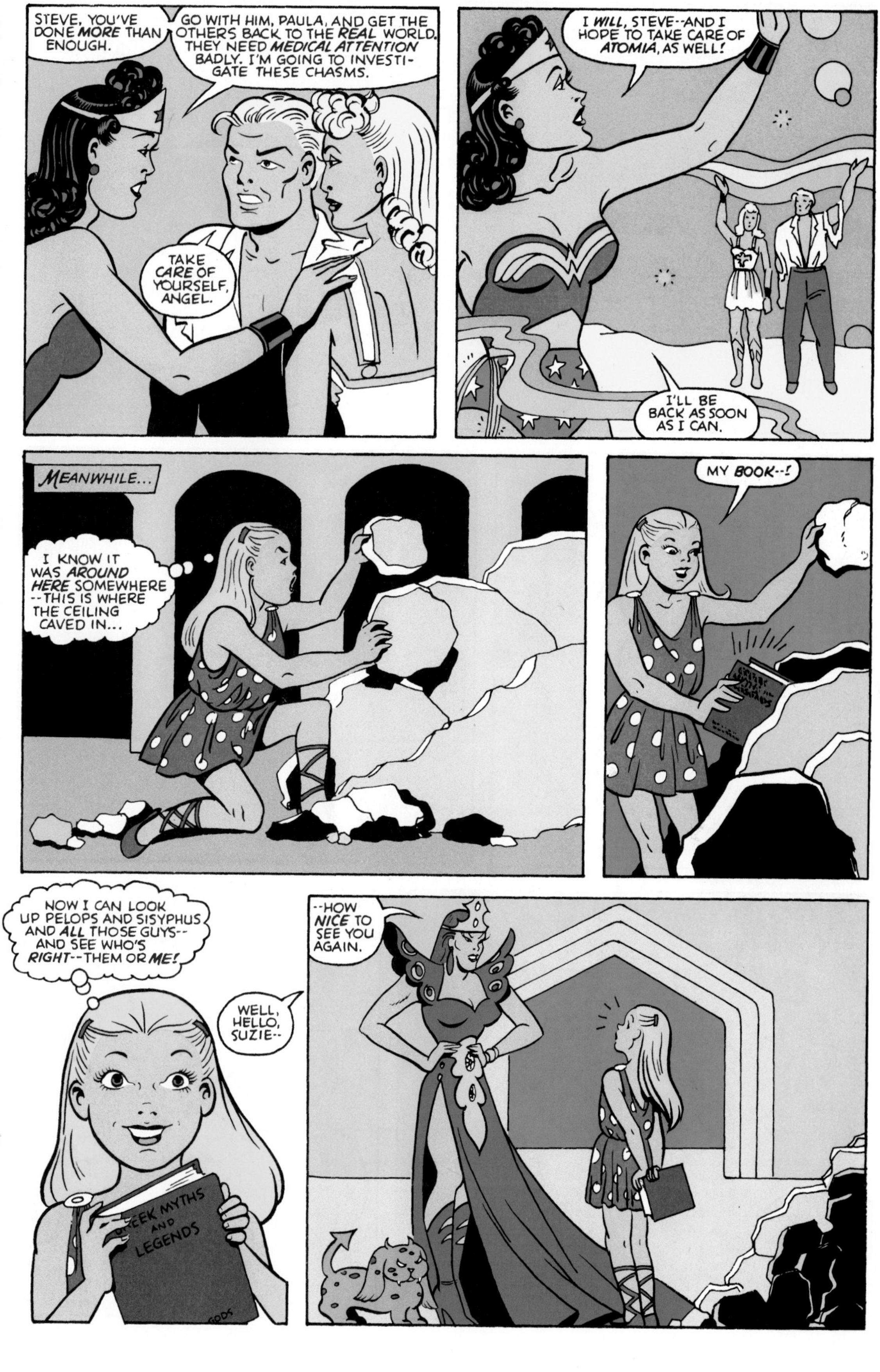
STEVE, YOU'VE DONE MORE THAN ENOUGH.
GO WITH HIM, PAULA, AND GET THE OTHERS BACK TO THE REAL WORLD. THEY NEED MEDICAL ATTENTION BADLY. I'M GOING TO INVESTI-GATE THESE CHASMS.
TAKE CARE OF YOURSELF, ANGEL.
I WILL, STEVE--AND I HOPE TO TAKE CARE OF ATOMIA, AS WELL!
I'LL BE BACK AS SOON AS I CAN.
MEANWHILE...
I KNOW IT WAS AROUND HERE SOMEWHERE--THIS IS WHERE THE CEILING CAVED IN...
MY BOOK--!
NOW I CAN LOOK UP PELOPS AND SISYPHUS AND ALL THOSE GUYS--AND SEE WHO'S RIGHT--THEM OR ME!
GREEK MYTHS AND LEGENDS
WELL, HELLO, SUZIE--
--HOW NICE TO SEE YOU AGAIN.

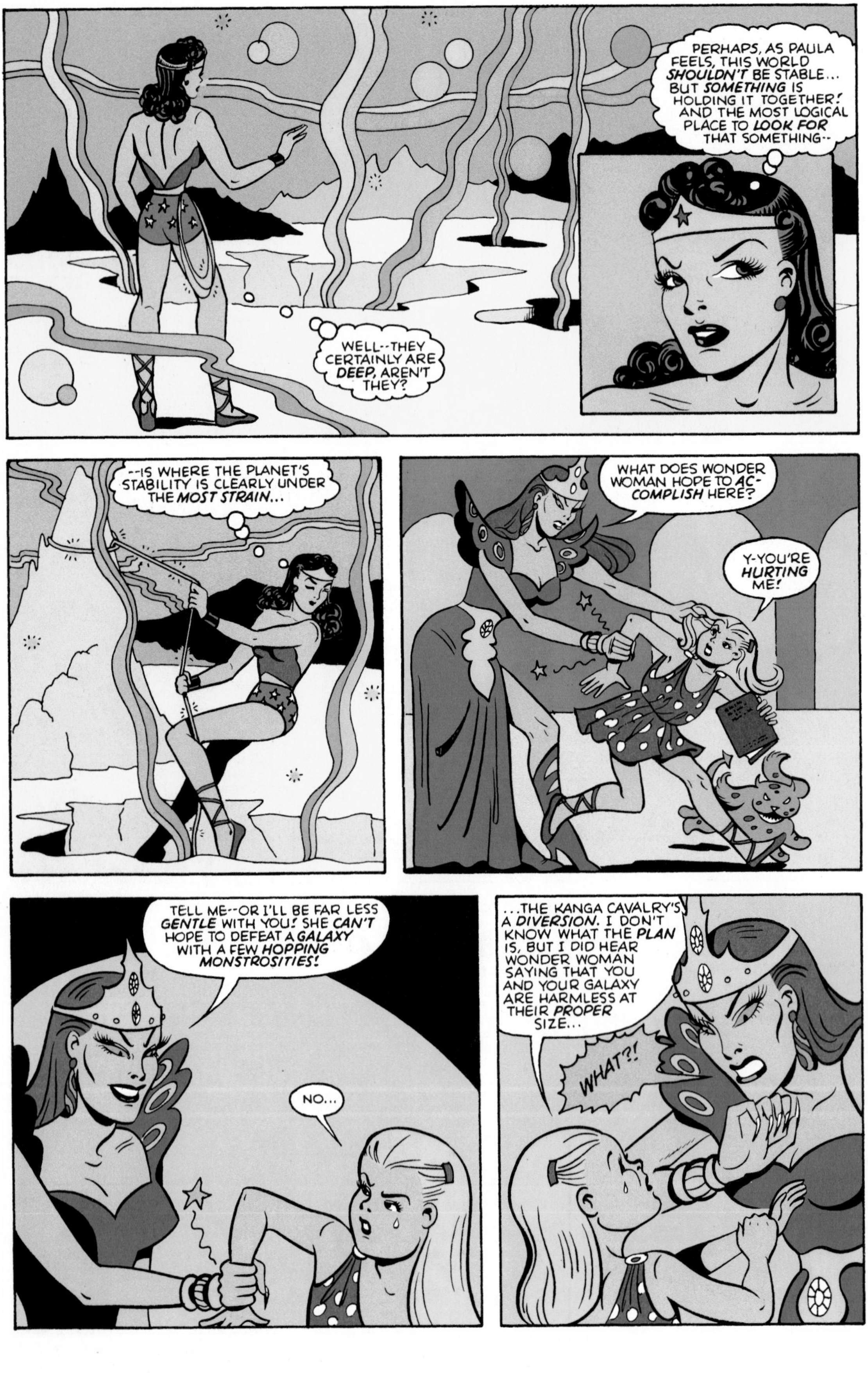
PERHAPS, AS PAULA FEELS, THIS WORLD SHOULDN'T BE STABLE... BUT SOMETHING IS HOLDING IT TOGETHER! AND THE MOST LOGICAL PLACE TO LOOK FOR THAT SOMETHING--
WELL--THEY CERTAINLY ARE DEEP, AREN'T THEY?
--IS WHERE THE PLANET'S STABILITY IS CLEARLY UNDER THE MOST STRAIN...
WHAT DOES WONDER WOMAN HOPE TO AC-COMPLISH HERE?
Y-YOU'RE HURTING ME!
TELL ME--OR I'LL BE FAR LESS GENTLE WITH YOU! SHE CAN'T HOPE TO DEFEAT A GALAXY WITH A FEW HOPPING MONSTROSITIES!
NO...
...THE KANGA CAVALRY'S A DIVERSION. I DON'T KNOW WHAT THE PLAN IS, BUT I DID HEAR WONDER WOMAN SAYING THAT YOU AND YOUR GALAXY ARE HARMLESS AT THEIR PROPER SIZE...
WHAT?!

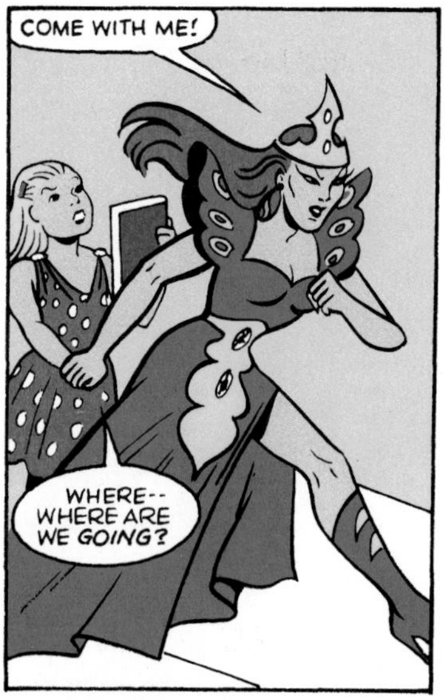
COME WITH ME!
WHERE-- WHERE ARE WE *GOING?*

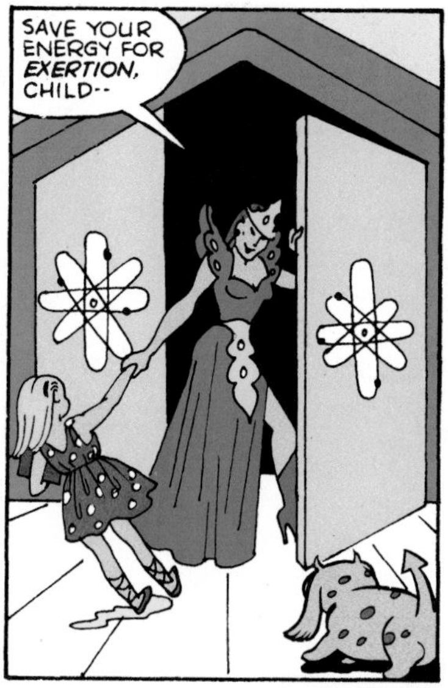
SAVE YOUR ENERGY FOR *EXERTION,* CHILD--

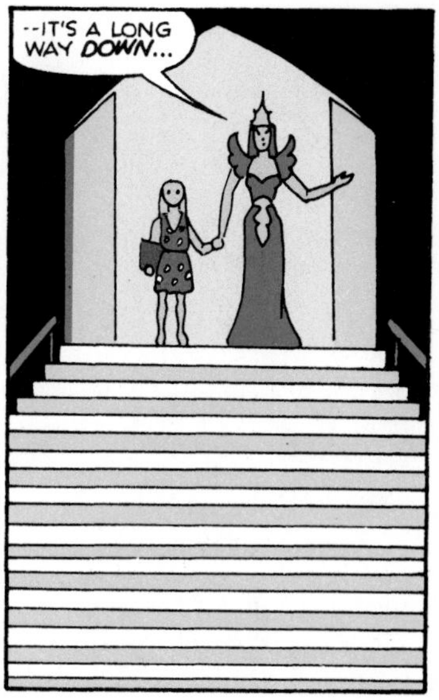
--IT'S A LONG WAY *DOWN...*

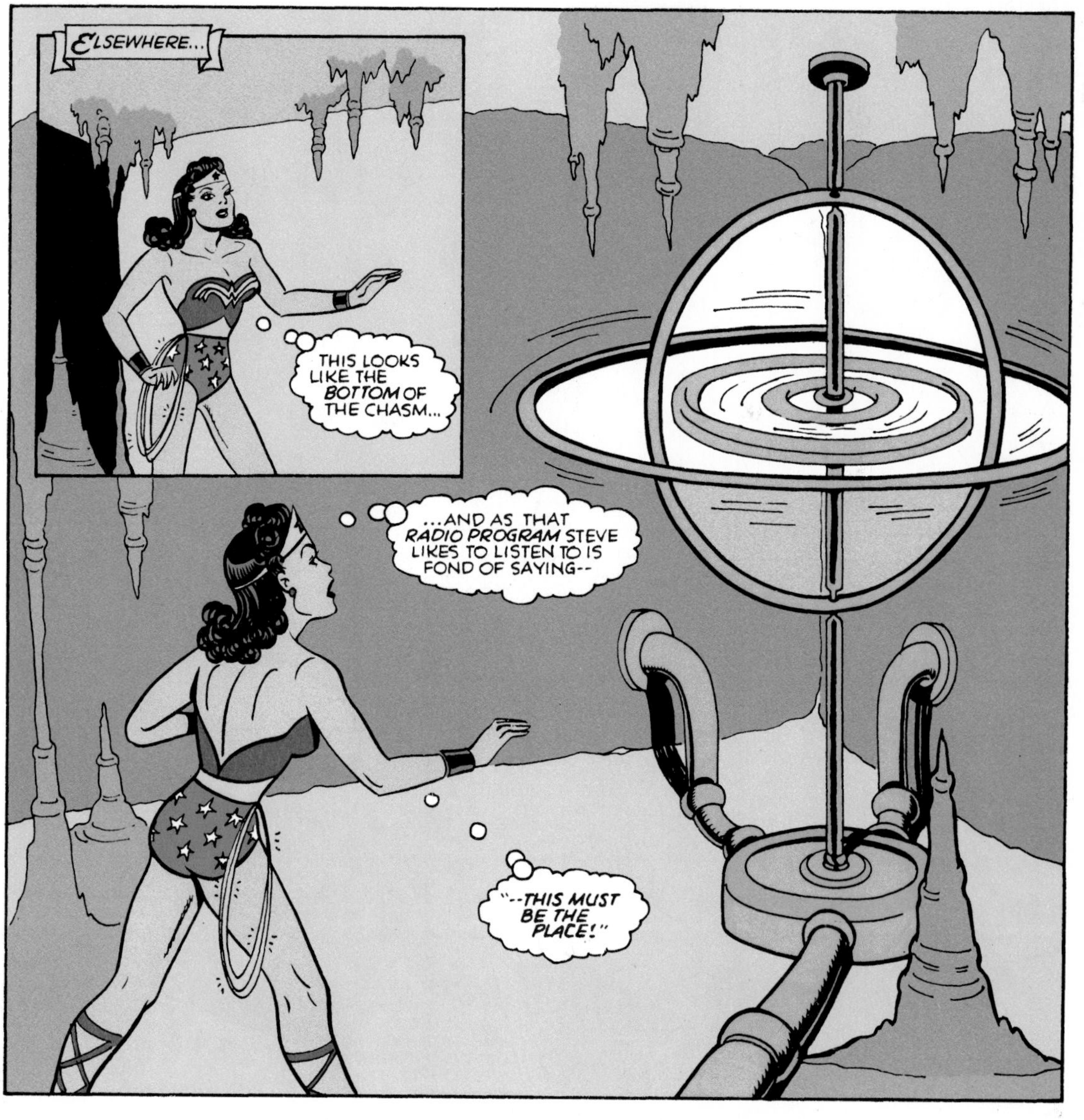
ELSEWHERE...
THIS LOOKS LIKE THE *BOTTOM* OF THE CHASM...
...AND AS THAT *RADIO PROGRAM* STEVE LIKES TO LISTEN TO IS FOND OF SAYING--
"--*THIS MUST BE THE PLACE!*"

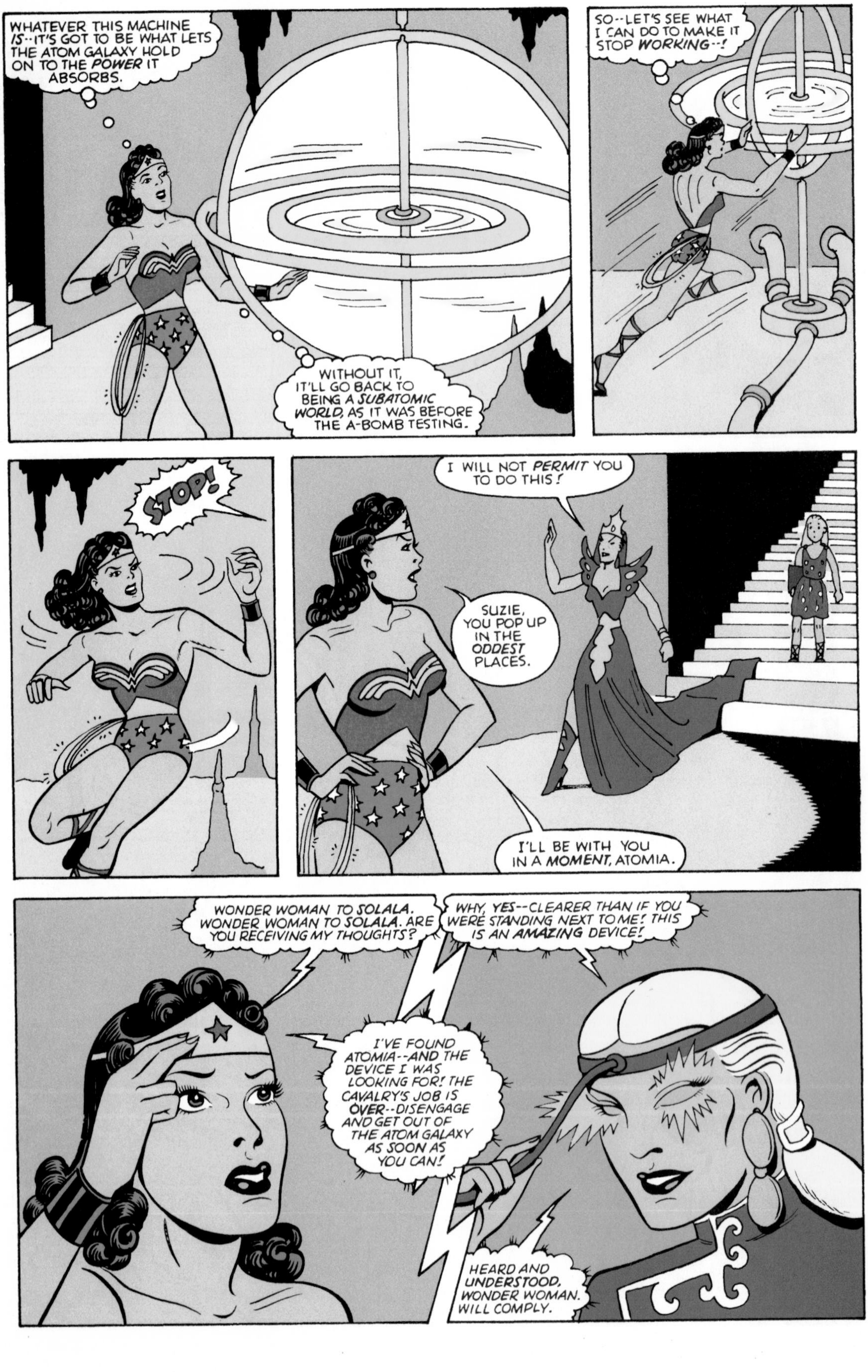

WHATEVER THIS MACHINE IS--IT'S GOT TO BE WHAT LETS THE ATOM GALAXY HOLD ON TO THE POWER IT ABSORBS.
WITHOUT IT, IT'LL GO BACK TO BEING A SUBATOMIC WORLD, AS IT WAS BEFORE THE A-BOMB TESTING.
SO--LET'S SEE WHAT I CAN DO TO MAKE IT STOP WORKING--!
STOP!
I WILL NOT PERMIT YOU TO DO THIS!
SUZIE, YOU POP UP IN THE ODDEST PLACES.
I'LL BE WITH YOU IN A MOMENT, ATOMIA.
WONDER WOMAN TO SOLALA. WONDER WOMAN TO SOLALA. ARE YOU RECEIVING MY THOUGHTS?
WHY, YES--CLEARER THAN IF YOU WERE STANDING NEXT TO ME! THIS IS AN AMAZING DEVICE!
I'VE FOUND ATOMIA--AND THE DEVICE I WAS LOOKING FOR! THE CAVALRY'S JOB IS OVER--DISENGAGE AND GET OUT OF THE ATOM GALAXY AS SOON AS YOU CAN!
HEARD AND UNDERSTOOD, WONDER WOMAN. WILL COMPLY.

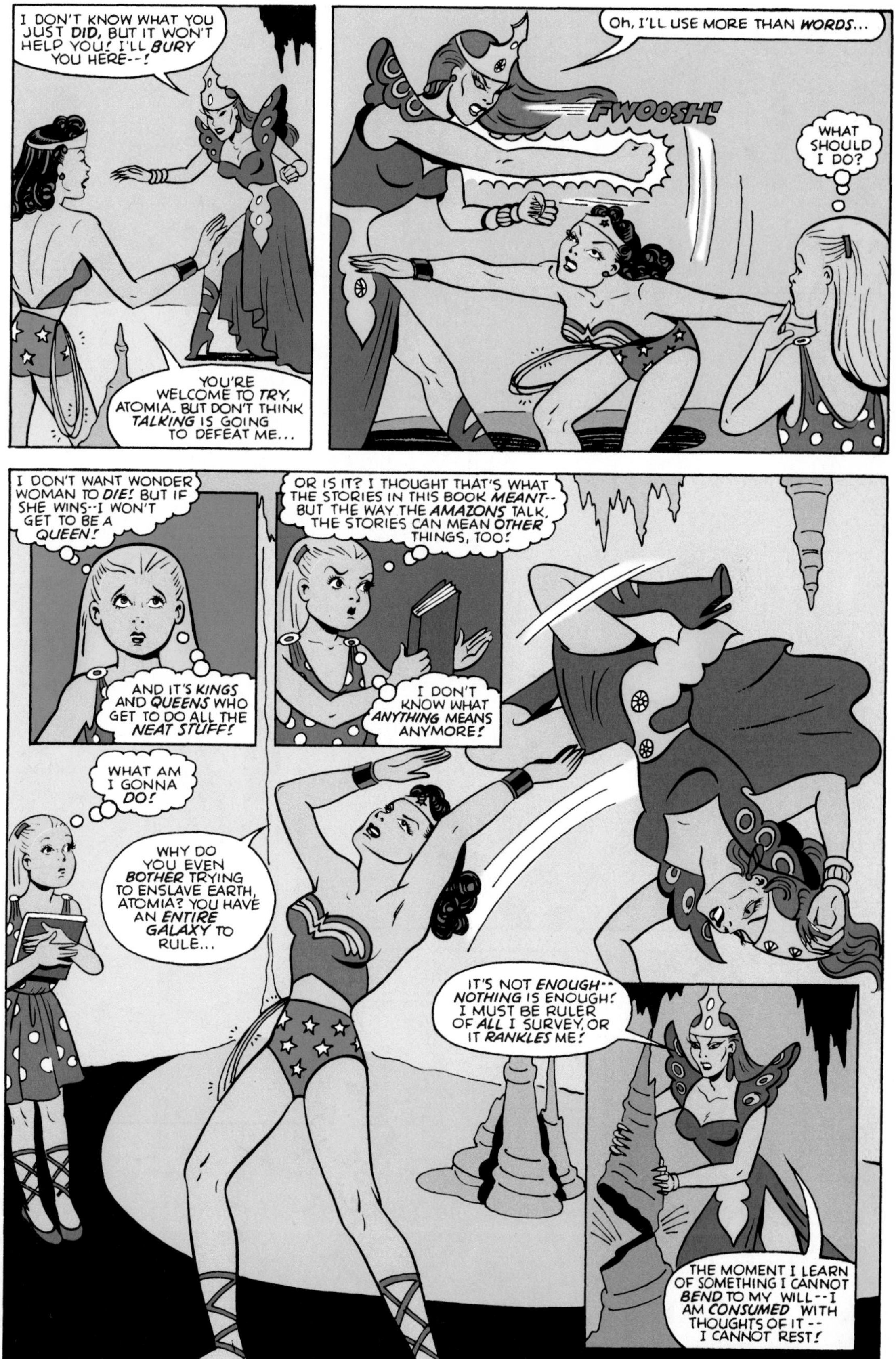
I DON'T KNOW WHAT YOU JUST DID, BUT IT WON'T HELP YOU! I'LL BURY YOU HERE--!
YOU'RE WELCOME TO TRY, ATOMIA. BUT DON'T THINK TALKING IS GOING TO DEFEAT ME...
Oh, I'LL USE MORE THAN WORDS...
FWOOSH!
WHAT SHOULD I DO?
I DON'T WANT WONDER WOMAN TO DIE! BUT IF SHE WINS--I WON'T GET TO BE A QUEEN!
AND IT'S KINGS AND QUEENS WHO GET TO DO ALL THE NEAT STUFF!
OR IS IT? I THOUGHT THAT'S WHAT THE STORIES IN THIS BOOK MEANT-- BUT THE WAY THE AMAZONS TALK, THE STORIES CAN MEAN OTHER THINGS, TOO!
I DON'T KNOW WHAT ANYTHING MEANS ANYMORE!
WHAT AM I GONNA DO!
WHY DO YOU EVEN BOTHER TRYING TO ENSLAVE EARTH, ATOMIA? YOU HAVE AN ENTIRE GALAXY TO RULE...
IT'S NOT ENOUGH-- NOTHING IS ENOUGH! I MUST BE RULER OF ALL I SURVEY, OR IT RANKLES ME!
THE MOMENT I LEARN OF SOMETHING I CANNOT BEND TO MY WILL--I AM CONSUMED WITH THOUGHTS OF IT-- I CANNOT REST!

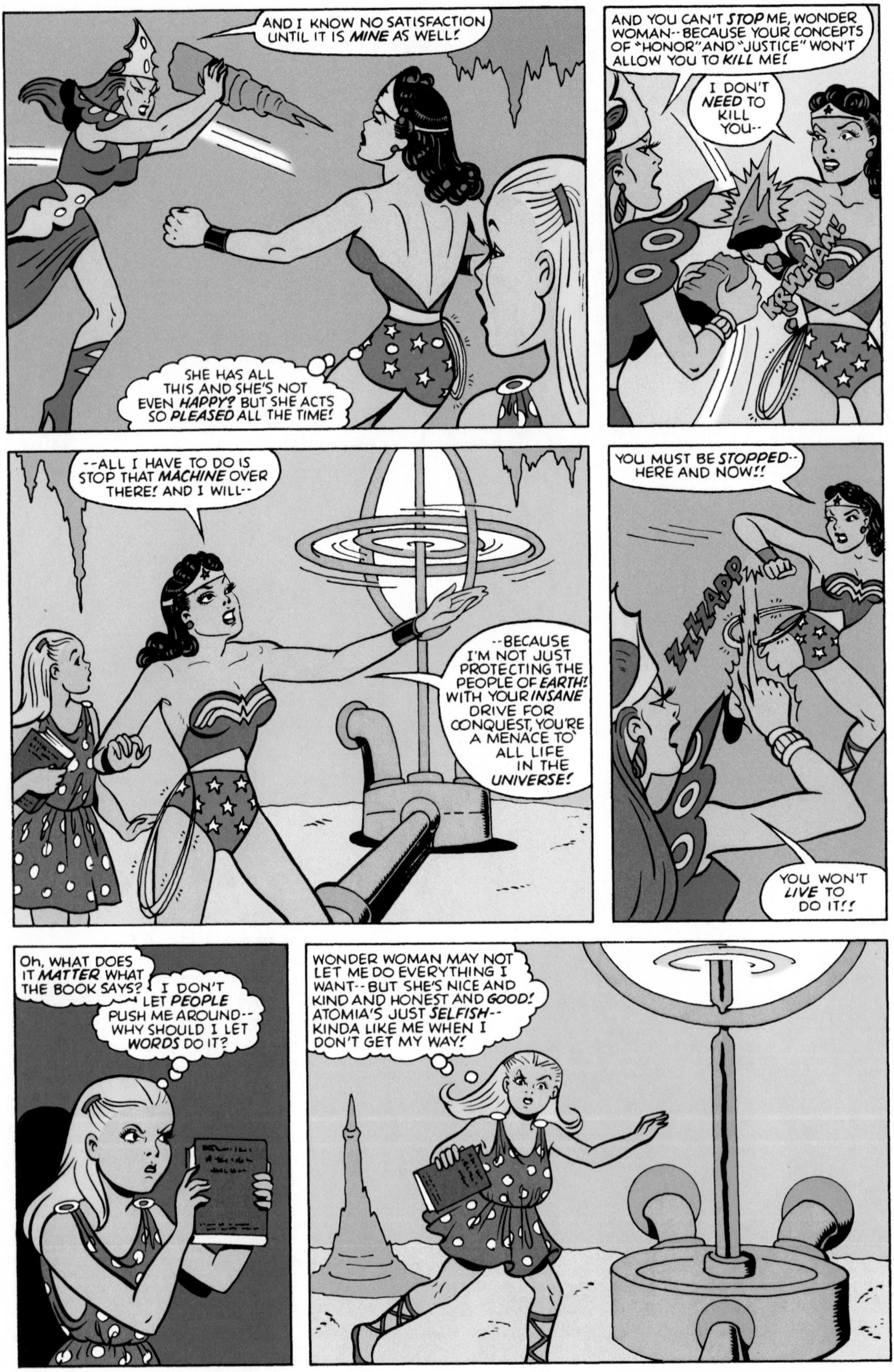
AND I KNOW NO SATISFACTION UNTIL IT IS *MINE* AS WELL!
SHE HAS ALL THIS AND SHE'S NOT EVEN *HAPPY?* BUT SHE ACTS SO *PLEASED* ALL THE TIME!
AND YOU CAN'T *STOP* ME, WONDER WOMAN--BECAUSE YOUR CONCEPTS OF "HONOR" AND "JUSTICE" WON'T ALLOW YOU TO *KILL* ME!
I DON'T *NEED* TO KILL YOU--
KRWHAM!
--ALL I HAVE TO DO IS STOP THAT *MACHINE* OVER THERE! AND I WILL--
--BECAUSE I'M NOT JUST PROTECTING THE PEOPLE OF *EARTH!* WITH YOUR *INSANE* DRIVE FOR CONQUEST, YOU'RE A MENACE TO ALL LIFE IN THE *UNIVERSE!*
YOU MUST BE *STOPPED*--HERE AND NOW!!
Z-ZZAPP
YOU WON'T *LIVE* TO DO IT!!
Oh, WHAT DOES IT *MATTER* WHAT THE BOOK SAYS?
I DON'T LET *PEOPLE* PUSH ME AROUND--WHY SHOULD I LET *WORDS* DO IT?
WONDER WOMAN MAY NOT LET ME DO EVERYTHING I WANT--BUT SHE'S NICE AND KIND AND HONEST AND *GOOD!* ATOMIA'S JUST *SELFISH*--KINDA LIKE ME WHEN I DON'T GET MY WAY!

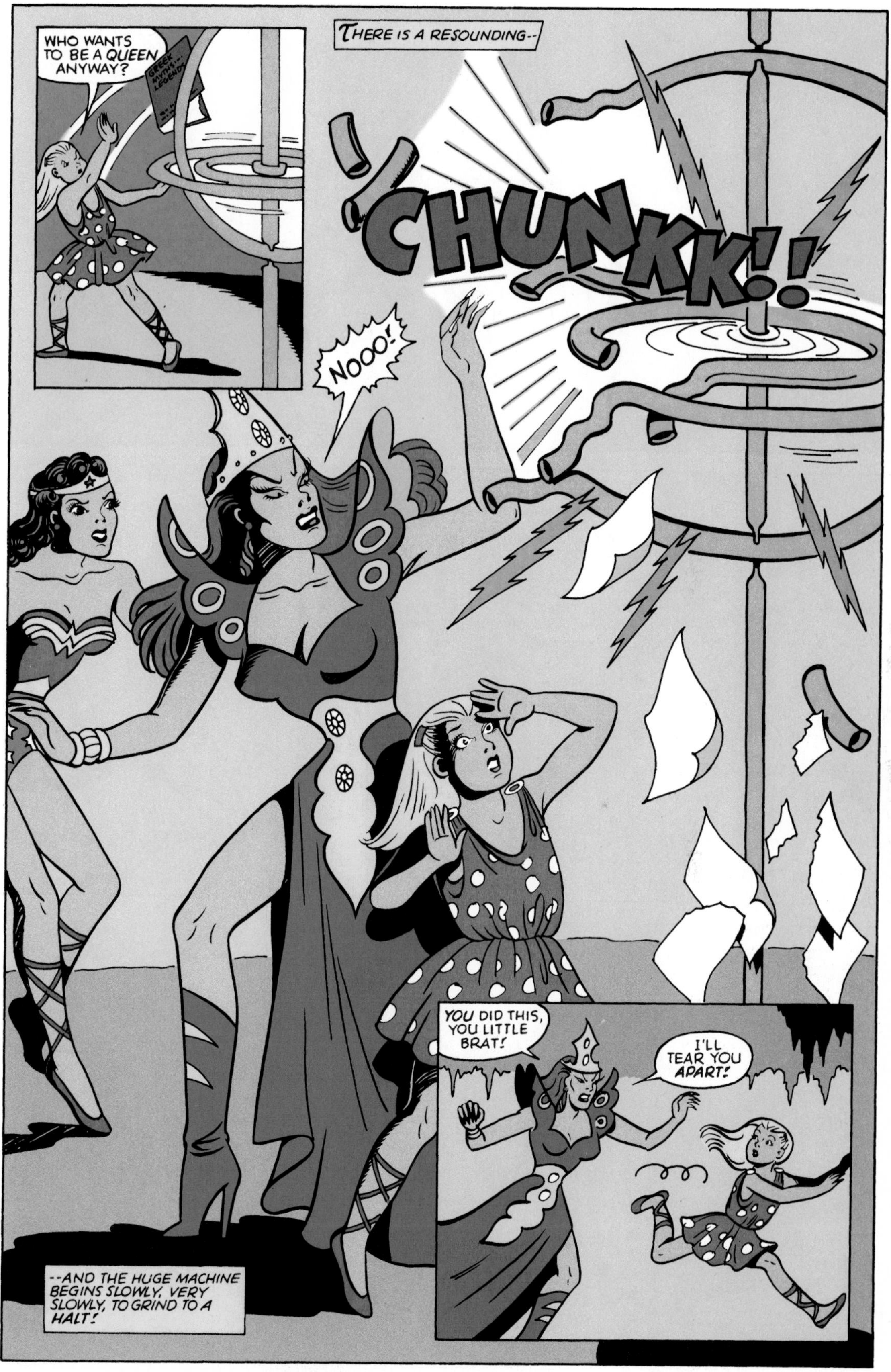
WHO WANTS TO BE A QUEEN ANYWAY?
GREEK MYTHS LEGENDS
THERE IS A RESOUNDING--
CHUNKK!!
NOOO!
--AND THE HUGE MACHINE BEGINS SLOWLY, VERY SLOWLY, TO GRIND TO A HALT!
YOU DID THIS, YOU LITTLE BRAT!
I'LL TEAR YOU APART!

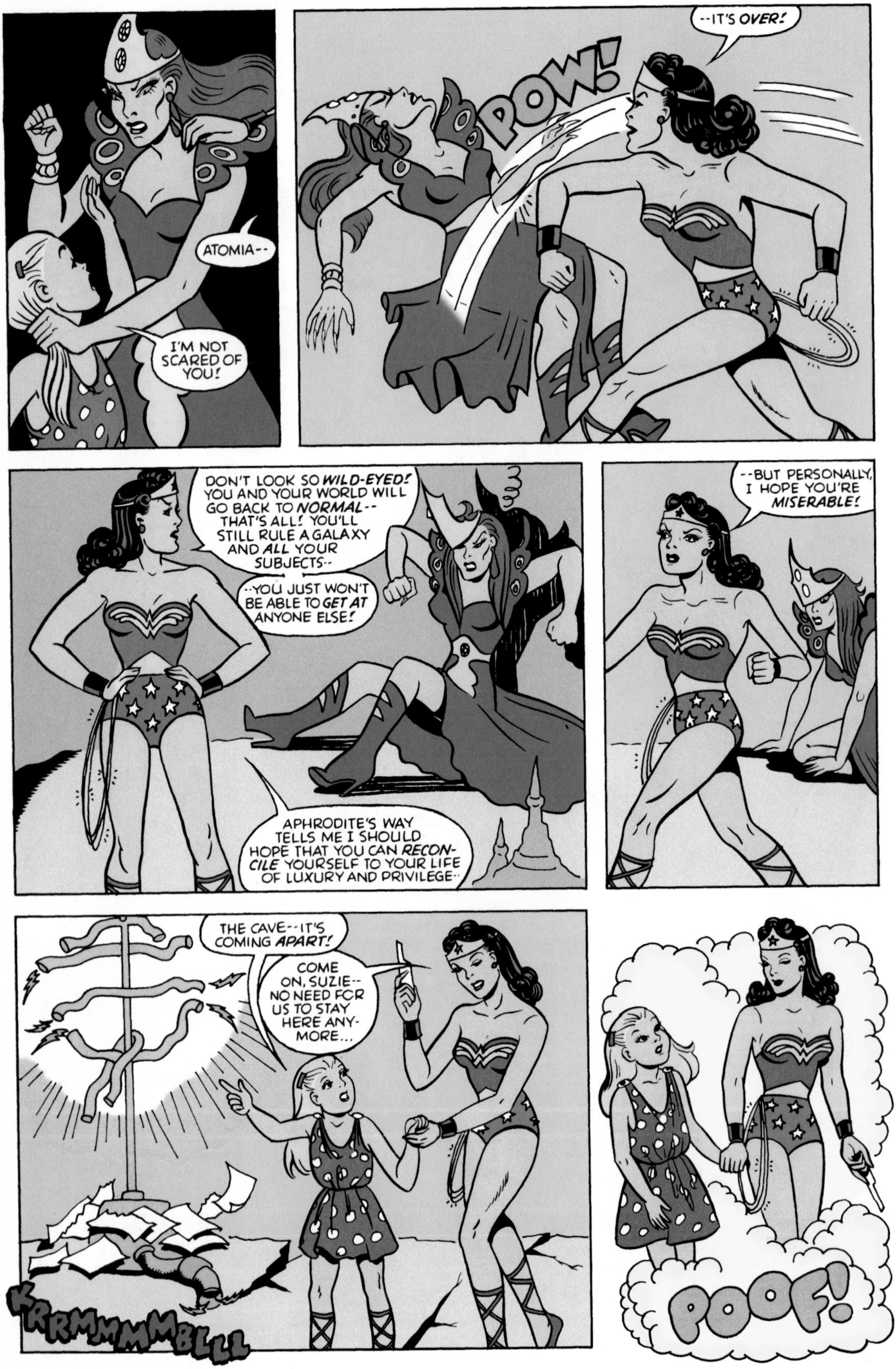
ATOMIA--
I'M NOT SCARED OF YOU!
POW!
--IT'S OVER!
DON'T LOOK SO WILD-EYED! YOU AND YOUR WORLD WILL GO BACK TO NORMAL-- THAT'S ALL! YOU'LL STILL RULE A GALAXY AND ALL YOUR SUBJECTS--
--YOU JUST WON'T BE ABLE TO GET AT ANYONE ELSE!
APHRODITE'S WAY TELLS ME I SHOULD HOPE THAT YOU CAN RECON-CILE YOURSELF TO YOUR LIFE OF LUXURY AND PRIVILEGE--
--BUT PERSONALLY, I HOPE YOU'RE MISERABLE!
THE CAVE--IT'S COMING APART!
COME ON, SUZIE-- NO NEED FOR US TO STAY HERE ANY-MORE...
KRRMMMMBLLL
POOF!

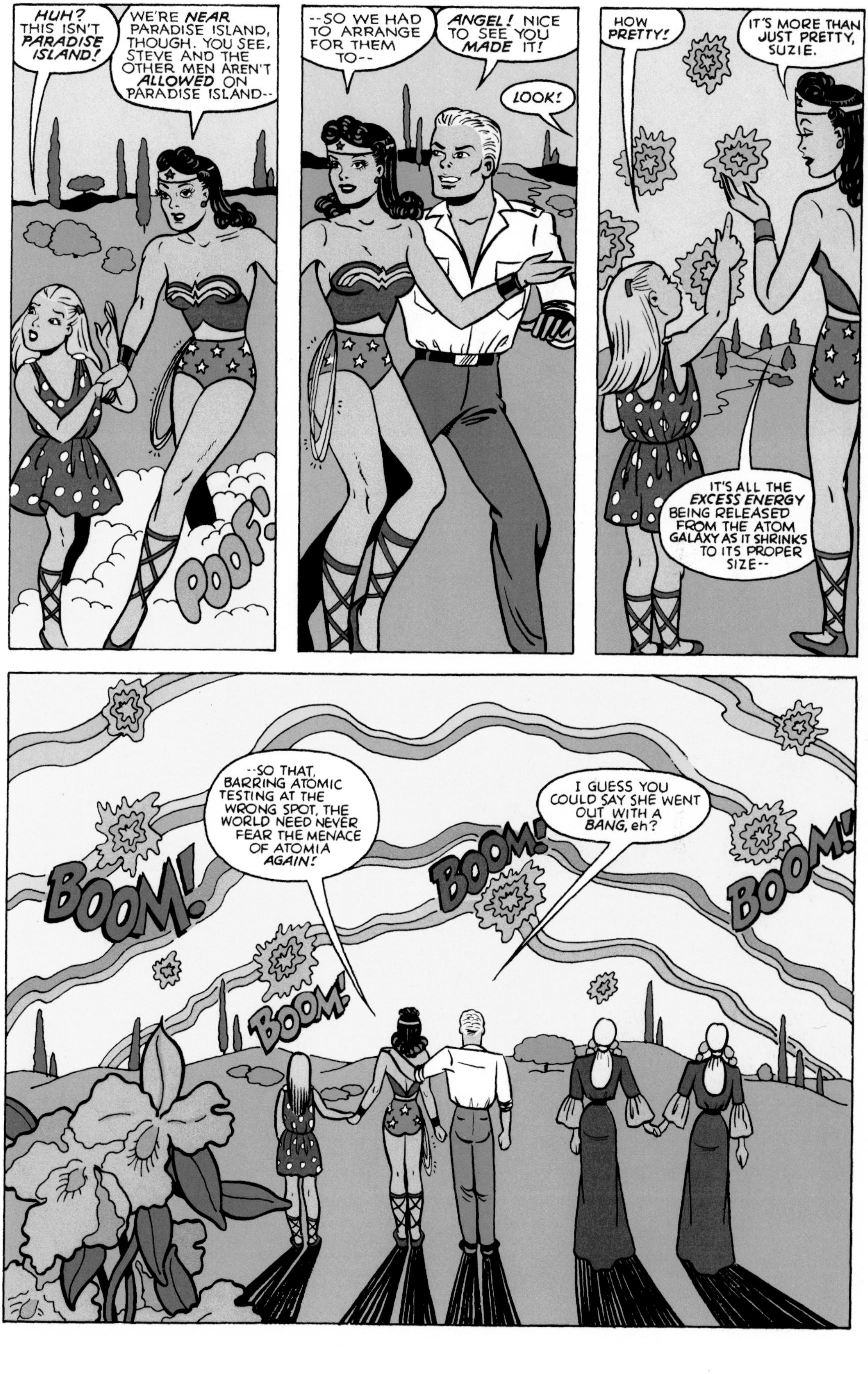

HUH? THIS ISN'T PARADISE ISLAND!
WE'RE NEAR PARADISE ISLAND, THOUGH. YOU SEE, STEVE AND THE OTHER MEN AREN'T ALLOWED ON PARADISE ISLAND--
POOF!
--SO WE HAD TO ARRANGE FOR THEM TO--
ANGEL! NICE TO SEE YOU MADE IT!
LOOK!
HOW PRETTY!
IT'S MORE THAN JUST PRETTY, SUZIE.
IT'S ALL THE EXCESS ENERGY BEING RELEASED FROM THE ATOM GALAXY AS IT SHRINKS TO ITS PROPER SIZE--
--SO THAT, BARRING ATOMIC TESTING AT THE WRONG SPOT, THE WORLD NEED NEVER FEAR THE MENACE OF ATOMIA AGAIN!
I GUESS YOU COULD SAY SHE WENT OUT WITH A BANG, eh?
BOOM!
BOOM!
BOOM!
BOOM!

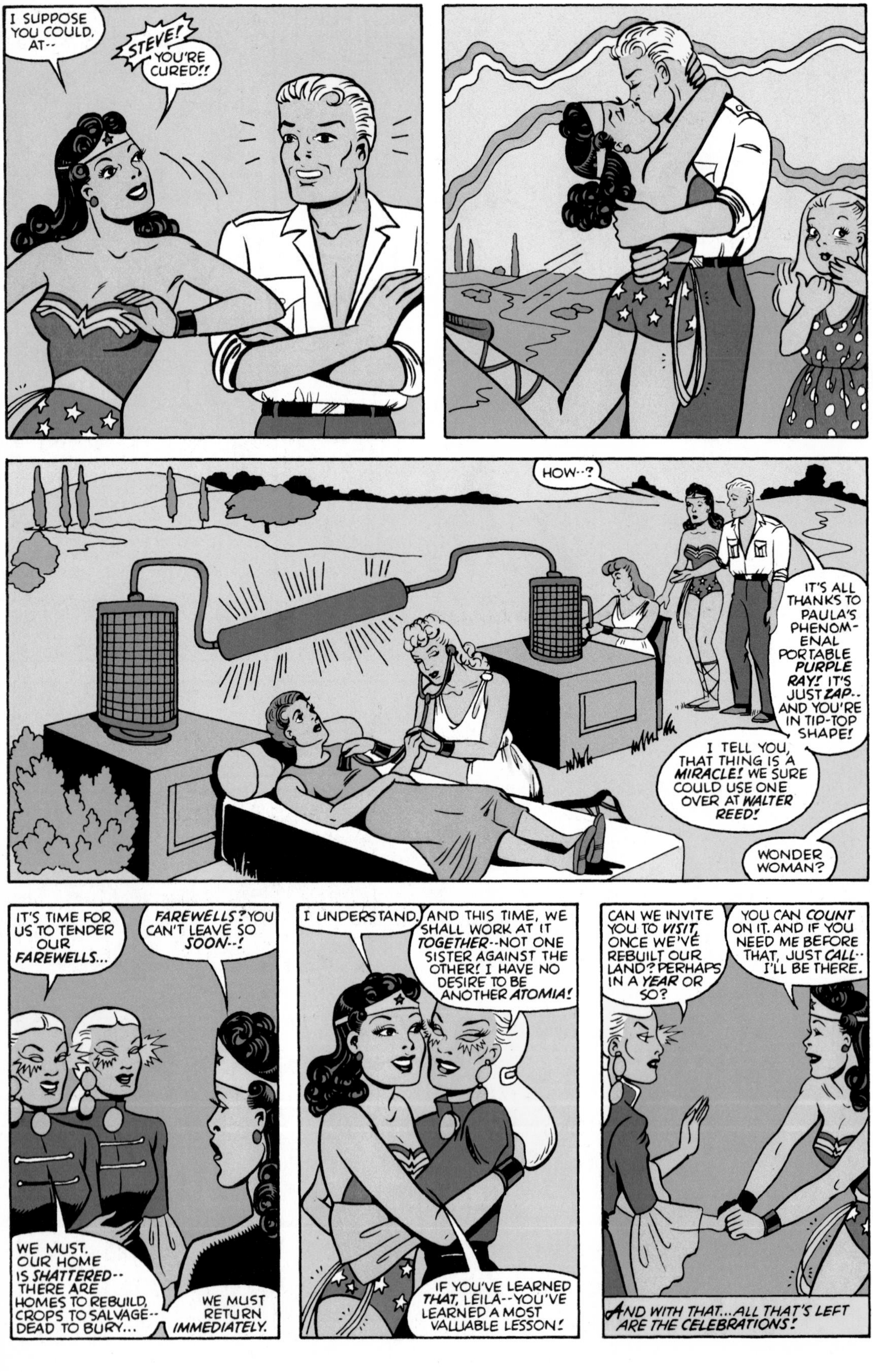
I SUPPOSE YOU COULD, AT--
STEVE! YOU'RE CURED!!
HOW--?
IT'S ALL THANKS TO PAULA'S PHENOMENAL PORTABLE PURPLE RAY! IT'S JUST ZAP.. AND YOU'RE IN TIP-TOP SHAPE!
I TELL YOU, THAT THING IS A MIRACLE! WE SURE COULD USE ONE OVER AT WALTER REED!
WONDER WOMAN?
IT'S TIME FOR US TO TENDER OUR FAREWELLS...
FAREWELLS? YOU CAN'T LEAVE SO SOON--!
WE MUST. OUR HOME IS SHATTERED-- THERE ARE HOMES TO REBUILD, CROPS TO SALVAGE-- DEAD TO BURY...
WE MUST RETURN IMMEDIATELY.
I UNDERSTAND.
AND THIS TIME, WE SHALL WORK AT IT TOGETHER--NOT ONE SISTER AGAINST THE OTHER! I HAVE NO DESIRE TO BE ANOTHER ATOMIA!
IF YOU'VE LEARNED THAT, LEILA--YOU'VE LEARNED A MOST VALUABLE LESSON!
CAN WE INVITE YOU TO VISIT, ONCE WE'VE REBUILT OUR LAND? PERHAPS IN A YEAR OR SO?
YOU CAN COUNT ON IT. AND IF YOU NEED ME BEFORE THAT, JUST CALL-- I'LL BE THERE.
AND WITH THAT... ALL THAT'S LEFT ARE THE CELEBRATIONS!

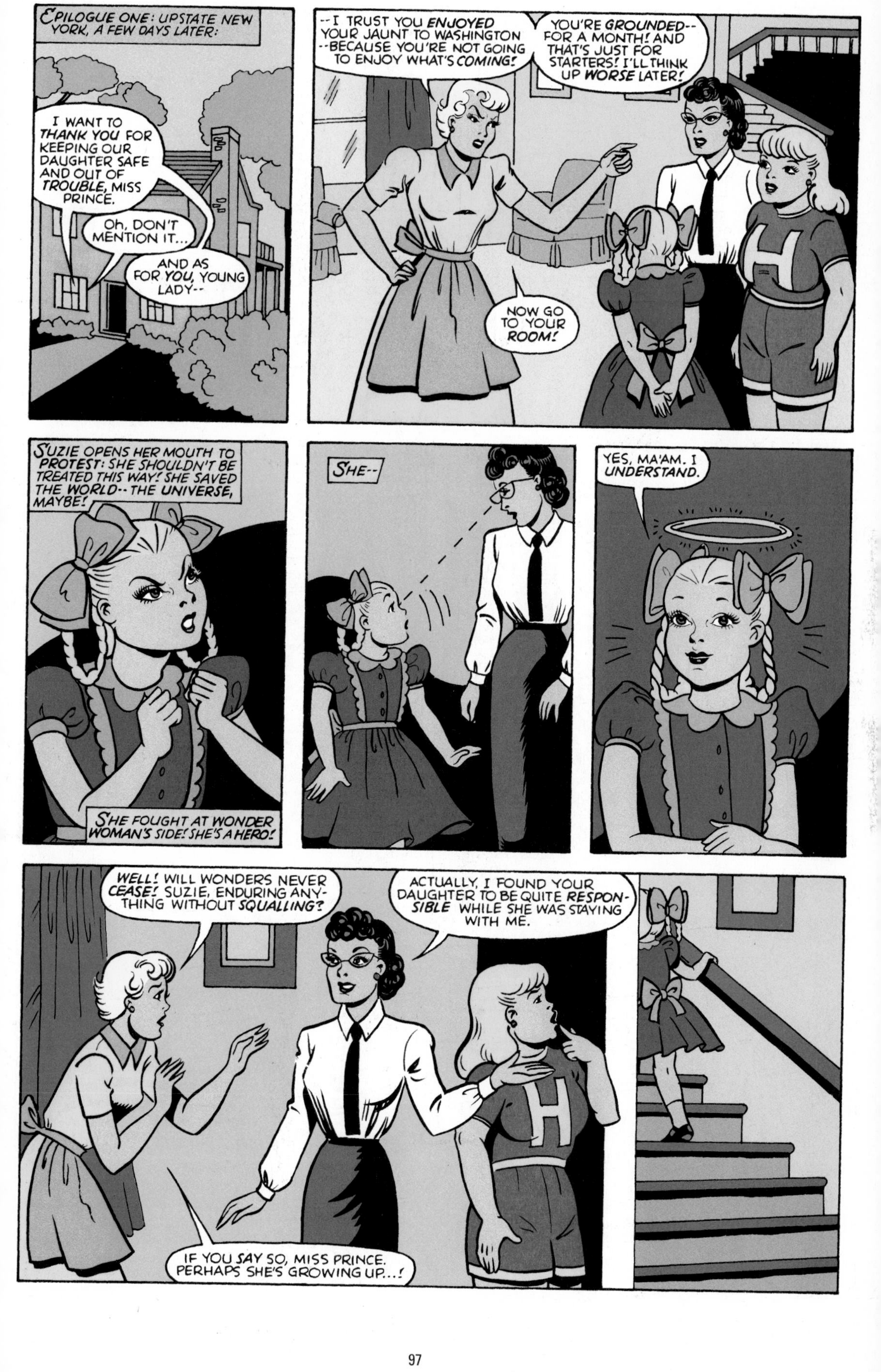
EPILOGUE ONE: UPSTATE NEW YORK, A FEW DAYS LATER:
I WANT TO THANK YOU FOR KEEPING OUR DAUGHTER SAFE AND OUT OF TROUBLE, MISS PRINCE.
Oh, DON'T MENTION IT...
AND AS FOR YOU, YOUNG LADY--
--I TRUST YOU ENJOYED YOUR JAUNT TO WASHINGTON --BECAUSE YOU'RE NOT GOING TO ENJOY WHAT'S COMING!
YOU'RE GROUNDED-- FOR A MONTH! AND THAT'S JUST FOR STARTERS! I'LL THINK UP WORSE LATER!
NOW GO TO YOUR ROOM!
SUZIE OPENS HER MOUTH TO PROTEST: SHE SHOULDN'T BE TREATED THIS WAY! SHE SAVED THE WORLD-- THE UNIVERSE, MAYBE!
SHE FOUGHT AT WONDER WOMAN'S SIDE! SHE'S A HERO!
SHE--
YES, MA'AM. I UNDERSTAND.
WELL! WILL WONDERS NEVER CEASE! SUZIE, ENDURING ANY-THING WITHOUT SQUALLING?
ACTUALLY, I FOUND YOUR DAUGHTER TO BE QUITE RESPON-SIBLE WHILE SHE WAS STAYING WITH ME.
IF YOU SAY SO, MISS PRINCE. PERHAPS SHE'S GROWING UP...!

EPILOGUE TWO: PARADISE ISLAND, TODAY:

THAT WAS *WONDERFUL*, MY QUEEN! THANK YOU FOR *SHOWING* IT TO US.

BUT--

--THE WOMAN IN COSTUME...WHO *WAS* THAT? WE'VE NEVER *SEEN* HER BEFORE.

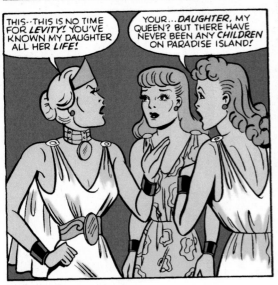

THIS--THIS IS NO TIME FOR *LEVITY!* YOU'VE KNOWN MY DAUGHTER ALL HER *LIFE!*

YOUR...*DAUGHTER*, MY QUEEN? BUT THERE HAVE NEVER BEEN ANY *CHILDREN* ON PARADISE ISLAND!

PAULA? PAULA, WHAT IS *HAPPENING?*

I...DON'T KNOW...

I'M SHOCKED *MYSELF* THAT OUR SISTER AMAZONS DON'T REMEMBER DIANA--BUT *MY* MEMORIES OF HER ARE HAZY--AS IF SHE WERE NOTHING MORE THAN A *DREAM*...

NO, PAULA-- NOT YOU, *TOO!*

98

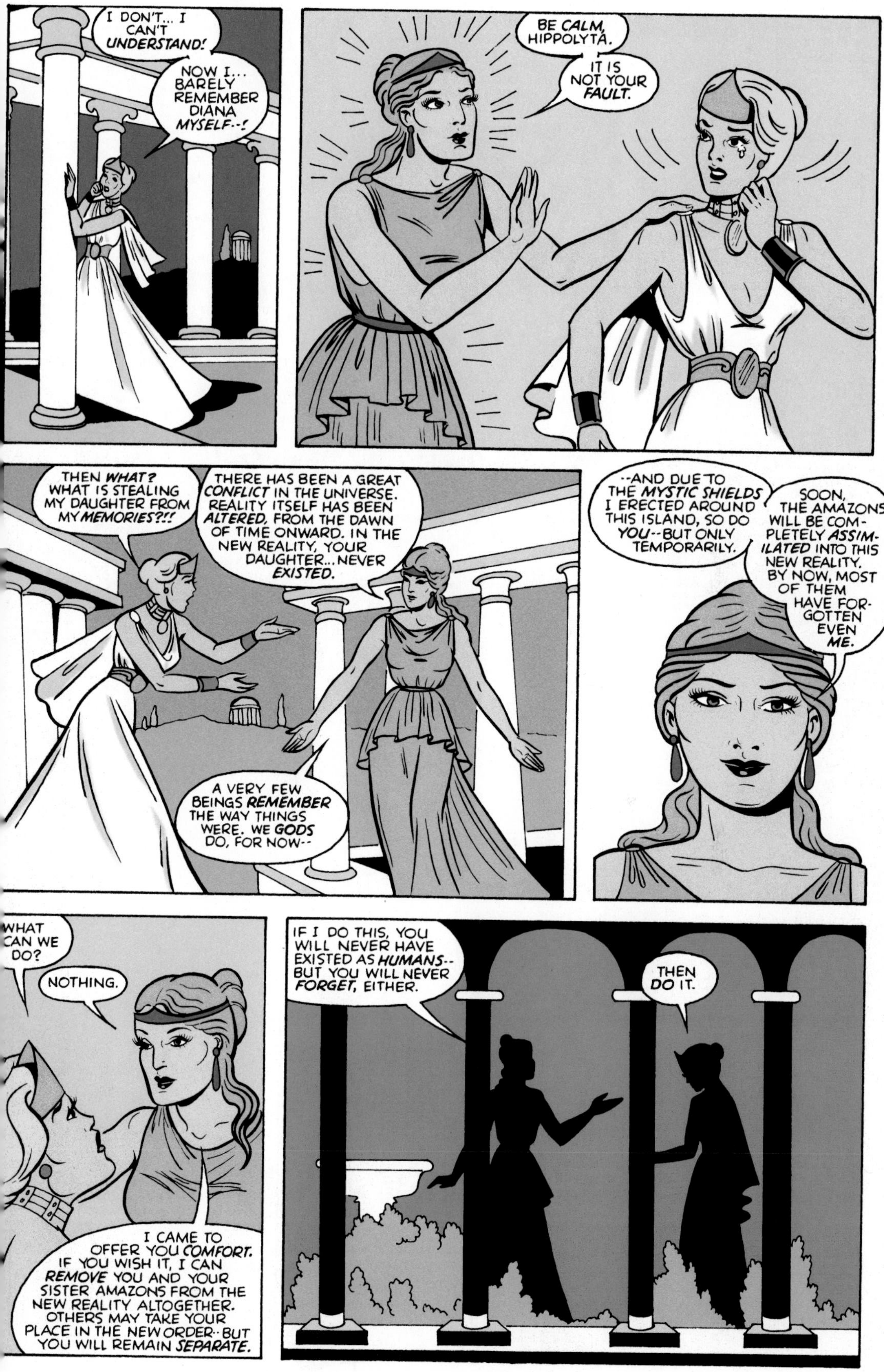

I DON'T... I CAN'T UNDERSTAND!
NOW I... BARELY REMEMBER DIANA MYSELF--!
BE CALM, HIPPOLYTA.
IT IS NOT YOUR FAULT.
THEN WHAT? WHAT IS STEALING MY DAUGHTER FROM MY MEMORIES?!!
THERE HAS BEEN A GREAT CONFLICT IN THE UNIVERSE. REALITY ITSELF HAS BEEN ALTERED, FROM THE DAWN OF TIME ONWARD. IN THE NEW REALITY, YOUR DAUGHTER... NEVER EXISTED.
A VERY FEW BEINGS REMEMBER THE WAY THINGS WERE. WE GODS DO, FOR NOW--
--AND DUE TO THE MYSTIC SHIELDS I ERECTED AROUND THIS ISLAND, SO DO YOU--BUT ONLY TEMPORARILY.
SOON, THE AMAZONS WILL BE COMPLETELY ASSIMILATED INTO THIS NEW REALITY. BY NOW, MOST OF THEM HAVE FORGOTTEN EVEN ME.
WHAT CAN WE DO?
NOTHING.
I CAME TO OFFER YOU COMFORT. IF YOU WISH IT, I CAN REMOVE YOU AND YOUR SISTER AMAZONS FROM THE NEW REALITY ALTOGETHER. OTHERS MAY TAKE YOUR PLACE IN THE NEW ORDER--BUT YOU WILL REMAIN SEPARATE.
IF I DO THIS, YOU WILL NEVER HAVE EXISTED AS HUMANS--BUT YOU WILL NEVER FORGET, EITHER.
THEN DO IT.

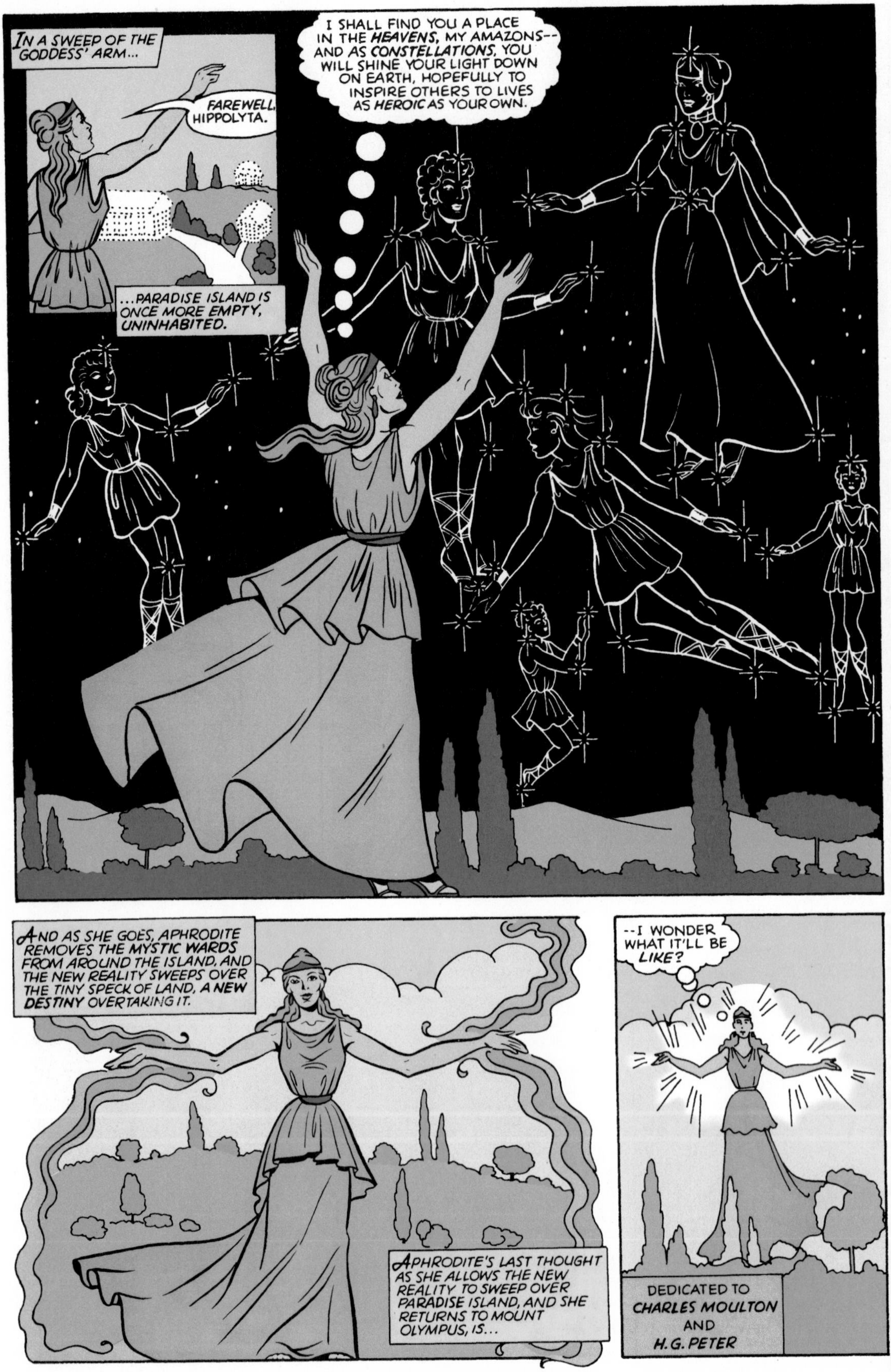
IN A SWEEP OF THE GODDESS' ARM...
FAREWELL, HIPPOLYTA.
...PARADISE ISLAND IS ONCE MORE EMPTY, UNINHABITED.
I SHALL FIND YOU A PLACE IN THE HEAVENS, MY AMAZONS--AND AS CONSTELLATIONS, YOU WILL SHINE YOUR LIGHT DOWN ON EARTH, HOPEFULLY TO INSPIRE OTHERS TO LIVES AS HEROIC AS YOUR OWN.
AND AS SHE GOES, APHRODITE REMOVES THE MYSTIC WARDS FROM AROUND THE ISLAND, AND THE NEW REALITY SWEEPS OVER THE TINY SPECK OF LAND, A NEW DESTINY OVERTAKING IT.
APHRODITE'S LAST THOUGHT AS SHE ALLOWS THE NEW REALITY TO SWEEP OVER PARADISE ISLAND, AND SHE RETURNS TO MOUNT OLYMPUS, IS...
--I WONDER WHAT IT'LL BE LIKE?
DEDICATED TO CHARLES MOULTON AND H.G. PETER

This portrait of the Amazon Princess by Trina Robbins (with color by Patricia Mulvihill) originally appeared in the 1996 *WONDER WOMAN GALLERY* one-shot.

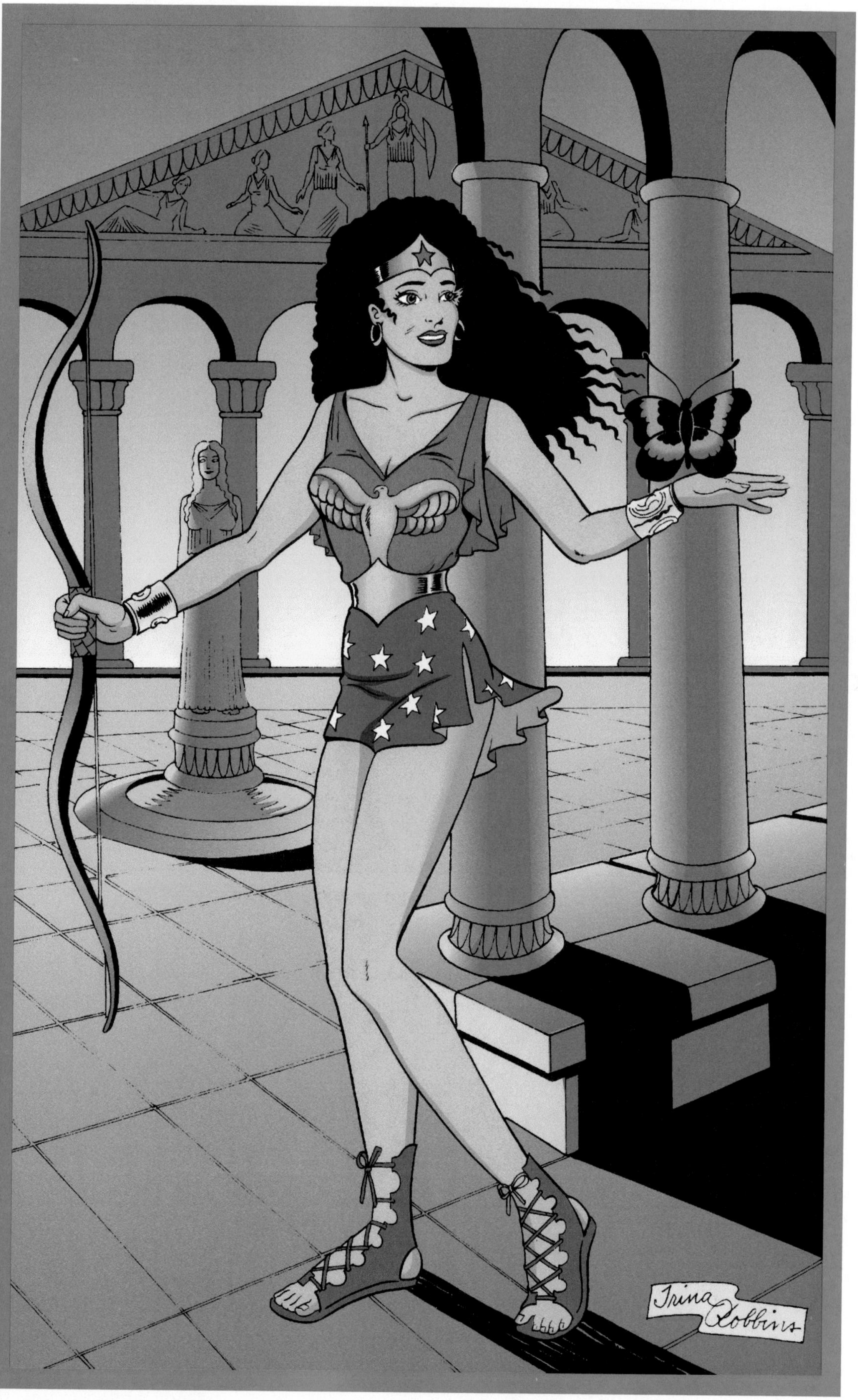
Trina Robbins

The following story originally appeared in 1989's WONDER WOMAN ANNUAL #2 (this first introductory page was written by George Pérez and lettered by Carrie Spiegle).

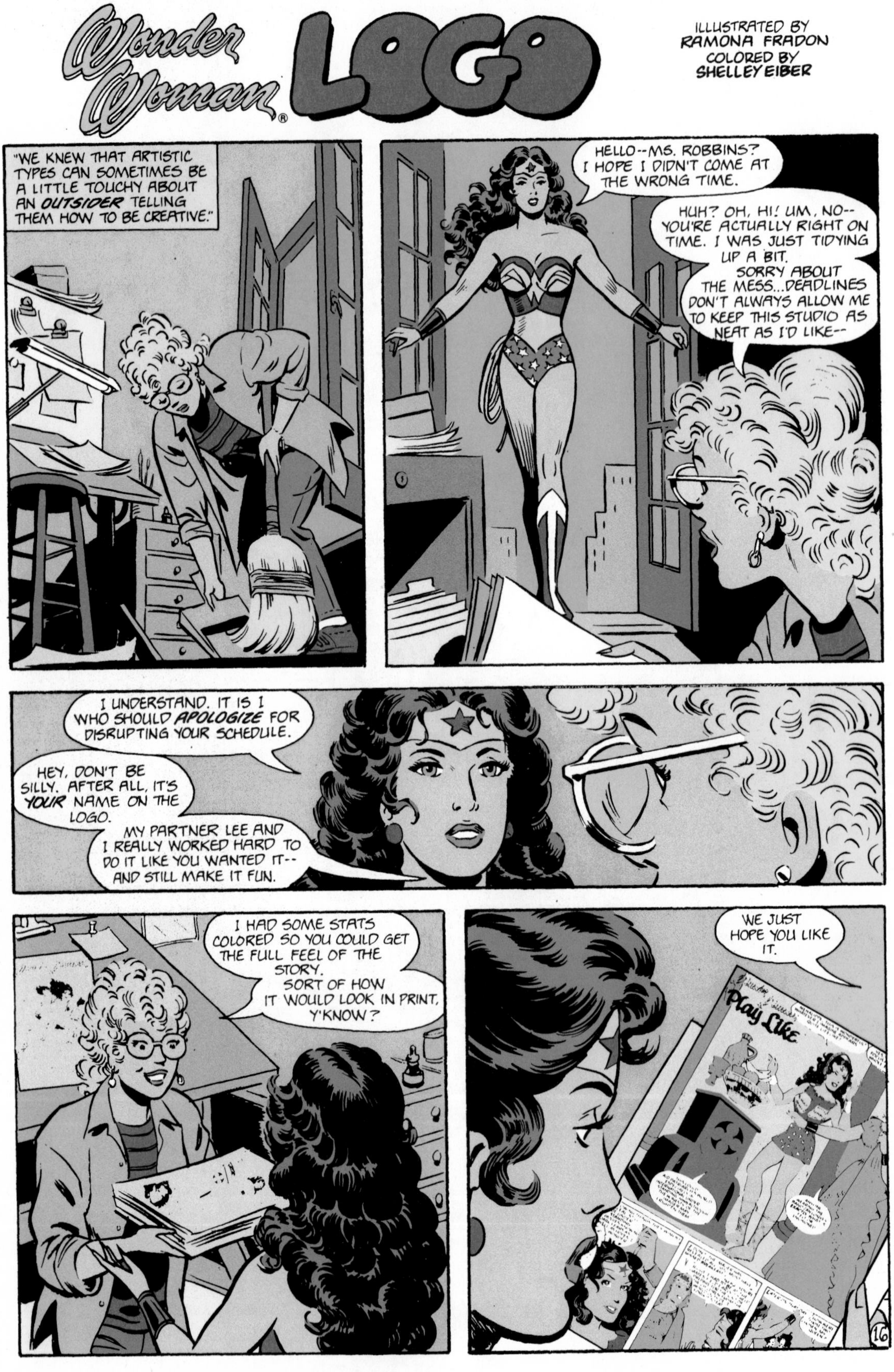

Wonder Woman® LOGO
ILLUSTRATED BY RAMONA FRADON
COLORED BY SHELLEY EIBER
"WE KNEW THAT ARTISTIC TYPES CAN SOMETIMES BE A LITTLE TOUCHY ABOUT AN OUTSIDER TELLING THEM HOW TO BE CREATIVE."
HELLO--MS. ROBBINS? I HOPE I DIDN'T COME AT THE WRONG TIME.
HUH? OH, HI! UM, NO-- YOU'RE ACTUALLY RIGHT ON TIME. I WAS JUST TIDYING UP A BIT.
SORRY ABOUT THE MESS...DEADLINES DON'T ALWAYS ALLOW ME TO KEEP THIS STUDIO AS NEAT AS I'D LIKE--
I UNDERSTAND. IT IS I WHO SHOULD APOLOGIZE FOR DISRUPTING YOUR SCHEDULE.
HEY, DON'T BE SILLY. AFTER ALL, IT'S YOUR NAME ON THE LOGO.
MY PARTNER LEE AND I REALLY WORKED HARD TO DO IT LIKE YOU WANTED IT-- AND STILL MAKE IT FUN.
I HAD SOME STATS COLORED SO YOU COULD GET THE FULL FEEL OF THE STORY.
SORT OF HOW IT WOULD LOOK IN PRINT, Y'KNOW?
WE JUST HOPE YOU LIKE IT.
Play Like
16

Wonder Woman
Play Like

MENALIPPE, THIS IS WONDERFUL! WHATEVER I IMAGINE APPEARS QUITE LIFELIKE!

YES, THIS IMAGER ENABLES YOU TO FOCUS AND PROJECT. YOU CAN CREATE WHOLE ENVIRONMENTS, TELL STORIES.

ANYONE WEARING THE BAND CAN CONVEY *EXACTLY* WHAT IS FELT OR ENVISIONED.

THIS COULD AID PATRIARCH'S WORLD, ESPECIALLY IN INTERNATIONAL UNDERSTANDING. *Hmm,* ALTHOUGH THE HONESTY OF THE IMAGER MAY FRIGHTEN THEM...

Story by
LEE MARRS
Art by
TRINA ROBBINS
Lettered by
L. LOIS BUHALIS
Colored by
SHELLEY EIBER

...SHOWING THINGS THEY WISH TO CONCEAL. STILL, TRUE UNDERSTANDING INVOLVES KNOWING DARK FEARS AS WELL AS HOPES. I WONDER...

I DON'T. THE IMAGER HAS REVEALED ALL: YOU MUST HAVE MISSED BREAKFAST.

Ha ha! YOU'RE RIGHT. I HAD TO BE AT THE GAMES FIELD EARLY TO HELP PREPARE FOR THE VISIT OF THE CHILDREN FROM THE WORLD OUTSIDE. I FORGOT TO EAT.

LATER ON THAT DAY... HOW WERE THOSE TWO CHOSEN, MY QUEEN?

A WRITING CONTEST WAS HELD ALL OVER THE WORLD. THE CHILD WHO WROTE THE BEST ESSAY ON PEACE WAS DECLARED THE WINNER.

⑰

103

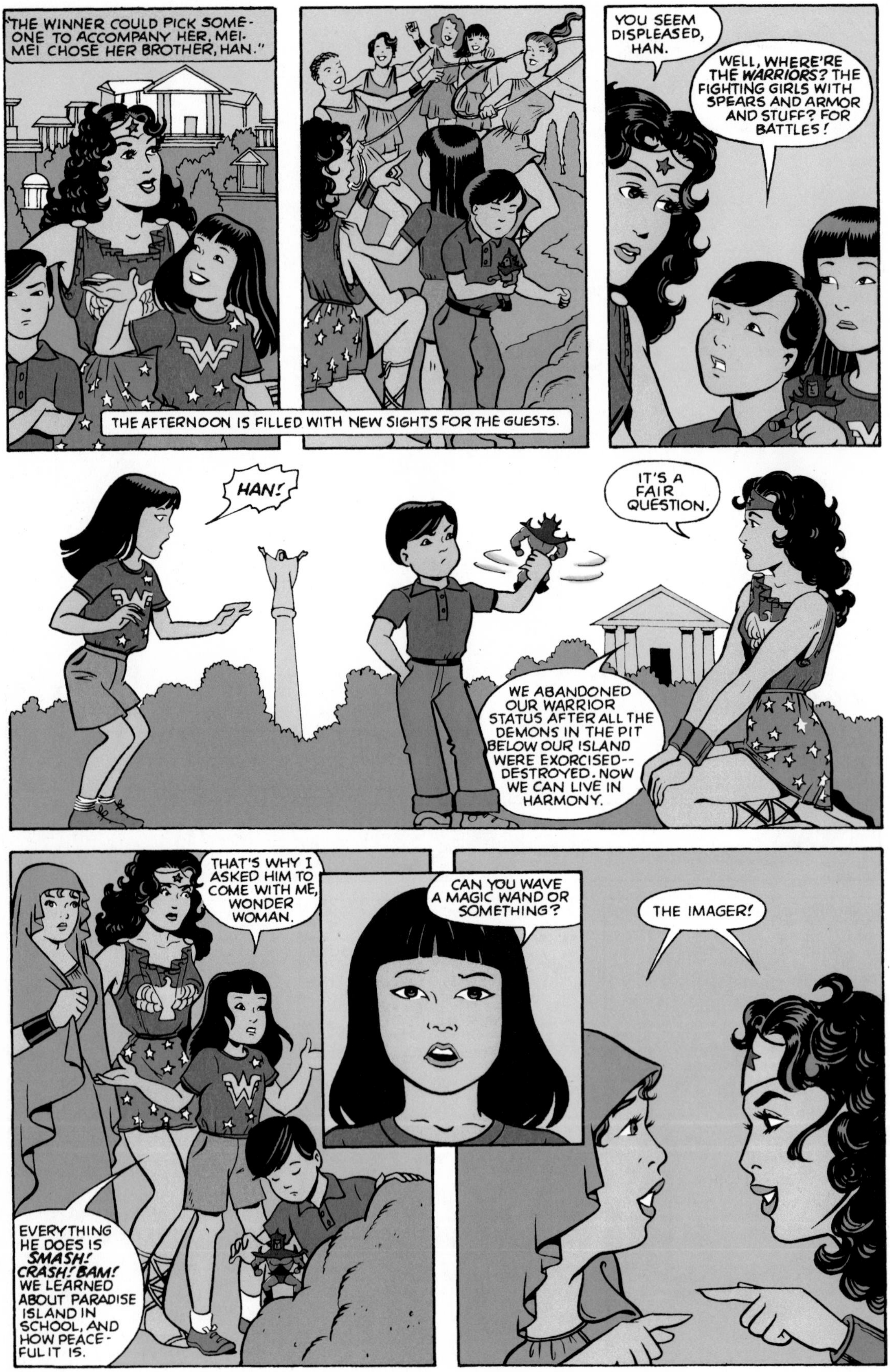

"THE WINNER COULD PICK SOMEONE TO ACCOMPANY HER. MEI-MEI CHOSE HER BROTHER, HAN."
THE AFTERNOON IS FILLED WITH NEW SIGHTS FOR THE GUESTS.
YOU SEEM DISPLEASED, HAN.
WELL, WHERE'RE THE WARRIORS? THE FIGHTING GIRLS WITH SPEARS AND ARMOR AND STUFF? FOR BATTLES!
HAN!
IT'S A FAIR QUESTION.
WE ABANDONED OUR WARRIOR STATUS AFTER ALL THE DEMONS IN THE PIT BELOW OUR ISLAND WERE EXORCISED--DESTROYED. NOW WE CAN LIVE IN HARMONY.
THAT'S WHY I ASKED HIM TO COME WITH ME, WONDER WOMAN.
EVERYTHING HE DOES IS SMASH! CRASH! BAM! WE LEARNED ABOUT PARADISE ISLAND IN SCHOOL, AND HOW PEACEFUL IT IS.
CAN YOU WAVE A MAGIC WAND OR SOMETHING?
THE IMAGER!

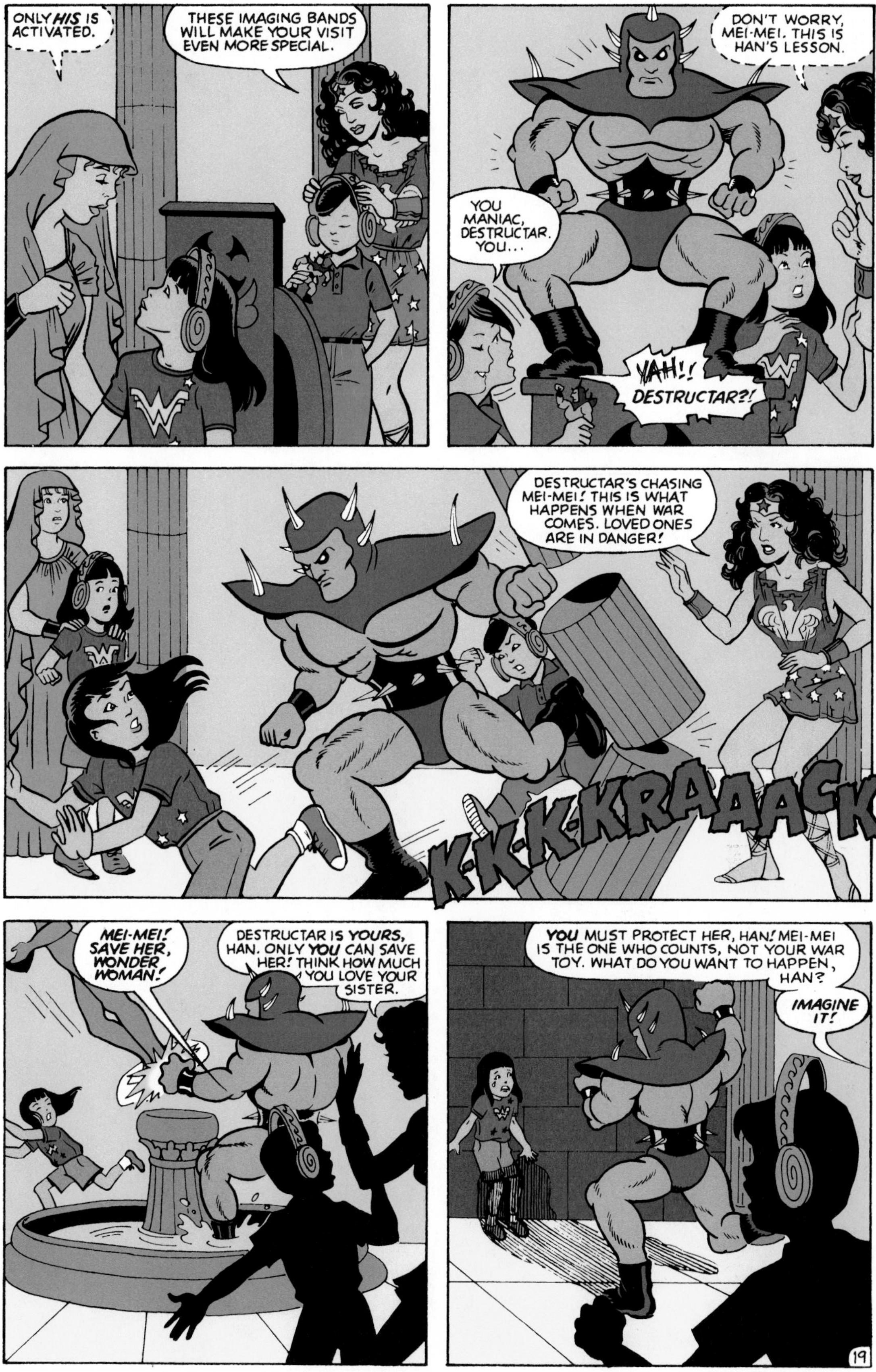
ONLY HIS IS ACTIVATED.
THESE IMAGING BANDS WILL MAKE YOUR VISIT EVEN MORE SPECIAL.
DON'T WORRY, MEI-MEI. THIS IS HAN'S LESSON.
YOU MANIAC, DESTRUCTAR. YOU...
YAH!! DESTRUCTAR?!
DESTRUCTAR'S CHASING MEI-MEI! THIS IS WHAT HAPPENS WHEN WAR COMES. LOVED ONES ARE IN DANGER!
K-K-K-KRAAAACK!
MEI-MEI! SAVE HER, WONDER WOMAN!
DESTRUCTAR IS YOURS, HAN. ONLY YOU CAN SAVE HER! THINK HOW MUCH YOU LOVE YOUR SISTER.
YOU MUST PROTECT HER, HAN! MEI-MEI IS THE ONE WHO COUNTS, NOT YOUR WAR TOY. WHAT DO YOU WANT TO HAPPEN, HAN?
IMAGINE IT!
19

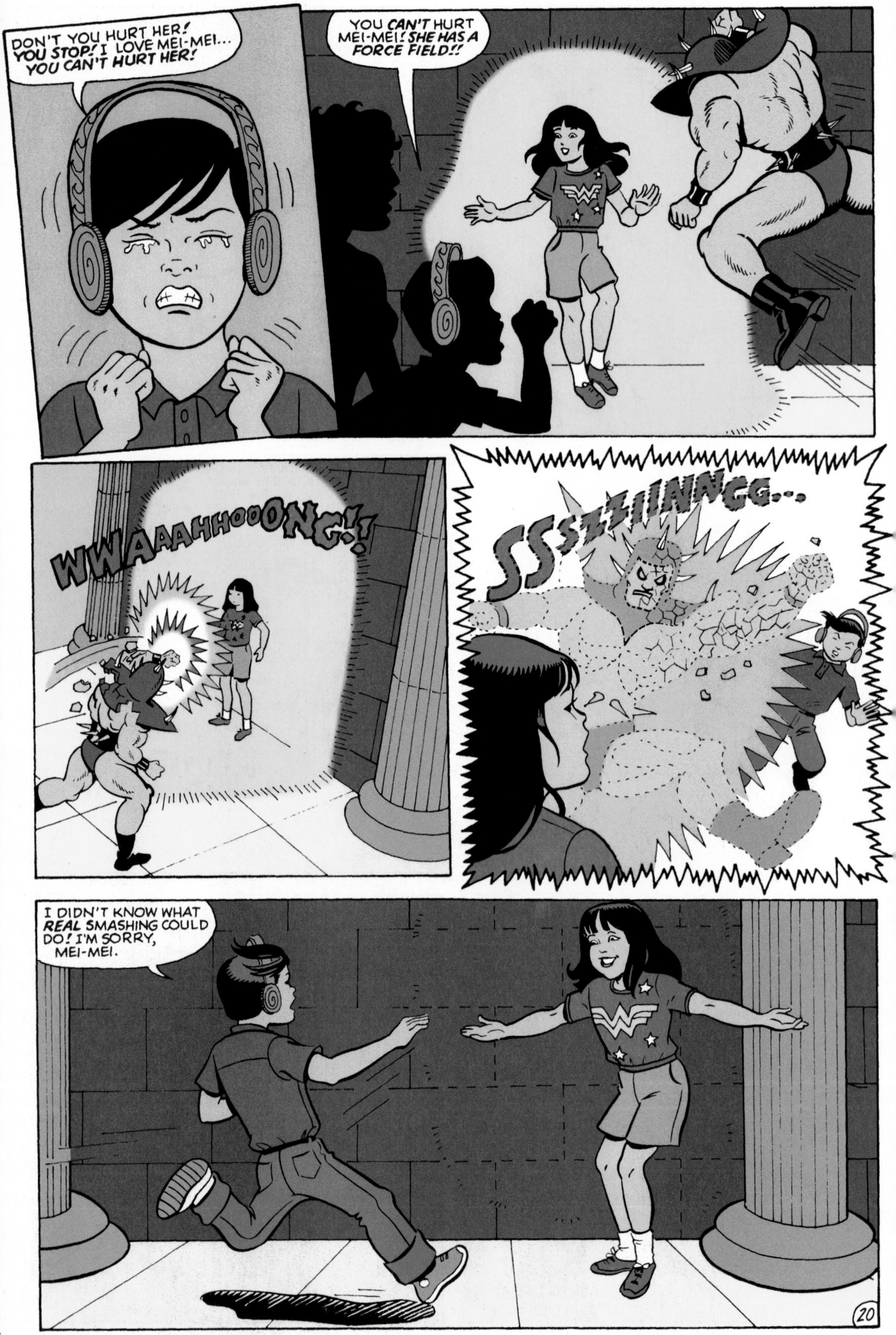
DON'T YOU HURT HER! YOU STOP! I LOVE MEI-MEI... YOU CAN'T HURT HER!
YOU CAN'T HURT MEI-MEI! SHE HAS A FORCE FIELD!!
WWAAAHHOOONG!!
SSSZZIIINNGG...
I DIDN'T KNOW WHAT REAL SMASHING COULD DO! I'M SORRY, MEI-MEI.
20

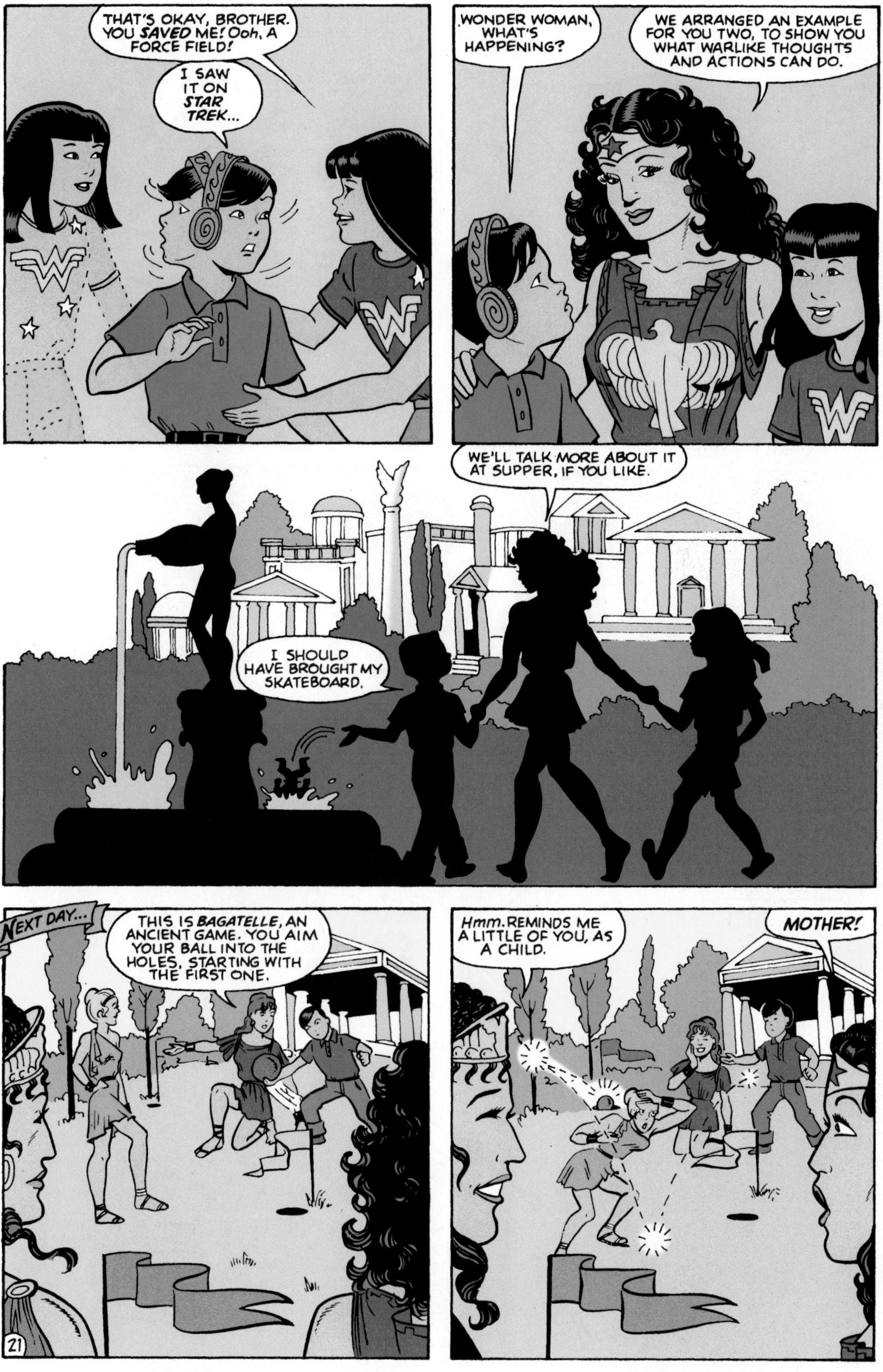
THAT'S OKAY, BROTHER. YOU SAVED ME! Ooh, A FORCE FIELD!
I SAW IT ON STAR TREK...
WONDER WOMAN, WHAT'S HAPPENING?
WE ARRANGED AN EXAMPLE FOR YOU TWO, TO SHOW YOU WHAT WARLIKE THOUGHTS AND ACTIONS CAN DO.
WE'LL TALK MORE ABOUT IT AT SUPPER, IF YOU LIKE.
I SHOULD HAVE BROUGHT MY SKATEBOARD.
NEXT DAY...
THIS IS BAGATELLE, AN ANCIENT GAME. YOU AIM YOUR BALL INTO THE HOLES, STARTING WITH THE FIRST ONE.
21
Hmm. REMINDS ME A LITTLE OF YOU, AS A CHILD.
MOTHER!

I LIKE IT. IT READS LIKE ONE OF THOSE FABLES MY MOTHER RECITED TO ME WHEN I WAS A LITTLE GIRL.

DO YOU THINK THE READERS WILL LIKE IT? WILL THEY LEARN FROM IT?

WELL, I'VE BEEN IN THIS BUSINESS A FEW YEARS.

IT WOULD BE GROSSLY NAIVE AND PRESUMPTUOUS TO THINK THAT A COMIC BOOK CAN CHANGE THE WORLD'S THINKING.

--BUT IT DOESN'T HURT TO TRY.

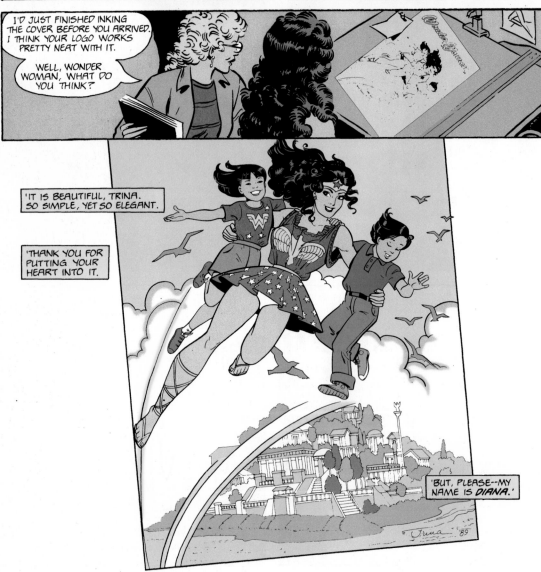

I'D JUST FINISHED INKING THE COVER BEFORE YOU ARRIVED. I THINK YOUR LOGO WORKS PRETTY NEAT WITH IT.

WELL, WONDER WOMAN, WHAT DO YOU THINK?

'IT IS BEAUTIFUL, TRINA. SO SIMPLE, YET SO ELEGANT.

'THANK YOU FOR PUTTING YOUR HEART INTO IT.

'BUT, PLEASE--MY NAME IS *DIANA*.'

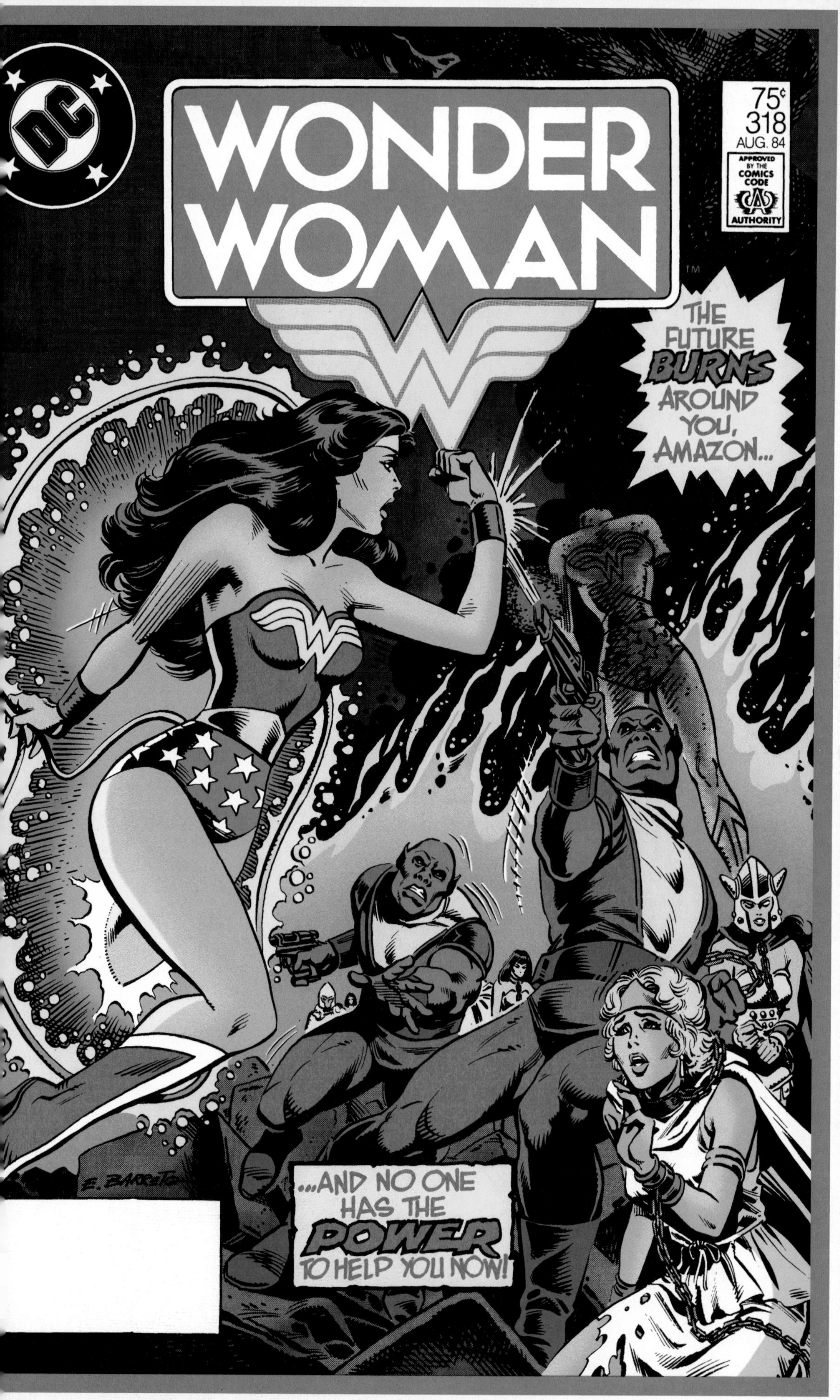

DC
WONDER WOMAN
75¢
318
AUG. 84
APPROVED BY THE COMICS CODE AUTHORITY
THE FUTURE BURNS AROUND YOU, AMAZON...
...AND NO ONE HAS THE POWER TO HELP YOU NOW!

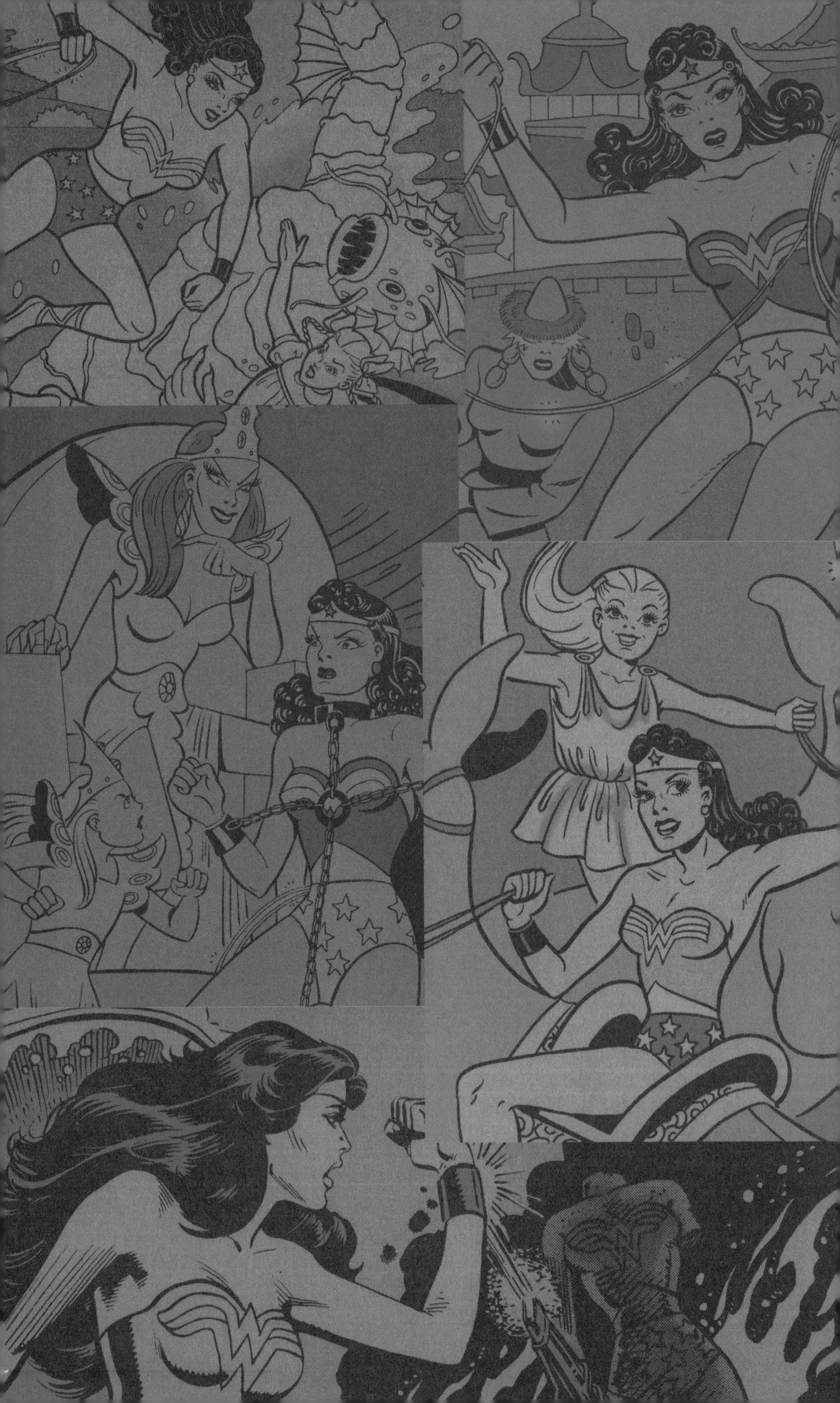

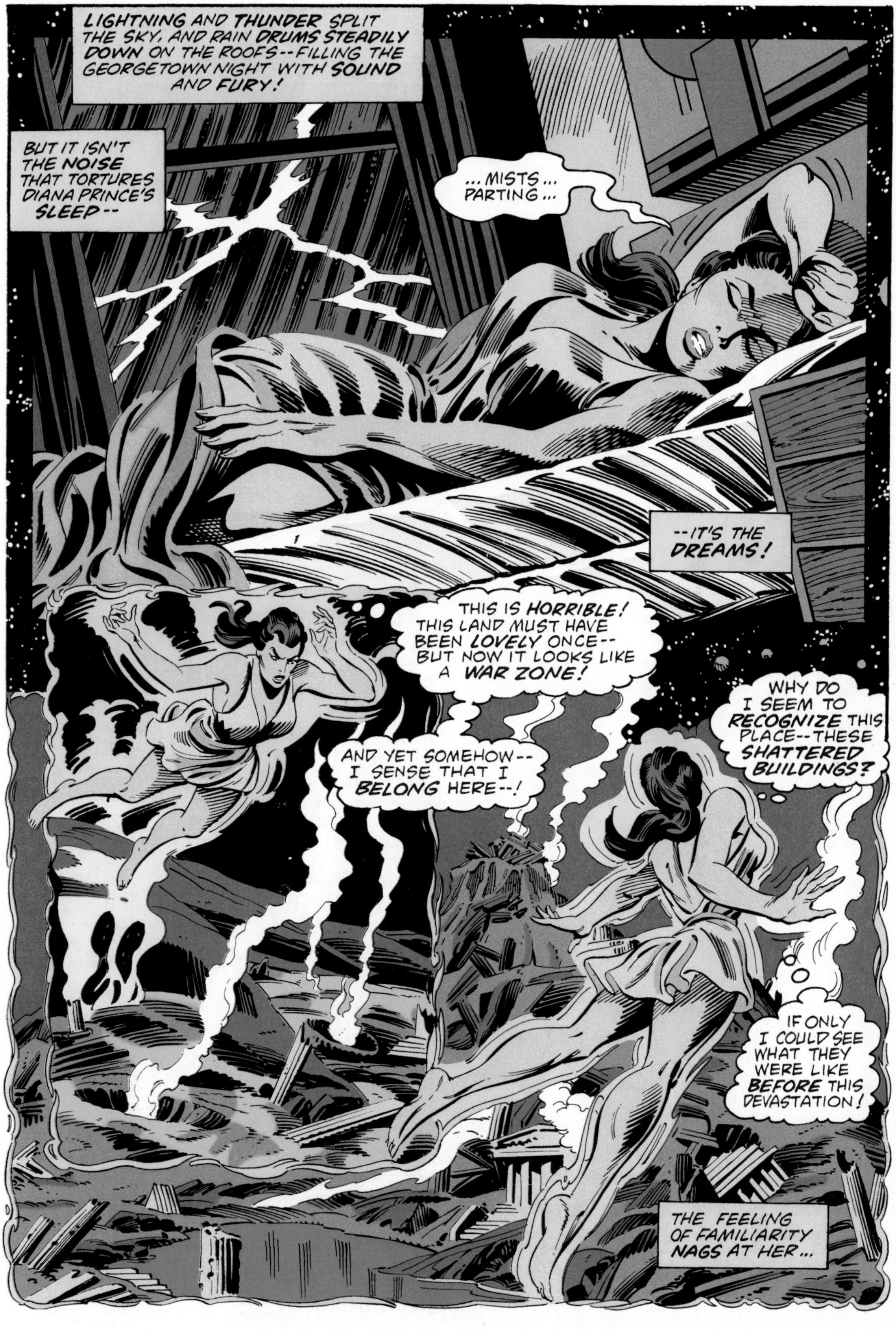
LIGHTNING AND THUNDER SPLIT THE SKY, AND RAIN DRUMS STEADILY DOWN ON THE ROOFS--FILLING THE GEORGETOWN NIGHT WITH SOUND AND FURY!
BUT IT ISN'T THE NOISE THAT TORTURES DIANA PRINCE'S SLEEP--
...MISTS... PARTING...
--IT'S THE DREAMS!
THIS IS HORRIBLE! THIS LAND MUST HAVE BEEN LOVELY ONCE--BUT NOW IT LOOKS LIKE A WAR ZONE!
AND YET SOMEHOW--I SENSE THAT I BELONG HERE--!
WHY DO I SEEM TO RECOGNIZE THIS PLACE--THESE SHATTERED BUILDINGS?
IF ONLY I COULD SEE WHAT THEY WERE LIKE BEFORE THIS DEVASTATION!
THE FEELING OF FAMILIARITY NAGS AT HER...

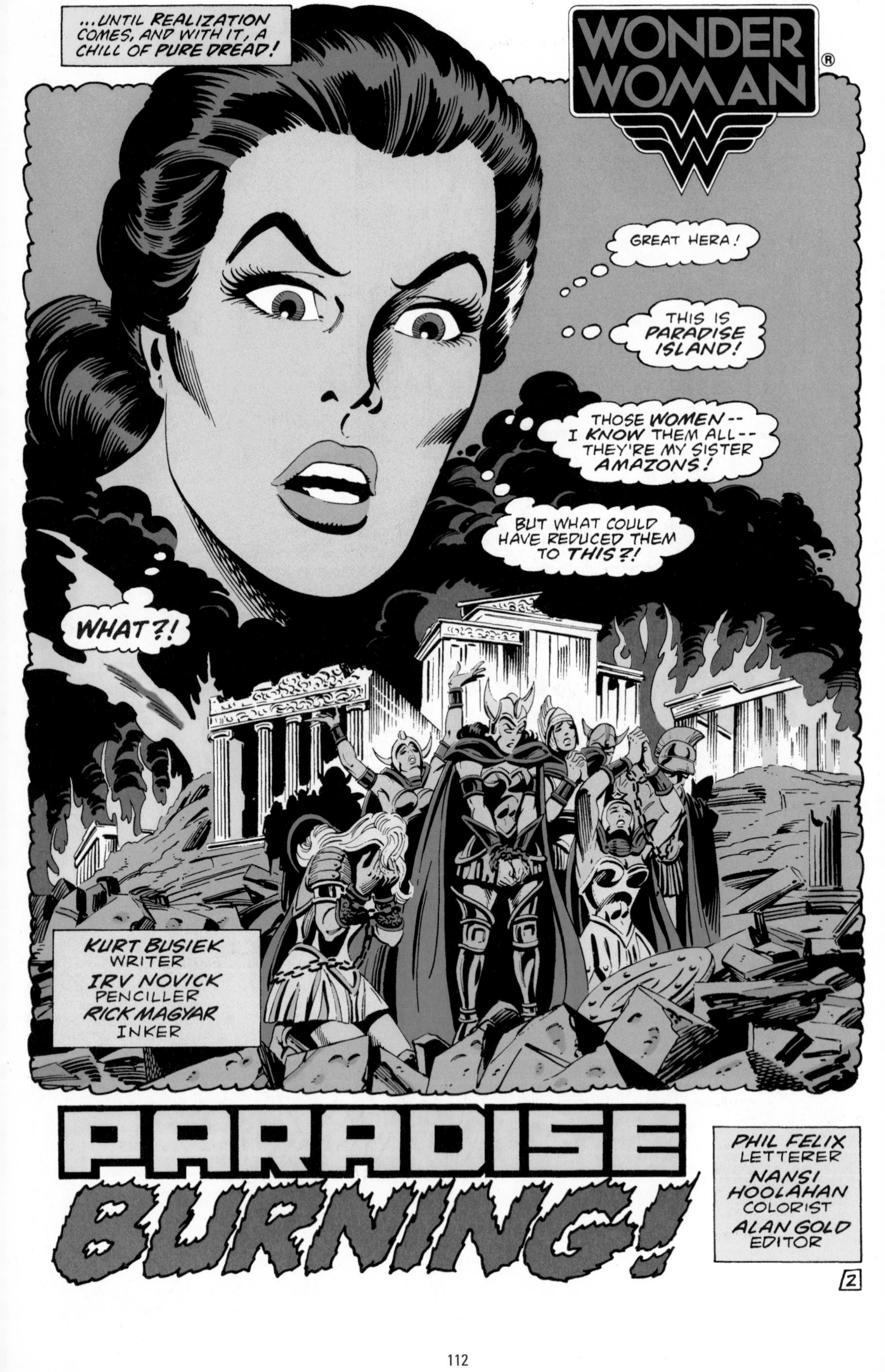
...UNTIL REALIZATION COMES, AND WITH IT, A CHILL OF PURE DREAD!
WONDER WOMAN
GREAT HERA!
THIS IS PARADISE ISLAND!
THOSE WOMEN -- I KNOW THEM ALL -- THEY'RE MY SISTER AMAZONS!
BUT WHAT COULD HAVE REDUCED THEM TO THIS?!
WHAT?!
KURT BUSIEK WRITER
IRV NOVICK PENCILLER
RICK MAGYAR INKER
PARADISE BURNING!
PHIL FELIX LETTERER
NANSI HOOLAHAN COLORIST
ALAN GOLD EDITOR
2

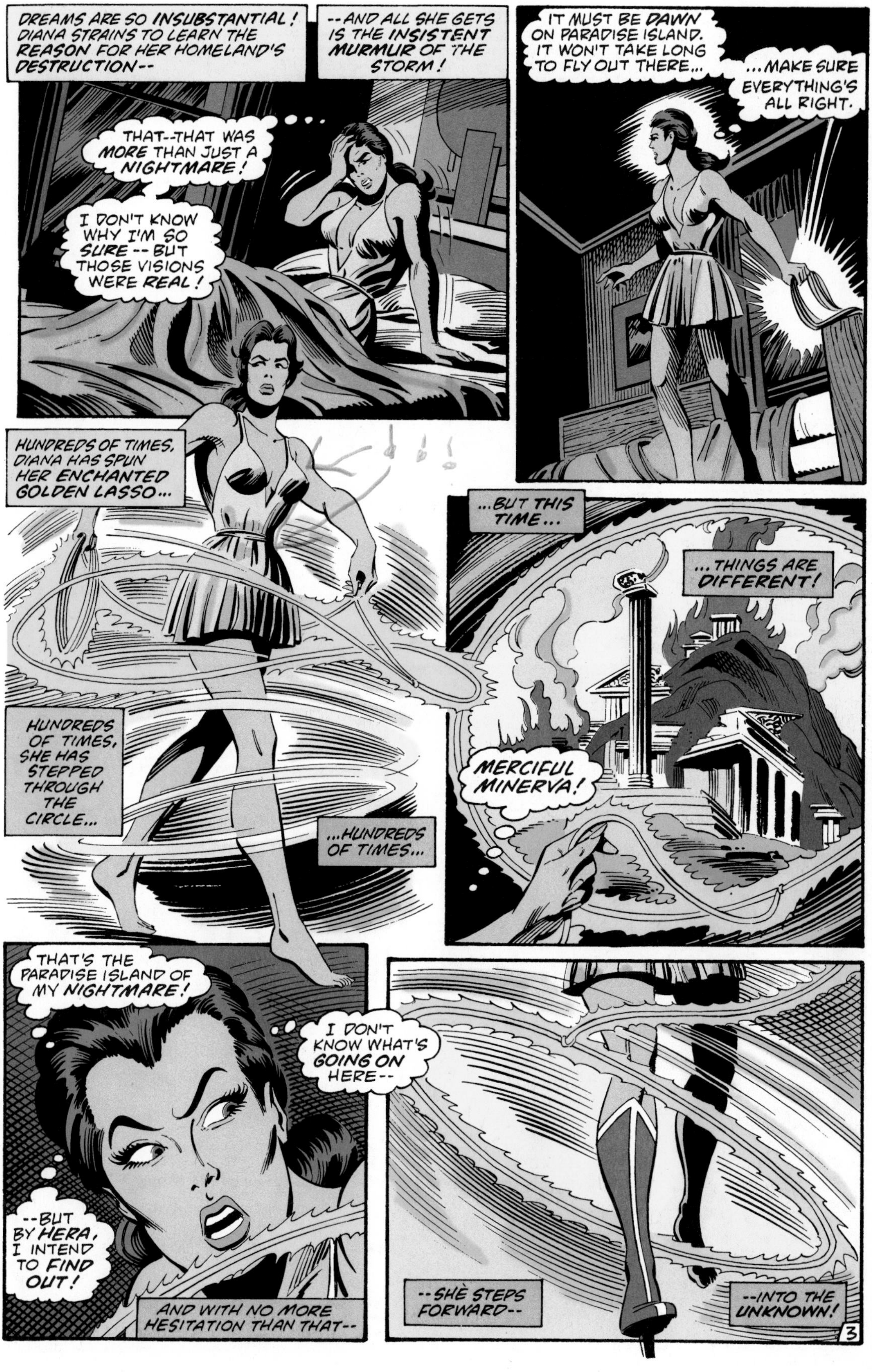
DREAMS ARE SO INSUBSTANTIAL! DIANA STRAINS TO LEARN THE REASON FOR HER HOMELAND'S DESTRUCTION--
--AND ALL SHE GETS IS THE INSISTENT MURMUR OF THE STORM!
THAT--THAT WAS MORE THAN JUST A NIGHTMARE!
I DON'T KNOW WHY I'M SO SURE -- BUT THOSE VISIONS WERE REAL!
IT MUST BE DAWN ON PARADISE ISLAND. IT WON'T TAKE LONG TO FLY OUT THERE...
...MAKE SURE EVERYTHING'S ALL RIGHT.
HUNDREDS OF TIMES, DIANA HAS SPUN HER ENCHANTED GOLDEN LASSO...
HUNDREDS OF TIMES, SHE HAS STEPPED THROUGH THE CIRCLE...
...HUNDREDS OF TIMES...
...BUT THIS TIME...
...THINGS ARE DIFFERENT!
MERCIFUL MINERVA!
THAT'S THE PARADISE ISLAND OF MY NIGHTMARE!
I DON'T KNOW WHAT'S GOING ON HERE--
--BUT BY HERA, I INTEND TO FIND OUT!
AND WITH NO MORE HESITATION THAN THAT--
--SHE STEPS FORWARD--
--INTO THE UNKNOWN!
3

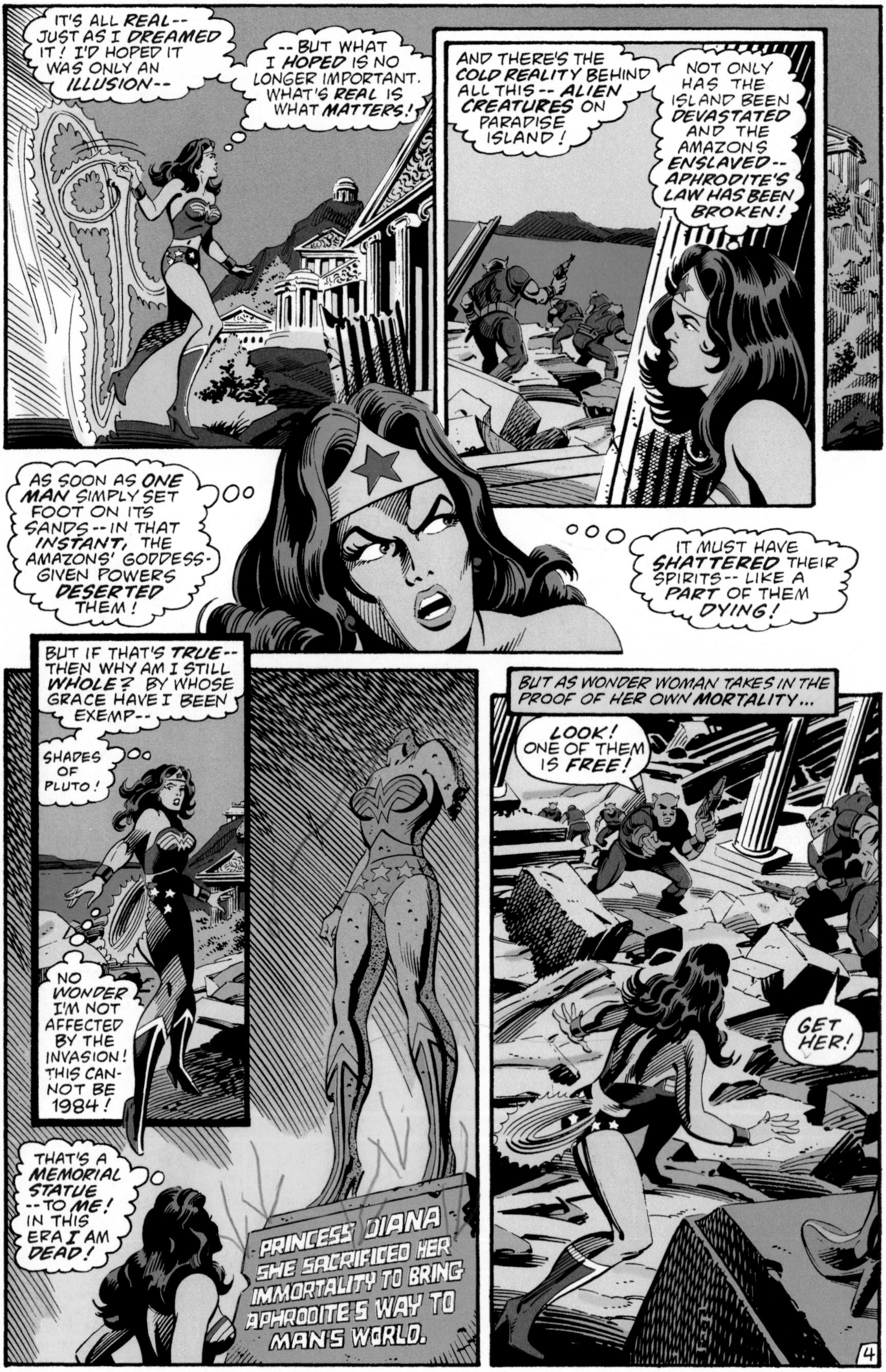
IT'S ALL REAL-- JUST AS I DREAMED IT! I'D HOPED IT WAS ONLY AN ILLUSION--
--BUT WHAT I HOPED IS NO LONGER IMPORTANT. WHAT'S REAL IS WHAT MATTERS!
AND THERE'S THE COLD REALITY BEHIND ALL THIS -- ALIEN CREATURES ON PARADISE ISLAND!
NOT ONLY HAS THE ISLAND BEEN DEVASTATED AND THE AMAZONS ENSLAVED-- APHRODITE'S LAW HAS BEEN BROKEN!
AS SOON AS ONE MAN SIMPLY SET FOOT ON ITS SANDS--IN THAT INSTANT, THE AMAZONS' GODDESS-GIVEN POWERS DESERTED THEM!
IT MUST HAVE SHATTERED THEIR SPIRITS-- LIKE A PART OF THEM DYING!
BUT IF THAT'S TRUE-- THEN WHY AM I STILL WHOLE? BY WHOSE GRACE HAVE I BEEN EXEMP--
SHADES OF PLUTO!
NO WONDER I'M NOT AFFECTED BY THE INVASION! THIS CANNOT BE 1984!
THAT'S A MEMORIAL STATUE --TO ME! IN THIS ERA I AM DEAD!
PRINCESS DIANA SHE SACRIFICED HER IMMORTALITY TO BRING APHRODITE'S WAY TO MAN'S WORLD.
BUT AS WONDER WOMAN TAKES IN THE PROOF OF HER OWN MORTALITY...
LOOK! ONE OF THEM IS FREE!
GET HER!
4

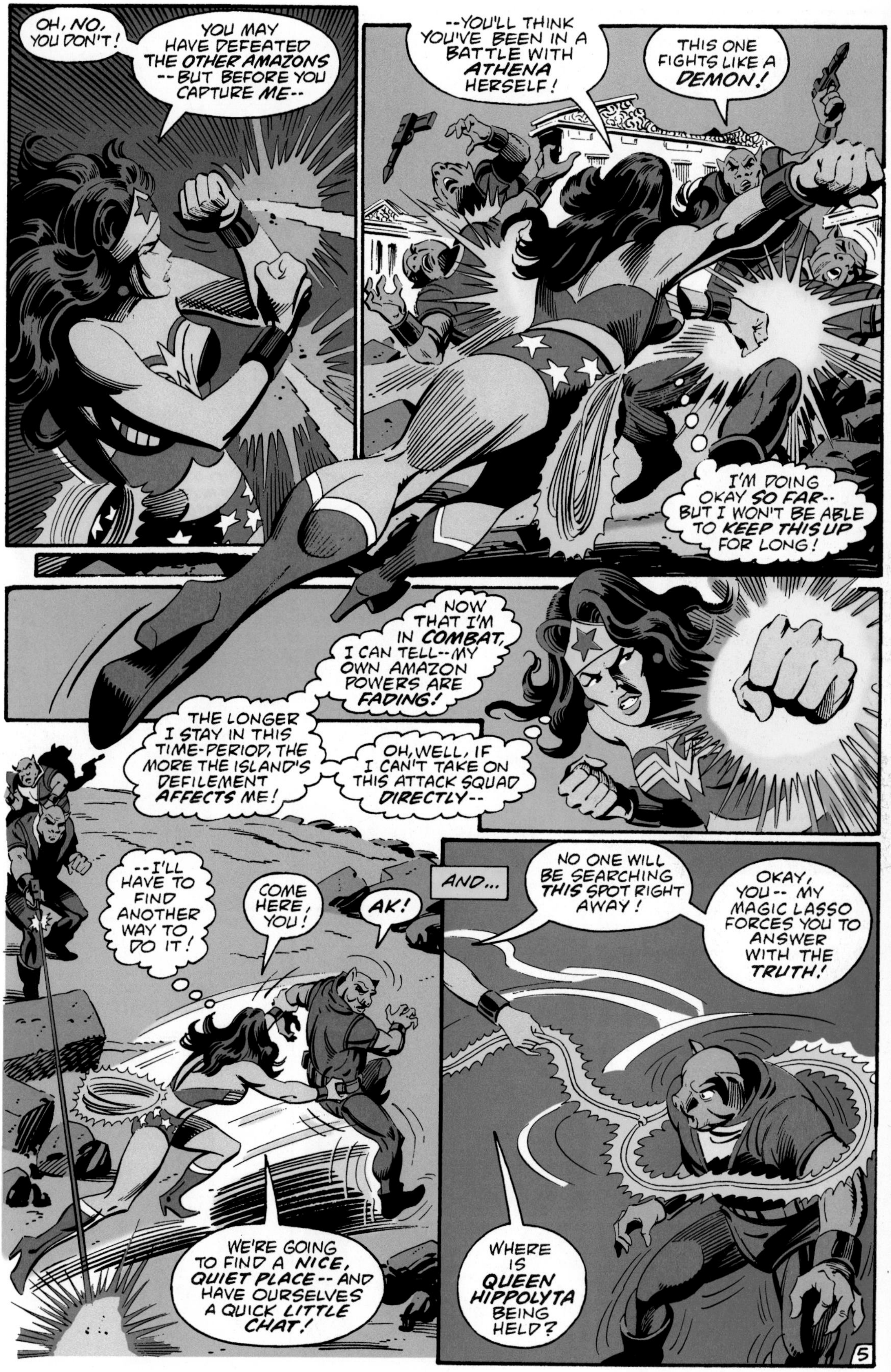
OH, NO, YOU DON'T!
YOU MAY HAVE DEFEATED THE OTHER AMAZONS --BUT BEFORE YOU CAPTURE ME--
--YOU'LL THINK YOU'VE BEEN IN A BATTLE WITH ATHENA HERSELF!
THIS ONE FIGHTS LIKE A DEMON!
I'M DOING OKAY SO FAR-- BUT I WON'T BE ABLE TO KEEP THIS UP FOR LONG!
NOW THAT I'M IN COMBAT, I CAN TELL--MY OWN AMAZON POWERS ARE FADING!
THE LONGER I STAY IN THIS TIME-PERIOD, THE MORE THE ISLAND'S DEFILEMENT AFFECTS ME!
OH, WELL, IF I CAN'T TAKE ON THIS ATTACK SQUAD DIRECTLY--
--I'LL HAVE TO FIND ANOTHER WAY TO DO IT!
COME HERE, YOU!
AK!
WE'RE GOING TO FIND A NICE, QUIET PLACE-- AND HAVE OURSELVES A QUICK LITTLE CHAT!
AND...
NO ONE WILL BE SEARCHING THIS SPOT RIGHT AWAY!
OKAY, YOU-- MY MAGIC LASSO FORCES YOU TO ANSWER WITH THE TRUTH!
WHERE IS QUEEN HIPPOLYTA BEING HELD?
5

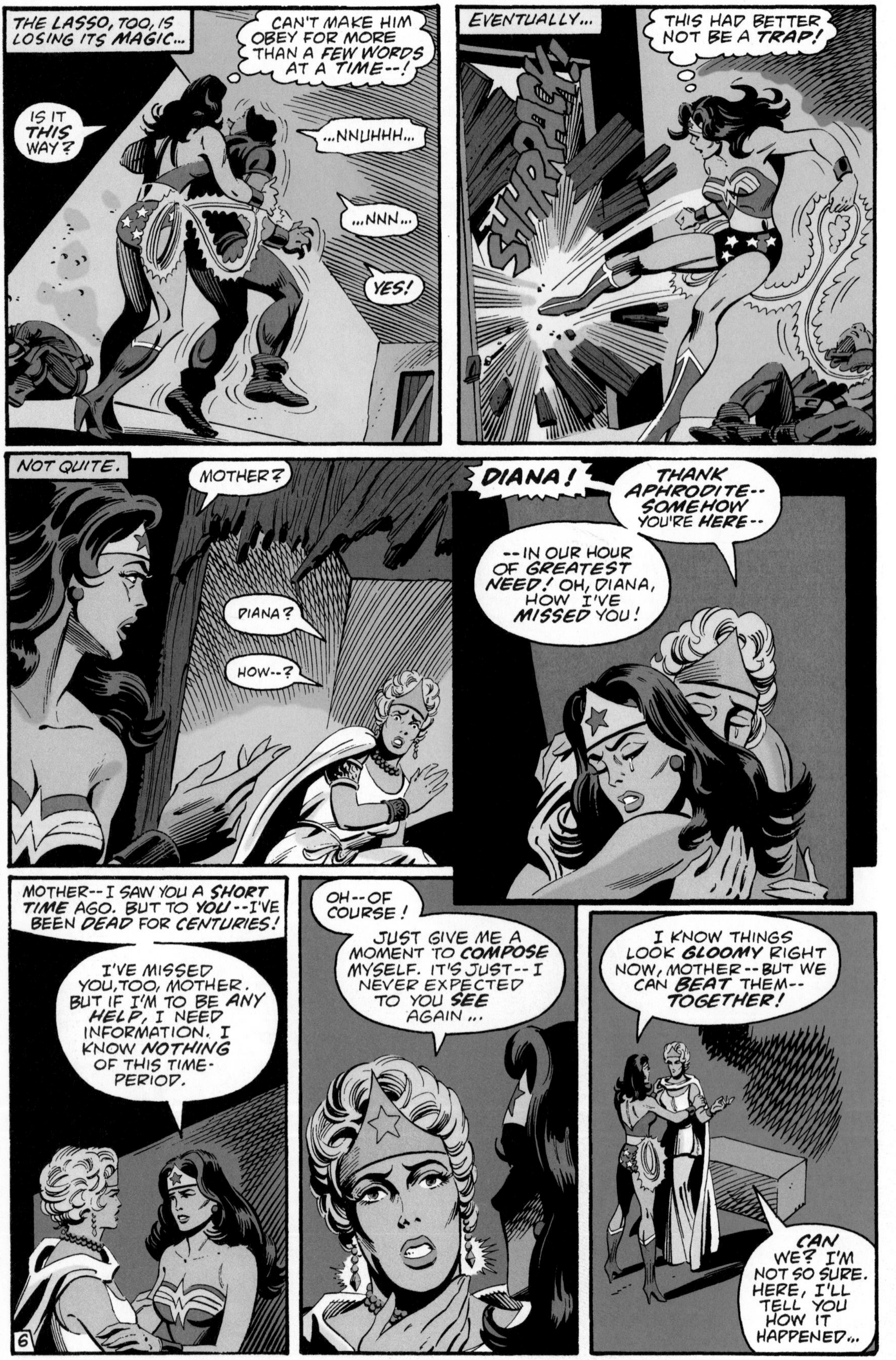
THE LASSO, TOO, IS LOSING ITS MAGIC...
CAN'T MAKE HIM OBEY FOR MORE THAN A FEW WORDS AT A TIME--!
IS IT THIS WAY?
...NNUHHH...
...NNN...
YES!
EVENTUALLY...
THIS HAD BETTER NOT BE A TRAP!
SHRAKK
NOT QUITE.
MOTHER?
DIANA?
HOW--?
DIANA!
THANK APHRODITE-- SOMEHOW YOU'RE HERE--
--IN OUR HOUR OF GREATEST NEED! OH, DIANA, HOW I'VE MISSED YOU!
MOTHER--I SAW YOU A SHORT TIME AGO. BUT TO YOU--I'VE BEEN DEAD FOR CENTURIES!
I'VE MISSED YOU, TOO, MOTHER. BUT IF I'M TO BE ANY HELP, I NEED INFORMATION. I KNOW NOTHING OF THIS TIME-PERIOD.
6
OH--OF COURSE!
JUST GIVE ME A MOMENT TO COMPOSE MYSELF. IT'S JUST--I NEVER EXPECTED TO YOU SEE AGAIN...
I KNOW THINGS LOOK GLOOMY RIGHT NOW, MOTHER--BUT WE CAN BEAT THEM-- TOGETHER!
CAN WE? I'M NOT SO SURE. HERE, I'LL TELL YOU HOW IT HAPPENED...

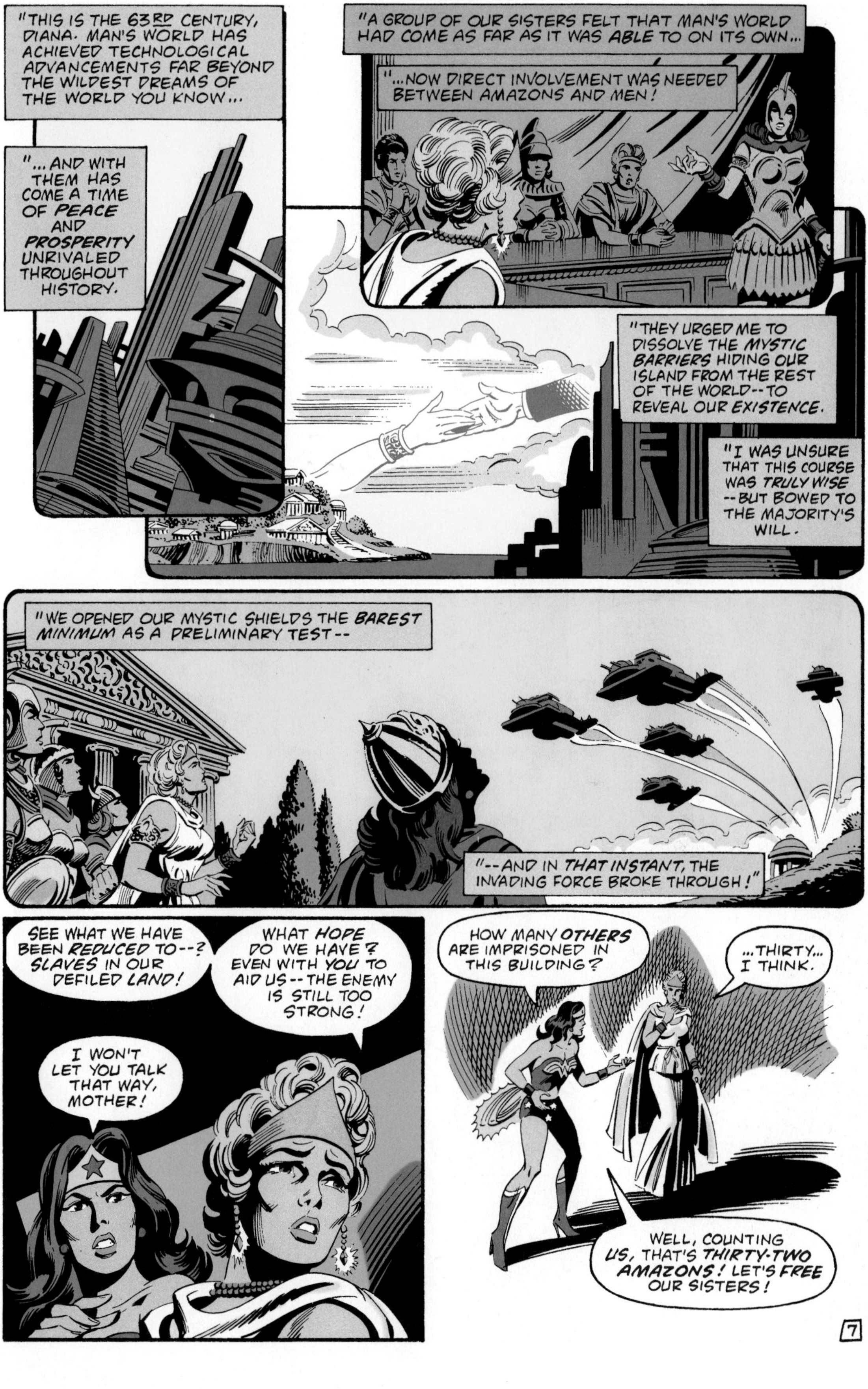
"THIS IS THE 63RD CENTURY, DIANA. MAN'S WORLD HAS ACHIEVED TECHNOLOGICAL ADVANCEMENTS FAR BEYOND THE WILDEST DREAMS OF THE WORLD YOU KNOW...
"...AND WITH THEM HAS COME A TIME OF PEACE AND PROSPERITY UNRIVALED THROUGHOUT HISTORY.
"A GROUP OF OUR SISTERS FELT THAT MAN'S WORLD HAD COME AS FAR AS IT WAS ABLE TO ON ITS OWN...
"...NOW DIRECT INVOLVEMENT WAS NEEDED BETWEEN AMAZONS AND MEN!
"THEY URGED ME TO DISSOLVE THE MYSTIC BARRIERS HIDING OUR ISLAND FROM THE REST OF THE WORLD--TO REVEAL OUR EXISTENCE.
"I WAS UNSURE THAT THIS COURSE WAS TRULY WISE --BUT BOWED TO THE MAJORITY'S WILL.
"WE OPENED OUR MYSTIC SHIELDS THE BAREST MINIMUM AS A PRELIMINARY TEST--
"--AND IN THAT INSTANT, THE INVADING FORCE BROKE THROUGH!"
SEE WHAT WE HAVE BEEN REDUCED TO--? SLAVES IN OUR DEFILED LAND!
WHAT HOPE DO WE HAVE? EVEN WITH YOU TO AID US--THE ENEMY IS STILL TOO STRONG!
I WON'T LET YOU TALK THAT WAY, MOTHER!
HOW MANY OTHERS ARE IMPRISONED IN THIS BUILDING?
...THIRTY... I THINK.
WELL, COUNTING US, THAT'S THIRTY-TWO AMAZONS! LET'S FREE OUR SISTERS!
7

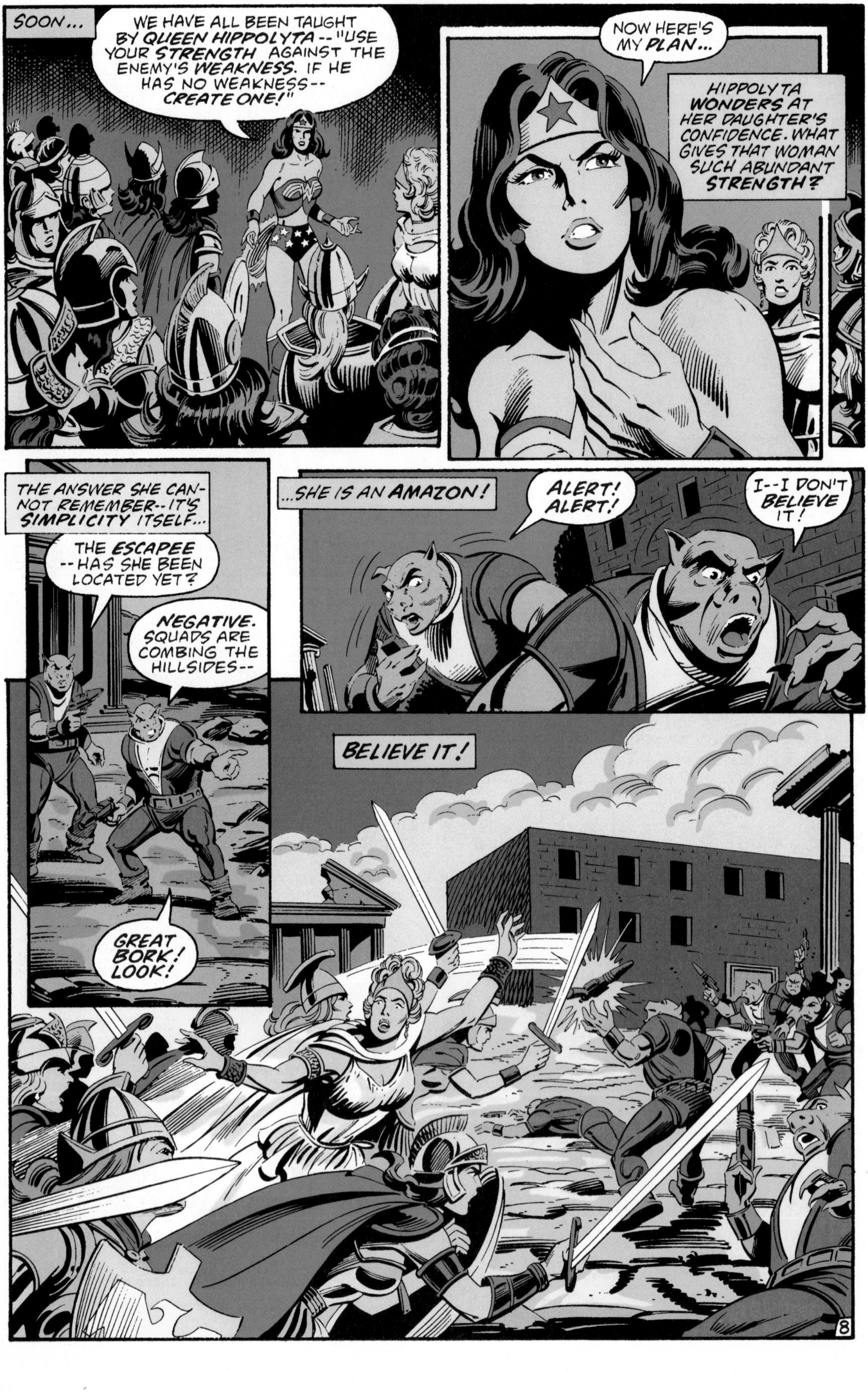
SOON...
WE HAVE ALL BEEN TAUGHT BY QUEEN HIPPOLYTA -- "USE YOUR STRENGTH AGAINST THE ENEMY'S WEAKNESS. IF HE HAS NO WEAKNESS -- CREATE ONE!"
NOW HERE'S MY PLAN...
HIPPOLYTA WONDERS AT HER DAUGHTER'S CONFIDENCE. WHAT GIVES THAT WOMAN SUCH ABUNDANT STRENGTH?
THE ANSWER SHE CAN-NOT REMEMBER--IT'S SIMPLICITY ITSELF...
THE ESCAPEE --HAS SHE BEEN LOCATED YET?
NEGATIVE. SQUADS ARE COMBING THE HILLSIDES--
...SHE IS AN AMAZON!
ALERT! ALERT!
I--I DON'T BELIEVE IT!
GREAT BORK! LOOK!
BELIEVE IT!
8

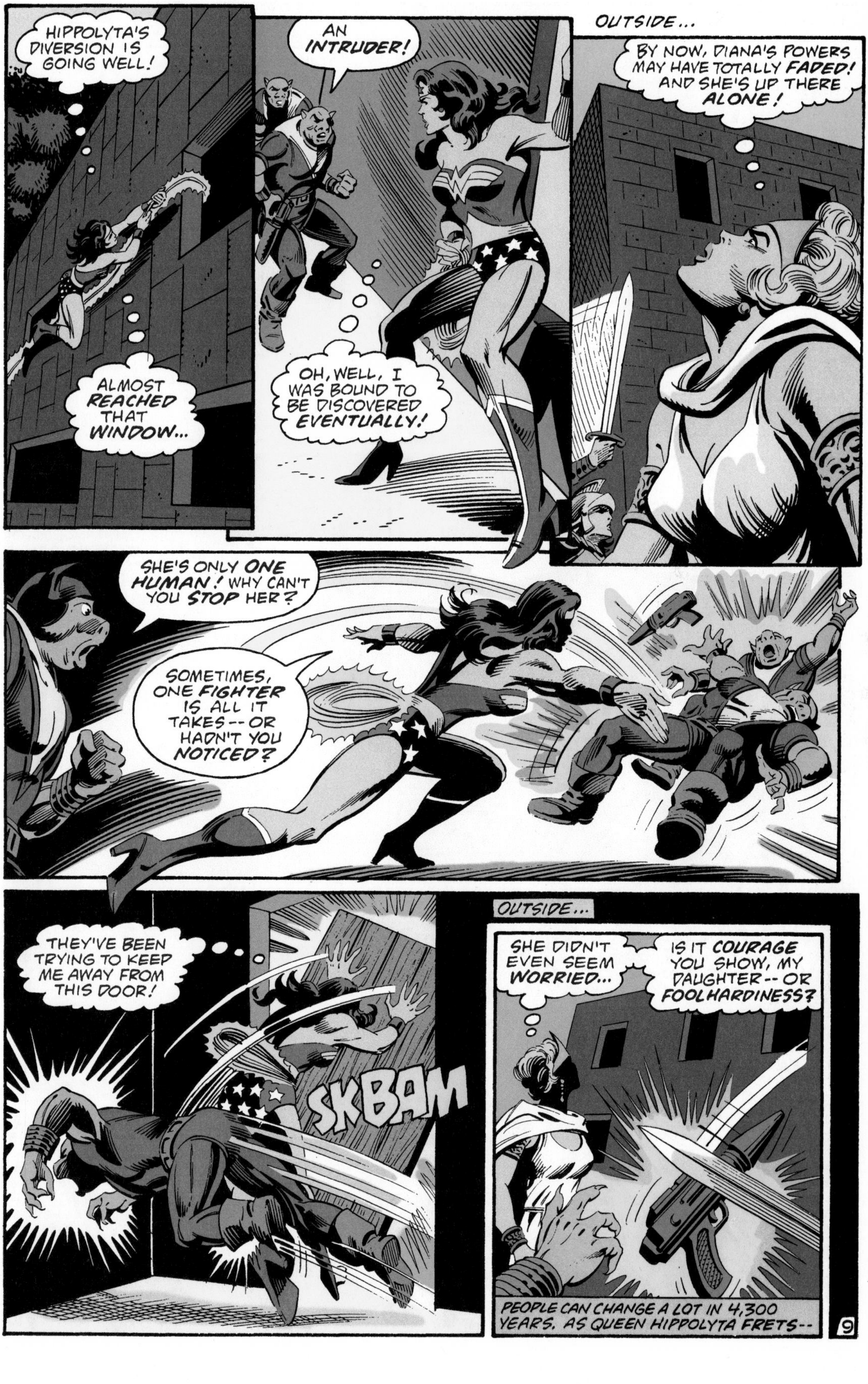
HIPPOLYTA'S DIVERSION IS GOING WELL!
ALMOST REACHED THAT WINDOW...
AN INTRUDER!
OH, WELL, I WAS BOUND TO BE DISCOVERED EVENTUALLY!
OUTSIDE...
BY NOW, DIANA'S POWERS MAY HAVE TOTALLY FADED! AND SHE'S UP THERE ALONE!
SHE'S ONLY ONE HUMAN! WHY CAN'T YOU STOP HER?
SOMETIMES, ONE FIGHTER IS ALL IT TAKES--OR HADN'T YOU NOTICED?
THEY'VE BEEN TRYING TO KEEP ME AWAY FROM THIS DOOR!
SKBAM
OUTSIDE...
SHE DIDN'T EVEN SEEM WORRIED...
IS IT COURAGE YOU SHOW, MY DAUGHTER--OR FOOLHARDINESS?
PEOPLE CAN CHANGE A LOT IN 4,300 YEARS. AS QUEEN HIPPOLYTA FRETS--
9

-- HER DAUGHTER PERSEVERES!

SHREEEE!

THE CEASE-FIRE SIREN! LAY DOWN YOUR ARMS!

GODDESS APHRODITE! SHE DID IT!

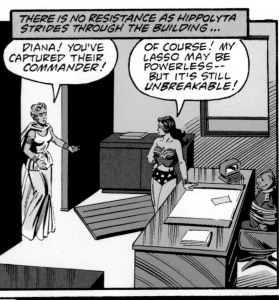

THERE IS NO RESISTANCE AS HIPPOLYTA STRIDES THROUGH THE BUILDING...

DIANA! YOU'VE CAPTURED THEIR COMMANDER!

OF COURSE! MY LASSO MAY BE POWERLESS-- BUT IT'S STILL UNBREAKABLE!

NOW, AS I WAS SAYING-- I COULD TURN YOU OVER TO THE PLANETARY GOVERNMENT, WHICH TAKES A DIM VIEW OF TECHNOLOGICALLY INFERIOR INVADERS--

--OR YOU COULD EVACUATE THIS ISLAND, LEAVE THIS PLANET, AND NEVER COME ANYWHERE NEAR IT AGAIN!

WHICH WILL IT BE?

UNDER THE CIRCUMSTANCES... AH... WE'RE NOT AN UNREASONABLE RACE-- HOW SOON DO YOU WANT US TO LEAVE?

GOOD THING HE DIDN'T CALL MY BLUFF! TO EXPOSE THE INVASION-- I'D HAVE TO REVEAL THE EXISTENCE OF PARADISE ISLAND-- AND THAT'S HARDLY MY SECRET TO TELL!

SO...

--AND ONCE YOUR MAIN FORCE HAS DEPARTED, WE'LL RELEASE YOU ... YOU CAN CATCH UP WITH THEM LATER.

IN THE MEANTIME, I'M CURIOUS-- HOW DID YOU KNOW TO ATTACK AT JUST THE RIGHT TIME?

I COULD REFUSE TO TELL YOU. BUT YOU ARE A GOOD WARRIOR AND A NOBLE OPPONENT. IT IS AN ODD TALE ...

10

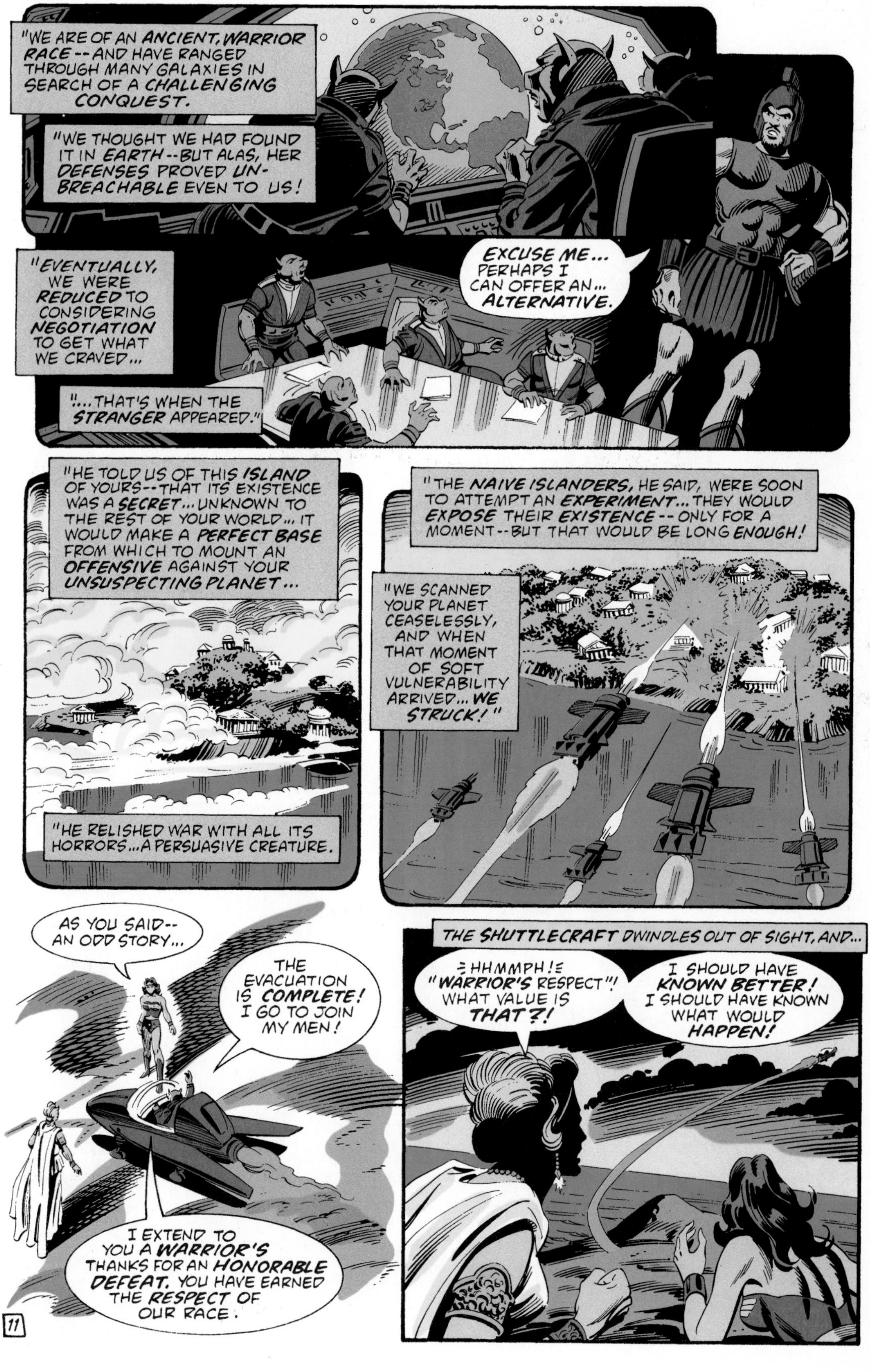

"WE ARE OF AN ANCIENT, WARRIOR RACE -- AND HAVE RANGED THROUGH MANY GALAXIES IN SEARCH OF A CHALLENGING CONQUEST.
"WE THOUGHT WE HAD FOUND IT IN EARTH -- BUT ALAS, HER DEFENSES PROVED UN-BREACHABLE EVEN TO US!
"EVENTUALLY, WE WERE REDUCED TO CONSIDERING NEGOTIATION TO GET WHAT WE CRAVED...
"...THAT'S WHEN THE STRANGER APPEARED."
EXCUSE ME... PERHAPS I CAN OFFER AN... ALTERNATIVE.
"HE TOLD US OF THIS ISLAND OF YOURS -- THAT ITS EXISTENCE WAS A SECRET... UNKNOWN TO THE REST OF YOUR WORLD... IT WOULD MAKE A PERFECT BASE FROM WHICH TO MOUNT AN OFFENSIVE AGAINST YOUR UNSUSPECTING PLANET...
"HE RELISHED WAR WITH ALL ITS HORRORS... A PERSUASIVE CREATURE.
"THE NAIVE ISLANDERS, HE SAID, WERE SOON TO ATTEMPT AN EXPERIMENT... THEY WOULD EXPOSE THEIR EXISTENCE -- ONLY FOR A MOMENT -- BUT THAT WOULD BE LONG ENOUGH!
"WE SCANNED YOUR PLANET CEASELESSLY, AND WHEN THAT MOMENT OF SOFT VULNERABILITY ARRIVED... WE STRUCK!"
AS YOU SAID -- AN ODD STORY...
THE EVACUATION IS COMPLETE! I GO TO JOIN MY MEN!
I EXTEND TO YOU A WARRIOR'S THANKS FOR AN HONORABLE DEFEAT. YOU HAVE EARNED THE RESPECT OF OUR RACE.
11
THE SHUTTLECRAFT DWINDLES OUT OF SIGHT, AND...
HHMMPH! "WARRIOR'S RESPECT"! WHAT VALUE IS THAT?!
I SHOULD HAVE KNOWN BETTER! I SHOULD HAVE KNOWN WHAT WOULD HAPPEN!

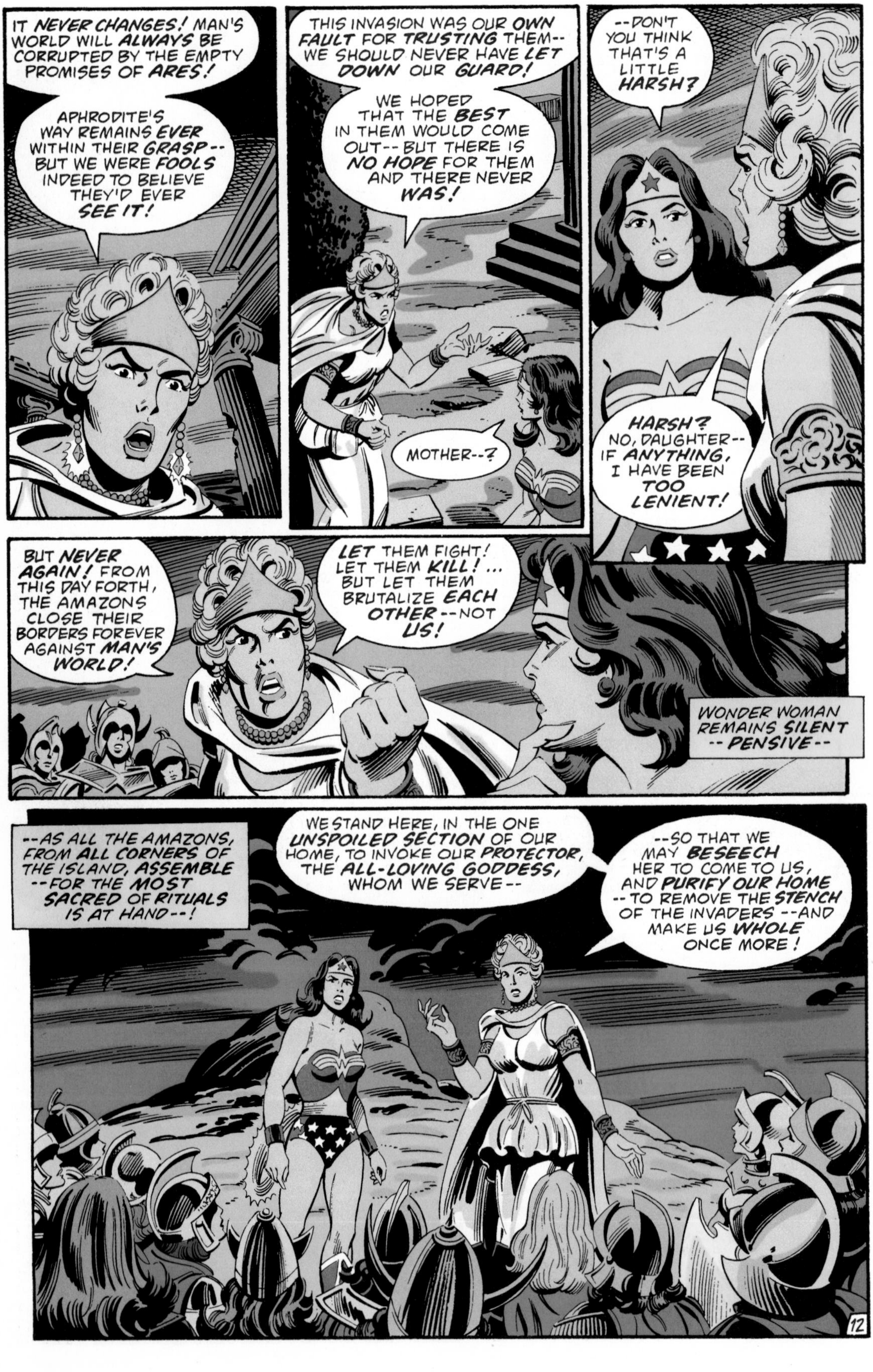
IT NEVER CHANGES! MAN'S WORLD WILL ALWAYS BE CORRUPTED BY THE EMPTY PROMISES OF ARES!
APHRODITE'S WAY REMAINS EVER WITHIN THEIR GRASP-- BUT WE WERE FOOLS INDEED TO BELIEVE THEY'D EVER SEE IT!
THIS INVASION WAS OUR OWN FAULT FOR TRUSTING THEM-- WE SHOULD NEVER HAVE LET DOWN OUR GUARD!
WE HOPED THAT THE BEST IN THEM WOULD COME OUT-- BUT THERE IS NO HOPE FOR THEM AND THERE NEVER WAS!
MOTHER--?
--DON'T YOU THINK THAT'S A LITTLE HARSH?
HARSH? NO, DAUGHTER-- IF ANYTHING, I HAVE BEEN TOO LENIENT!
BUT NEVER AGAIN! FROM THIS DAY FORTH, THE AMAZONS CLOSE THEIR BORDERS FOREVER AGAINST MAN'S WORLD!
LET THEM FIGHT! LET THEM KILL! ... BUT LET THEM BRUTALIZE EACH OTHER --NOT US!
WONDER WOMAN REMAINS SILENT -- PENSIVE--
--AS ALL THE AMAZONS, FROM ALL CORNERS OF THE ISLAND, ASSEMBLE --FOR THE MOST SACRED OF RITUALS IS AT HAND--!
WE STAND HERE, IN THE ONE UNSPOILED SECTION OF OUR HOME, TO INVOKE OUR PROTECTOR, THE ALL-LOVING GODDESS, WHOM WE SERVE--
--SO THAT WE MAY BESEECH HER TO COME TO US, AND PURIFY OUR HOME --TO REMOVE THE STENCH OF THE INVADERS --AND MAKE US WHOLE ONCE MORE!
12

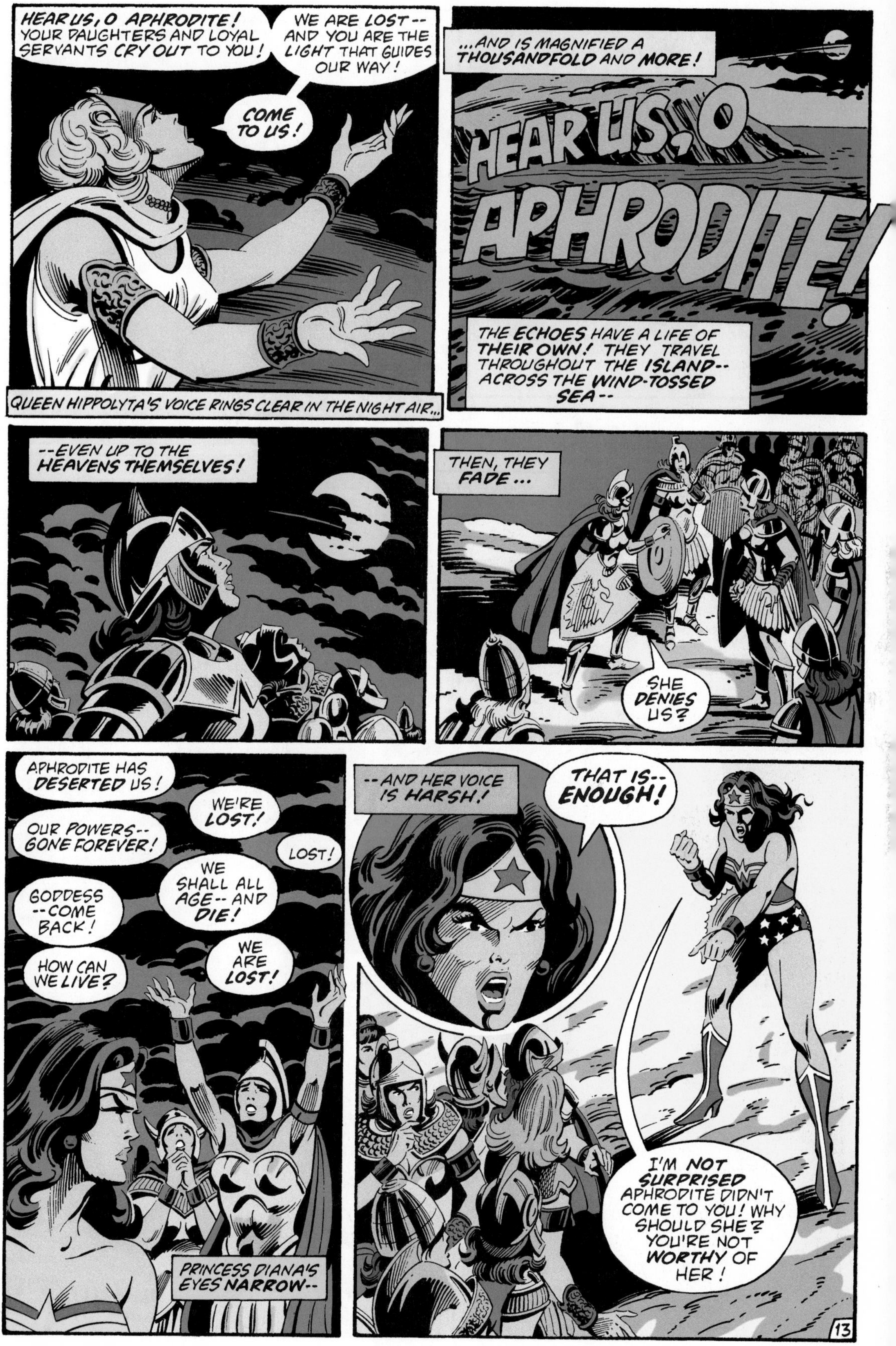
HEAR US, O APHRODITE! YOUR DAUGHTERS AND LOYAL SERVANTS CRY OUT TO YOU!
WE ARE LOST-- AND YOU ARE THE LIGHT THAT GUIDES OUR WAY!
COME TO US!
QUEEN HIPPOLYTA'S VOICE RINGS CLEAR IN THE NIGHT AIR...
...AND IS MAGNIFIED A THOUSANDFOLD AND MORE!
HEAR US, O APHRODITE!
THE ECHOES HAVE A LIFE OF THEIR OWN! THEY TRAVEL THROUGHOUT THE ISLAND-- ACROSS THE WIND-TOSSED SEA--
--EVEN UP TO THE HEAVENS THEMSELVES!
THEN, THEY FADE...
SHE DENIES US?
APHRODITE HAS DESERTED US!
WE'RE LOST!
OUR POWERS-- GONE FOREVER!
LOST!
WE SHALL ALL AGE-- AND DIE!
GODDESS --COME BACK!
HOW CAN WE LIVE?
WE ARE LOST!
PRINCESS DIANA'S EYES NARROW--
--AND HER VOICE IS HARSH!
THAT IS-- ENOUGH!
I'M NOT SURPRISED APHRODITE DIDN'T COME TO YOU! WHY SHOULD SHE? YOU'RE NOT WORTHY OF HER!
13

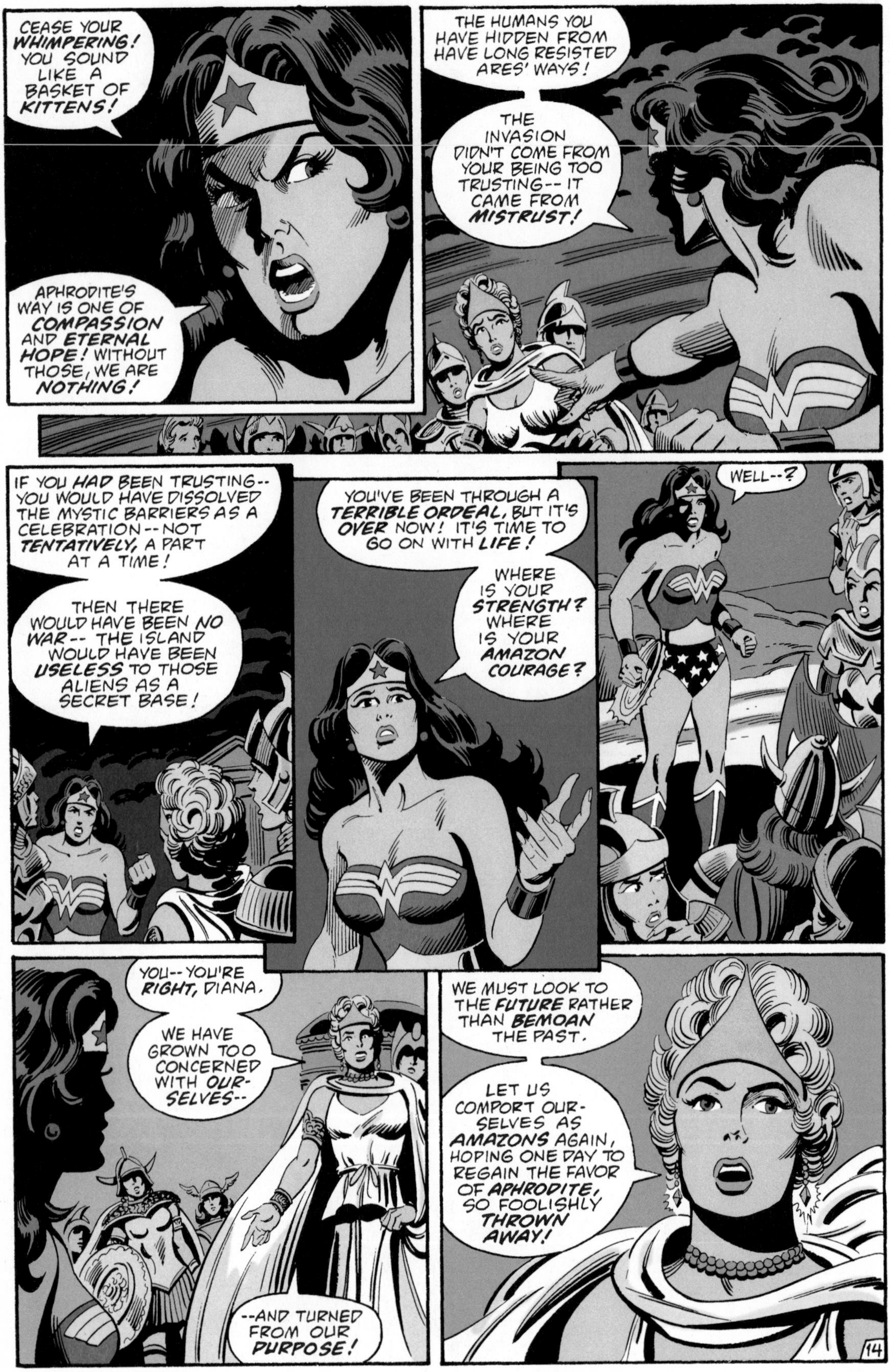
CEASE YOUR WHIMPERING! YOU SOUND LIKE A BASKET OF KITTENS!
APHRODITE'S WAY IS ONE OF COMPASSION AND ETERNAL HOPE! WITHOUT THOSE, WE ARE NOTHING!
THE HUMANS YOU HAVE HIDDEN FROM HAVE LONG RESISTED ARES' WAYS!
THE INVASION DIDN'T COME FROM YOUR BEING TOO TRUSTING-- IT CAME FROM MISTRUST!
IF YOU HAD BEEN TRUSTING-- YOU WOULD HAVE DISSOLVED THE MYSTIC BARRIERS AS A CELEBRATION--NOT TENTATIVELY, A PART AT A TIME!
THEN THERE WOULD HAVE BEEN NO WAR-- THE ISLAND WOULD HAVE BEEN USELESS TO THOSE ALIENS AS A SECRET BASE!
YOU'VE BEEN THROUGH A TERRIBLE ORDEAL, BUT IT'S OVER NOW! IT'S TIME TO GO ON WITH LIFE!
WHERE IS YOUR STRENGTH? WHERE IS YOUR AMAZON COURAGE?
WELL--?
YOU--YOU'RE RIGHT, DIANA.
WE HAVE GROWN TOO CONCERNED WITH OUR-SELVES--
--AND TURNED FROM OUR PURPOSE!
WE MUST LOOK TO THE FUTURE RATHER THAN BEMOAN THE PAST.
LET US COMPORT OUR-SELVES AS AMAZONS AGAIN, HOPING ONE DAY TO REGAIN THE FAVOR OF APHRODITE, SO FOOLISHLY THROWN AWAY!
14

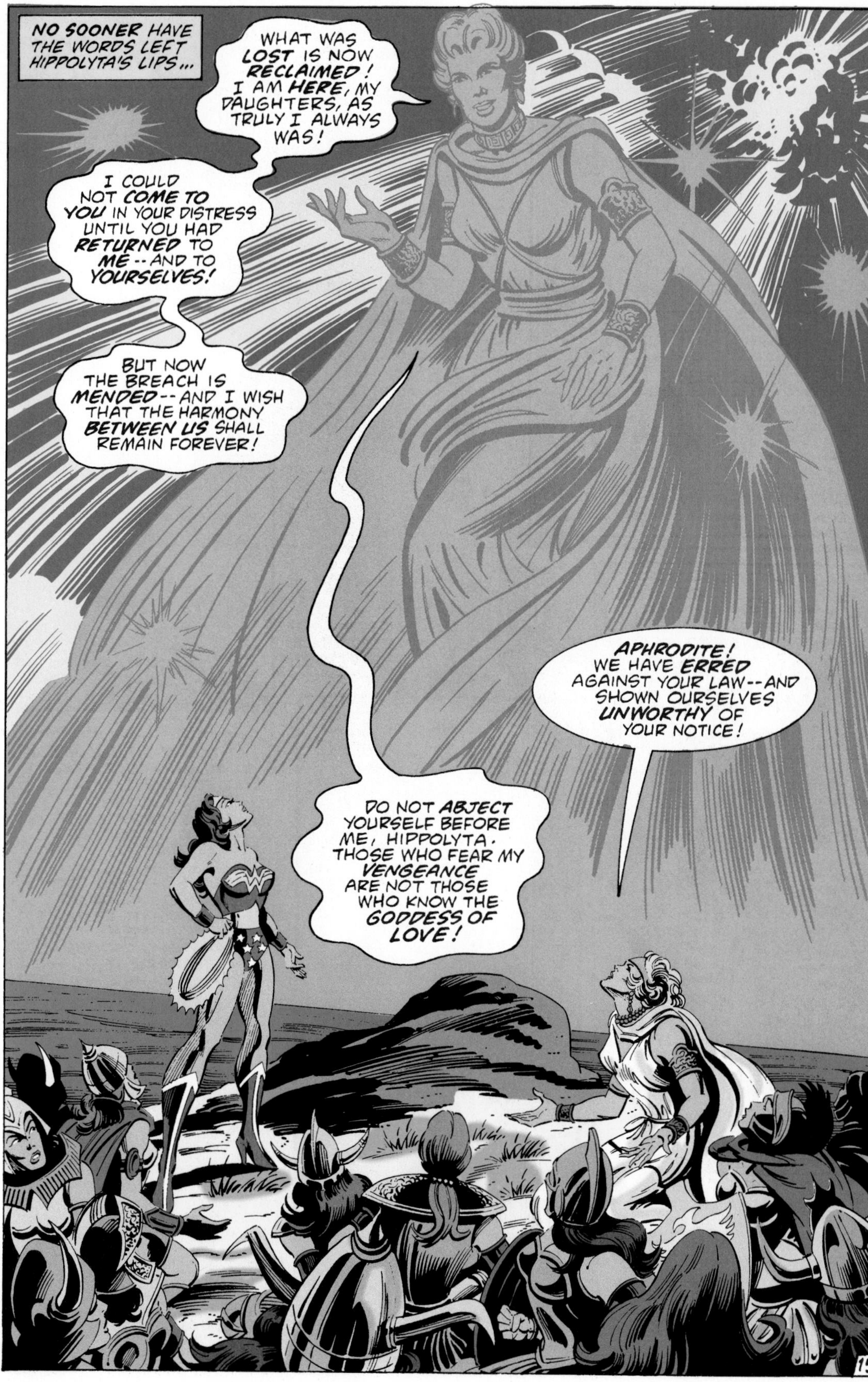
NO SOONER HAVE THE WORDS LEFT HIPPOLYTA'S LIPS...
WHAT WAS LOST IS NOW RECLAIMED! I AM HERE, MY DAUGHTERS, AS TRULY I ALWAYS WAS!
I COULD NOT COME TO YOU IN YOUR DISTRESS UNTIL YOU HAD RETURNED TO ME--AND TO YOURSELVES!
BUT NOW THE BREACH IS MENDED--AND I WISH THAT THE HARMONY BETWEEN US SHALL REMAIN FOREVER!
APHRODITE! WE HAVE ERRED AGAINST YOUR LAW--AND SHOWN OURSELVES UNWORTHY OF YOUR NOTICE!
DO NOT ABJECT YOURSELF BEFORE ME, HIPPOLYTA. THOSE WHO FEAR MY VENGEANCE ARE NOT THOSE WHO KNOW THE GODDESS OF LOVE!
15

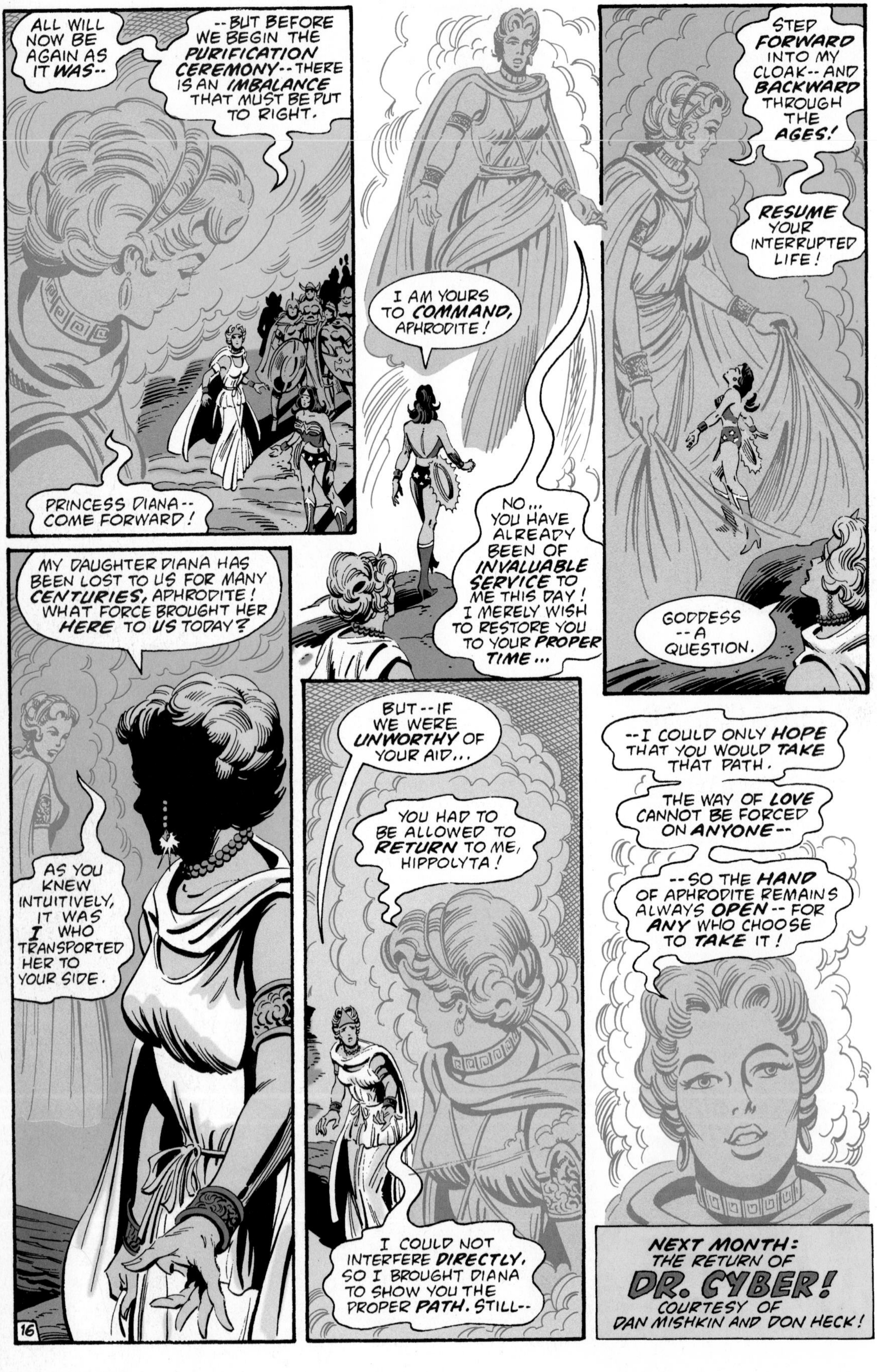
ALL WILL NOW BE AGAIN AS IT WAS--
--BUT BEFORE WE BEGIN THE PURIFICATION CEREMONY--THERE IS AN IMBALANCE THAT MUST BE PUT TO RIGHT.
PRINCESS DIANA--COME FORWARD!
I AM YOURS TO COMMAND, APHRODITE!
NO... YOU HAVE ALREADY BEEN OF INVALUABLE SERVICE TO ME THIS DAY! I MERELY WISH TO RESTORE YOU TO YOUR PROPER TIME...
STEP FORWARD INTO MY CLOAK--AND BACKWARD THROUGH THE AGES!
RESUME YOUR INTERRUPTED LIFE!
GODDESS--A QUESTION.
MY DAUGHTER DIANA HAS BEEN LOST TO US FOR MANY CENTURIES, APHRODITE! WHAT FORCE BROUGHT HER HERE TO US TODAY?
AS YOU KNEW INTUITIVELY, IT WAS I WHO TRANSPORTED HER TO YOUR SIDE.
16
BUT--IF WE WERE UNWORTHY OF YOUR AID...
YOU HAD TO BE ALLOWED TO RETURN TO ME, HIPPOLYTA!
I COULD NOT INTERFERE DIRECTLY, SO I BROUGHT DIANA TO SHOW YOU THE PROPER PATH. STILL--
--I COULD ONLY HOPE THAT YOU WOULD TAKE THAT PATH.
THE WAY OF LOVE CANNOT BE FORCED ON ANYONE--
--SO THE HAND OF APHRODITE REMAINS ALWAYS OPEN--FOR ANY WHO CHOOSE TO TAKE IT!
NEXT MONTH: THE RETURN OF DR. CYBER! COURTESY OF DAN MISHKIN AND DON HECK!

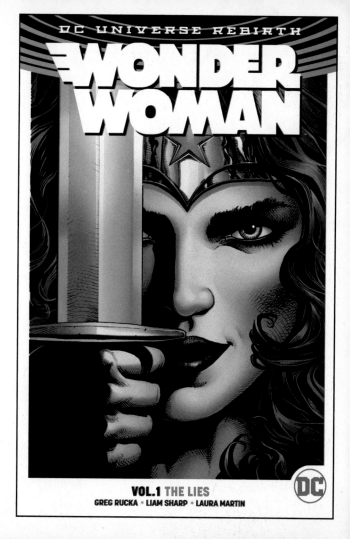

"Clear storytelling at its best. It's an intriguing concept and easy to grasp."
– THE NEW YORK TIMES

"Azzarello is rebuilding the mythology of Wonder Woman."
– CRAVE ONLINE

WONDER WOMAN
VOL. 1: BLOOD
BRIAN AZZARELLO
with CLIFF CHIANG

**WONDER WOMAN
VOL. 2: GUTS**

**WONDER WOMAN
VOL. 3: IRON**

READ THE ENTIRE EPIC

WONDER WOMAN VOL.
WA

WONDER WOMAN VOL.
FLES

WONDER WOMAN VOL.
BON

WONDER WOMAN VOL.
WAR-TOR

WONDER WOMAN VOL.
A TWIST OF FA

WONDER WOMAN VOL.
RESURRECTIO